W9-DDD-218

Affirmative Action
and the Stalled Quest
for Black Progress

Affirmative Action
and the Stalled Quest
for Black Progress

W. AVON DRAKE

AND

ROBERT D. HOLSWORTH

University of Illinois Press   URBANA AND CHICAGO

© 1996 by the Board of Trustees of the University of Illinois
Manufactured in the United States of America
1 2 3 4 5 C P 5 4 3 2 1

This book is printed on acid-free paper.

Library of Congress Cataloging-in-Publication Data
Drake, Willie Avon, 1946–
Affirmative action and the stalled quest for Black progress / W. Avon
Drake and Robert D. Holsworth.
p.   cm.
Includes bibliographical references and index.
ISBN 0-252-02238-6 (acid-free paper). — ISBN 0-252-06539-5 (pbk. : acid-free
paper)
1. Affirmative action programs—United States. 2. Afro-Americans—
Employment. 3. Public contracts—United States. 4. Letting of contracts—
United States. 5. Minority business enterprises—United States.
I. Holsworth, Robert D. II. Title.
HF5549.5.A34D73   1996
331.13'3'0973—dc20   95-41799
                                                               CIP

Contents

Introduction   1

1   The Affirmative Action Debate   11

2   Black Politics in Richmond, 1945–89   37

3   Set-Aside Politics   70

4   Set-Asides and the Broader Strategy for Black Progress   95

5   White Responses to Affirmative Action   115

6   *Richmond v. Croson* in the Courts   138

7   Urban Politics after *Croson*   161

Notes   185

Bibliography   201

Index   209

Acknowledgments

We want to thank a number of people who were especially helpful in researching and preparing this book. Our former students Melissa L. King and Joy Green Stenner combed back copies of the *Richmond Afro-American,* the *Richmond News Leader,* and the *Richmond Times-Dispatch* for relevant articles. Marianne Graves of the political science department and Stephanie Lofton, Peggy Thompson, and Priscilla Wallace of the African-American Studies Program expertly prepared the various versions of the manuscript. Kemberley Papoy helped to develop the index. Margaret Edds shared with us transcripts of the interviews that she conducted with Richmond leaders for her own book *Free at Last.*

In addition to these individuals, we are grateful to the city officials who consented to be interviewed, who provided us with useful leads, and who took the time to go back through their own files to provide us with documentation. The comments offered by the reviewers selected by the University of Illinois Press enabled us to make this a better book. We are also appreciative of the general helpfulness and patience of Dick Martin and the entire staff at the University of Illinois Press.

Introduction

In the spring of 1995, the issue of affirmative action took center stage in American political debate. A widely publicized effort was started in California on behalf of a ballot initiative that would prohibit the state and localities from using race, sex, color, ethnicity, or national origin as a criterion for either discriminating against or granting preferential treatment to individuals or groups in public employment, education, and contracting. Emboldened by their success in the elections of 1994, congressional Republicans vowed to introduce similar legislation at the federal level. A number of Republican presidential hopefuls placed their opposition to affirmative action at the heart of their platforms. Torn between his "New Democrat" loyalties and the recognition that affirmative action was vitally important to the leadership of core Democratic constituencies, President Bill Clinton appeared to move simultaneously in a number of different directions. His administration criticized Republicans for trying to divide the nation and reiterated its commitment in principle to affirmative action. Yet the administration also insisted that it was reviewing all federal affirmative action programs to identify those that should be retained and practices that should be discarded.

More than thirty years of presidential decrees, congressional laws, local actions, court decisions, and administrative rulings preceded the debate of 1995. One of the most important paths to this debate, particularly about the use of economic set-asides, came through the city of Richmond, Virginia. In 1977, a black majority city council was elected for the first time in Richmond's history. The election was the culmination of a tumultuous decade in which litigation over an annexation plan had resulted in a court order that prevented the city from holding councilmanic elections for seven years. From 1977 to 1982, the new majority attempted to reshape the city's governance structure to redress what it considered the racially exclu-sionary practices of the old system. African American council members used their appointment power to select a black city manager; they recruited a new superintendent of schools; and they altered the composition of city boards and commissions.

By the early 1980s, African American leaders in Richmond had turned their attention to ways of rectifying the consequences of racially based economic discrimination. They believed that it was time, as one political figure was fond of saying, to "integrate the money." After a period of ini-tial disagreement, the black civic elite focused ultimately on utilizing set-aside policies as a means of demonstrating their commitment. Given the historic exclusion of African Americans from development opportunities, they believed that the city should use its economic leverage to promote greater minority involvement in city projects and other undertakings where the municipality had a direct financial stake. Indeed, set-asides became a core feature in the establishment and legitimation of the entire econom-ic development strategy pursued by the city.

In April 1983, the Richmond City Council passed a set-aside ordinance by a vote of 6-2, requiring whites who received city construction contracts to utilize minority subcontractors and suppliers for at least 30 percent of the total dollar amount.[1] The ordinance was passed after a lengthy debate in the council and over the objection of the local chapter of the Associa-tion of General Contractors.[2] Despite the opposition to the measure, it was evident that the set-aside program was by no means as controversial as other issues addressed by the council. Members who voted for the bill felt that they were on strong legal ground. They were aware that other cities, such as Atlanta, had implemented this kind of affirmative action. Perhaps more importantly, the U.S. Supreme Court in *H. Earl Fullilove et al., petition-ers v. Philip M. Klutznick, Secretary of Commerce of the United States, et al.* (1980) had upheld a similar congressional set-aside ordinance in which states and localities were required to utilize minority contractors for at least 10 percent of the dollar amounts given from a federal program to the states. One council member, Andrew Gillespie, voted against the ordinance because he feared that the city would incur large legal bills in "establish-ing law for the entire country."[3] Despite Gillespie's warning, few Richmond residents believed that the city had started down the path that would lead to one of the most significant Supreme Court opinions of the 1980s.

Supporters of the set-aside program pointed to a study that indicated that minority business people received less than 1 percent of the money spent on city contracts. They believed that this piece of evidence was so compelling that the courts would certainly approve the council's remedial action. But a major legal challenge to the city's position was initiated less than six months after the program's passage. In September 1983, J. A. Croson Company, an Ohio-based business, submitted a bid for installing stainless steel plumbing fixtures, requesting a waiver from the set-aside requirement on the grounds that there were no qualified minority suppliers. A minority-owned firm disputed Croson's claim and asserted that it was willing to supply the fixtures, though Croson maintained that the minority firm's bid was substantially over market price. After reviewing the documents submitted by Croson, the city announced that it would rebid the contract. Croson then filed suit, alleging that the city had violated several laws of the Commonwealth of Virginia as well as the protections inherent in the Fourteenth Amendment to the U.S. Constitution.

Over the next three years, the city of Richmond went on a legal roller-coaster ride in the federal court system. The case was first heard in the U.S. District Court where the city was upheld in a strongly worded opinion. The decision was appealed to the Fourth Circuit Court of Appeals where the program was supported by a 2-1 vote. Croson then appealed to the U.S. Supreme Court, which reviewed and sent the case back to the circuit court with instructions to reconsider in light of a decision in which the high court had recently struck down a local affirmative action policy. The circuit court reversed itself, ruling against the city and overturning the program. At this time, the city of Richmond appealed. The Supreme Court, however, not only agreed with Croson but also established a criterion of "strict scrutiny" as the yardstick by which all future affirmative action claims should be evaluated. Thus, a dispute over plumbing fixtures had culminated in a major policy statement that reverberated across the nation.

The Supreme Court's decision in *City of Richmond v. J. A. Croson Co.* provoked a vigorous reaction across the American political spectrum. At first, many liberals attempted to downplay the significance of the Court's decision. They suggested that the Court's opinion should not be viewed as a repudiation of affirmative action in general but merely as a rejection of an ill-conceived set-aside plan by the Richmond City Council. According to this position, the Richmond City Council had not done its homework. In other words, the council had not provided adequate evidence of discrimination that made the program necessary, nor had it justified its selection of the 30 percent requirement for minority subcontracting on city construction work. This stance was initially elaborated by the leaders of many cities that had also instituted affirmative action programs in hiring and contracting.[4] Moreover, a coalition of law school deans and prominent professors, convened by Laurence Tribe at the request of the Organization for a New Equality, issued a similar statement in response to the Court's decision. They argued that "while it would be irresponsible for local governments to avoid whatever steps are necessary to adjust their minority contract programs to the Supreme Court's ruling in the *Croson* decision, it would be equally irresponsible for others to claim that this opinion casts doubt on the overall constitutionality of properly constructed race-conscious remedies."[5]

Conservatives responded by asserting that the implications of *Richmond v. Croson* were far more extensive than liberals would acknowledge. Charles Fried, who had been solicitor general during Ronald Reagan's second term, called the decision "the justification of our four years of work in this regard." Responding in the *Yale Law Journal* to the members of Tribe's alliance, Fried dismissed their commentary as predictable "spin control" and described their perspective as a combination of "Chicken Little and Dr. Pangloss. Something terrible has happened, but it is not so bad after all."[6] He added, "*Croson* is not a disaster to be deplored and explained away. It is a firm and noble affirmation that in this area, too, the end does not justify the means" (160). In Richmond itself, the initial reaction of the daily papers' conservative editorial pages echoed Fried's approbation. Quoting Martin Luther King Jr.'s comment that he dreamed of the day when people would be judged by the "content of their character, not by the color of their skin," the *Richmond News Leader* claimed that the Court's decision brought America "almost home, home to the vision of Martin Luther King."[7]

The heated nature of the controversy that accompanied the decision in *Richmond v. Croson* was itself an indication of the gathering storm that had been brewing about affirmative action in American society. By the 1980s the term itself had taken on a symbolic importance in the nation's political debate. To many Americans, the continued pursuit of affirmative action was the absolute minimum required to demonstrate that the society remained committed to the goals of racial equality. It was the natural extension of the civil rights movement. From this perspective, the Reagan administration's efforts to challenge affirmative action in the courts were an attempt to "turn back the clock" and placed the government on record against civil rights. To other citizens, affirmative action was shorthand for "reverse discrimination," a policy by which liberals advanced the interests of minority groups by discriminating against white males. Indeed, some civil rights movement supporters claimed that preferential treatment was antithetical to the goals of color-blind justice, which had been central to the original meaning of civil rights. Writing in *Harper's* in 1983, Michael Kinsley contended that "no single development of the past fifteen years has turned more liberals into former liberals than affirmative action."[8]

From a scholarly perspective, the debate about affirmative action was unsatisfactory in a number of important respects. While the controversy recognized affirmative action's importance to proposals about black progress, the debate had a highly abstract character. First, discussion frequently occurred without any reference—beyond the self-serving anecdote—to the actual practice of affirmative action. Hardly anyone responded to *Richmond v. Croson*, for example, by referring to what was occurring with the Richmond program as a way of corroborating their position. Perhaps more importantly, the lack of concrete research on the development and practice of affirmative action programs left the debate about the policy confined within unduly narrow parameters. In many American cities, for instance, affirmative action was part of black leaders' response to the political and economic conditions that confronted them in the late twentieth century. But, with the notable exceptions of scholars such as Adolph Reed Jr. and William Julius Wilson, there appeared to be little interest in relating the discussion of "civil rights" policy to the challenges facing urban political leaders as the country shifted from an industrial to a service- and information-based economy that was increasingly international in character.

This book addresses what we view as the central deficiencies in the study of affirmative action. In one sense, our work is very narrowly focused. We want to illuminate the context in which an historically important affirmative action policy emerged, investigate its actual operation, and consider alternative options that might have been pursued. We thus examine extensively the details of the set-aside program in Richmond that led to the Supreme Court's historic decision. We describe the politics that gave rise to the program, probe the intentions and ideology of decision makers in Richmond, and explore the policy's effect on various groups within the black community. We also describe the response (or lack of) to the set-aside program in the city's white and black communities.

At the same time, we utilize this study of *Richmond v. Croson* to make a more general argument about affirmative action. We think that the standard debate about the policy has, in some instances, actually hindered public understanding of it. We maintain that the discussion of set-asides and other affirmative action policies pursued in American cities can only be properly understood and evaluated by connecting the discussion of civil rights issues to the historical, economic, and political contexts of these matters. Thus, we must explain the decisions that faced African American leaders as they became part of a governing coalition, examine the economic and demographic shifts that influenced the choices available in urban America, and evaluate the policies pursued by black leadership not only in terms of the economic outcomes but also in respect to the contribution these programs did or did not make to the political development of the African American community. In other words, scholars need to adopt an historical approach that demonstrates why affirmative action programs were initiated, whose interests these policies typically serve, and how they are related to the ongoing political conflicts within urban America.

Finally, we want to utilize our study of affirmative action as a way of entering the broader intellectual debate about black progress in the United States in the 1990s. We will examine an important set of questions in this regard. To what extent does the strategic package that contains affirmative action as a central element advance or hinder black progress? Are there economic and political options that would be more advantageous to pursue? What is the appropriate framework for evaluating the performance of black leadership? What are the possible economic and political relationships that can be developed between blacks and whites in the United States? And how can we employ democratic practices to address the problems of urban America? We do not profess to have answers to all these questions, but we hope to illuminate the dimensions of the issues in which these queries are based.

Chapter 1 begins with a synthesis of theoretical perspectives on affirmative action, explaining the liberal defense of affirmative action and examining the key theoretical critiques of this position. We present arguments drawn from not only the most visible opponents of the policy, such as Thomas Sowell, but also from authors such as William Julius Wilson, Adolph Reed Jr., and Harold Cruse, whose work has only recently received much attention. The first chapter also illustrates how the discussion of affirmative action necessarily entails exploring a wider set of issues concerning the policies pursued by contemporary black leadership, the opportunities available to all people (though especially minorities) in the existing American economy, and the most desirable political strategy for pursuing African American advancement. We suggest that the criticisms of affirmative action have considerable merit, though we do not believe that the alternative perspectives have yet furnished a workable strategic alternative.

Chapter 2 explains the struggle for black political power in Richmond in the post–World War II era. We begin by examining how the most important black political organization in the city, the Crusade for Voters, demonstrated that black Richmonders could hold the balance of power in city elections. The chapter also describes the transformation of black politics in the sixties and the quest that emerged for independent black political power. We show how the ultimate success of this quest led to a new set of dilemmas associated with actually governing the city, how black politics in Richmond became divided internally in the 1980s, and how this division ultimately contributed to an ossification of black leadership and a loss of strategic purpose in African American politics.

Chapter 3 examines the origins, development, and outcome of the set-aside program that was the centerpiece of the *Croson v. Richmond* challenge. It begins by analyzing the political context in which the set-aside policy arose and shows how the program was the result of an accommodation reached between a recently elected black majority city council in the early 1980s and prominent spokespersons for Main Street business interests. The chapter then describes the actual operation of the program and examines the companies that benefited from it. We also investigate city contracting in the post-*Croson* era. We argue that the program had, at best, only limited success. While a few well-positioned companies were able to take advantage of the program, set-asides had a limited impact in promoting black business development. Finally, the chapter introduces the concept of "elite racial reconciliation" as a way of analyzing the Richmond affirmative action policy. This strategy provided a means for the black leadership to argue that the program was meeting their constituents' needs, simultaneously enabling the white corporate leadership to demonstrate its commitment to the community and its willingness to dissolve the racial bitterness that had characterized city politics since the emergence of a black majority city council.

The fourth chapter elaborates on the connection between the formation of the set-aside program and the city's general strategy for African American advance. The chapter shows how the set-aside program was part of a broader strategy for black progress pursued by African American leadership. We examine the success of this general approach in areas such as city employment, budgetary priorities, the use of downtown revitalization strategies to enhance economic opportunities for African Americans, and the political development of the wider African American community. We argue that performance in these areas resembles that which occurred in the set-aside program inasmuch as success was much more limited than official rhetoric indicates. We suggest that numerous reasons can be advanced to explain the lack of success, some of which have very little to do with the decisions of black leadership. Nonetheless, we maintain that the decisions and choices made by the political elite contributed to the city's difficulties.

Chapter 5 discusses white reactions to Richmond's affirmative action program. We demonstrate how these have been a mixture of resistance, accommodation, and indifference. A significant part of the white elite, particularly those involved with downtown redevelopment, have embraced affirmative action as a useful and relatively innocuous policy. On the other hand, a substantial portion of the white population in the city has remained largely indifferent to the policy. We suggest that the latter's response stems from both the general economic trends that have made their jobs less dependent on local political decisions and the general political demobilization that currently characterizes Richmond politics. At the same time, certain groups of whites resisted the first African American mayor and his supporters in the late seventies and early eighties. For example, Teams for Progress, a predominantly white political organization, successfully replaced one member of the liberal black majority with a more conservative black member, thus changing the balance of power on the council.

As those most affected by the program, white contractors resisted almost from the moment of the policy's inception. We argue that the partial demobilization and the indifference of the white population in Richmond had both advantages and disadvantages for black progress. On the one hand, demobilization furnished greater leeway for black leaders to define policy in the city. At the same time, it reduced the possibility that development priorities and the city's social agenda could be influenced by neighborhood-based organizations. It also ensured that Richmond would not develop an interracial political coalition that could establish a policy agenda for the city, and it made regional cooperation across jurisdictions more problematic.

In Chapter 6, we turn to some of the broader questions that emerged from the Richmond set-aside program. We first concentrate on the Supreme Court's treatment of the *Richmond v. Croson* case and other affirmative action issues. Unlike the group convened by Tribe, we believe that the Court's decision was more far-reaching and indicative of the direction the Court is likely to pursue in future cases, particularly those involving state and local government decisions. We reach this conclusion through an analysis of the voting records and opinions on affirmative action of the justices presently on the Court. Given enough appointments, a Democratic president could shape a new Court more favorably disposed to set-asides than are the current justices. Barring this, however, it appears that the Court has given even greater urgency to the task of reconsidering the standard liberal policies for promoting the interests of African Americans.

The final chapter examines the broader questions raised by the *Croson* decision and the practice of set-aside politics in Richmond. We suggest that although the Richmond experience is not perfectly representative of affirmative action in all urban locales, reports from other cities indicate that the Richmond case is more typical than aberrant. We argue that black progress strategies that rely on set-asides and similar forms of affirmative action are vulnerable to challenge on legal, political, and economic grounds, as recent elections in urban America have indicated. The challenge for black leadership is to create a mix of strategies, informed by a common theme, that can respond more effectively to contemporary circumstances than that which guided African American politics in Richmond. We conclude by describing the strengths and weaknesses of an emerging alternative that we label the politics of development.

ONE

The Affirmative Action Debate

Those who have participated in a conversation about affirmative action recognize how emotionally charged such discussions can become. Unlike some political issues that never gain currency outside of Washington, D.C., almost everyone has an opinion on affirmative action. Everyone has a story to tell about why the policy is needed or how it has been corrupted into reverse discrimination. Clearly, discussions of affirmative action—whether in respect to admissions policies in educational institutions, hiring in the private sector, or promotion in government agencies—often become a vehicle for expressing contending views on the critical issues of our time. Affirmative action can hardly be mentioned without exposing people's beliefs about the proper meaning of civil rights, the extent to which historical discrimination should influence current policy, the openness of the American economic system to individual initiative, and the role of race in the United States. It is unsurprising that many scholars point to beliefs about affirmative action as one of the prime examples of persisting racial cleavages in the nation.

This chapter examines the intellectual positions that have been advanced on these questions. We begin with a presentation of the most common defenses of affirmative action as developed in judicial opinions and the policy arena as well as by various philosophers. We show how proponents have come to believe that affirmative action is both a justifiable and necessary component of African American progress. We then summarize the major critiques of affirmative action. We explore the arguments presented by American conservatives and the critiques advanced by progressive and nationalist scholars. The final section of the chapter delineates the key themes that emerge from the debate between the supporters and critics of affirmative action.

Defending Affirmative Action

The defense of affirmative action normally begins with the claim that these programs are a legitimate extension of the civil rights movement. According to the standard argument, civil rights leaders recognized that overturning the legal basis of segregation and removing barriers to voting rights had to be complemented eventually by policies that eliminated obstacles to economic advancement. They believed that the persistence of racial discrimination, manifested in both crude and subtle forms, hindered the capacity of African Americans to climb the ladder of economic opportunity. The development of affirmative action policies for admission to educational institutions and hiring procedures in the public and private sectors was one of the standard ways that civil rights leaders and black elected officials attempted to combat this problem. Supporters thus maintain that affirmative action policies represent an effort to ensure that, as Justice Thurgood Marshall has phrased it, equality of opportunity is a living reality, not an empty promise, in modern America.

Affirmative action's origins reside in a series of executive orders that were issued by Presidents John F. Kennedy and Lyndon B. Johnson and in legislation passed during their administrations. In March 1961, Kennedy issued Executive Order 10925 which, for the first time, "placed the full prestige of the presidency behind the moral imperative of non-discrimination."[1] Kennedy outlawed discrimination in federal contracting, gave the attorney general the power to bring suit against violators, and called for "affirmative action" to counter the effects of discrimination (40). Title VII of the 1964 Civil Rights Act forbade discrimination in "hiring, promotion, firing, transfer, training and pay, among all employers, employment agencies and labor unions engaged in industry effecting commerce."[2] A year after the passage of Title VII, Johnson signed Executive Order 11246 which "enjoined government contractors and others receiving government funds to promote hiring of blacks and other minorities." In addition, section 8A of the Small Business Act (1965) established minority set-asides by requiring that a portion of government contracts be reserved for minority-owned firms.

From the outset, an unresolved tension marked the concept of affirmative action. On the one hand, Kennedy, Johnson, and their allies in Congress insisted that it had nothing to do with preferential treatment or the establishment of quotas based on race and gender. They argued that it was simply an aggressive means of promoting and enforcing the principle of nondiscrimination. On the other hand, receipt of federal funds required employers to demonstrate their compliance with the law. This led to the gathering of statistical information about the racial and gender composition of an employer's workforce. In later years, the emphasis on statistical results would result in a more expansive interpretation of affirmative action in which the criteria for compliance required employers to set specific numerical targets as an indication of their commitment to nondiscrimination.

Ironically, the more expansive notion of affirmative action took root in Richard M. Nixon's administration in the late 1960s and early 1970s. During this period, the Equal Employment Opportunity Commission (EEOC) and the Department of Labor began to issue regulations that further refined the meaning of Executive Order 11246. The Department of Labor required every major government contractor and subcontractor to provide an "evaluation of utilization" of minority group members that included "an analysis of minority group representation" by job category.[3] By 1971, the guidelines also included a requirement that contractors have goals with specific timetables to improve performance in the areas in which their utilization of minority personnel was deficient. In the same period, the EEOC started to file amicus briefs in court cases that sought to promote "specific hiring goals and timetables" as a policy consistent with Executive Order 11246.[4] Moreover, in the early 1970s, Congress amended the Civil Rights Act (1964) to bring the policies of local municipalities under the jurisdiction of the EEOC.

From 1980 to 1995, the public and intellectual defense of affirmative action was carried on primarily (though not exclusively) by organizations, individuals, and elected officials on the more liberal side of the political spectrum. Support for affirmative action has come from traditional civil rights organizations, such as the National Association for the Advancement of Colored People (NAACP), that have defended the policy in the courts and have worked to establish hiring and promotion programs in the private sector through their informal contacts with corporate America. Affirmative action has also been an integral part of the programs developed by African Americans upon their election to office in urban America. Preferential treatment in city hiring and contracting has been used as a method to pursue a "black agenda" just as, its supporters note, other ethnic groups pursued similar agendas when they obtained political power. Affirmative action has also been employed at many state institutions, particularly universities and professional programs, in order to increase minority representation in higher education and the professions. And there are many social theorists, philosophers, and journalists who have defended the program in scholarly and popular outlets.

The courts have played an important role in the adjudication of affirmative action claims. Until the Reagan administration succeeded in altering the ideological composition of the federal courts, proponents of affirmative action believed that litigation was an important element in the continuation of the civil rights struggle. In the judicial system, supporters have typically employed a variant of what Bernard Boxill has called the "backward looking argument," maintaining that the history of slavery and discrimination has prevented blacks from "being more nearly equal in income, education and well-being to other groups who did not suffer from slavery or the extent and kind of discrimination from which blacks have suffered."[5] Most of the briefs supporting affirmative action that have come to the Supreme Court include a claim about the necessity of using the policy to remedy past discrimination. And most of the justices who have regularly supported affirmative action plans have argued that it is a necessary remedial step in response to a discriminatory history. The writings of Harry Blackmun, William Brennan, and Thurgood Marshall frequently refer to the American past in their opinions supporting affirmative action programs.

In philosophical terms, both utilitarian and rights-based liberals have published justifications of preferential treatment. The utilitarian argument is a forward-looking perspective that typically focuses on the benefits presumably derived from the implementation of affirmative action policies. Utilitarians concentrate on the good that society as a whole will eventually obtain from the passage of affirmative action. Thus, a utilitarian might suggest that affirmative action provides role models for minority youth that may well increase their opportunities in the future. A utilitarian might also contend that affirmative action will promote interaction among the races and eventually lead to a less segregated society. Or they might argue that affirmative action is a way of ensuring that the talents of a segment of the population are not squandered, but eventually employed for the benefit of the entire population. On the Supreme Court, Justice John Paul Stevens has sometimes suggested that this criterion ought to replace the historical argument as the principal justification for these policies.[6]

Rights-based liberals such as Ronald Dworkin have also defended affirmative action but on different and more complicated grounds. Writing about the Defunis case on admission to law school, Dworkin notes that all individuals have a right to "treatment as an equal" in which their "interests be treated as fully and sympathetically as the interests of any others when the law school decides whether to count race as a pertinent criterion for admission."[7] This does not necessarily mean that individuals also have a right to perfectly "equal treatment." As Dworkin puts it, "An individual's right to be treated as an equal means that his [sic] potential loss must be treated as a matter of concern, but that loss may nevertheless be outweighed by the gain to the community as a whole" (227). Further, Dworkin asserts that "any admissions policy must put some applicants at a disadvantage, and a policy preference for minority applicants can reasonably be supposed to benefit the community as a whole, even when the loss to candidates . . . is taken into account" (228).

Dworkin's conception of "gain to the community" is not a utilitarian one. Whether affirmative action actually increases the general welfare is an empirical question that he believes should be at the core of the debate about particular policies. Dworkin's "gain to the community" is an ideal conception not connected to empirical arguments about the furtherance of individual preferences. He suggests that it is related to the conception of equality which, in the long term, would allow more citizens to be treated with equal respect. Overall, he contends that "racial criteria are not necessarily the right standards for deciding which applicants should be accepted by law schools. But neither are intellectual criteria, nor indeed, any other set of criteria. The fairness—and constitutionality—of any admissions program must be tested in the same way. It is justified if it serves a proper policy that respects the right of all members of the community to be treated as equals, but not otherwise."[8]

Two assumptions embedded in the defense of affirmative action in the political arena are especially significant for our discussion. First, most supporters have come to argue that affirmative action is indispensable to promoting black economic progress. In the minds of those who support affirmative action, it is a link in the chain of minority advancement, a necessary if insufficient condition for economic progress. Affirmative action proponents believe that its elimination would be, on a practical level, a major setback to the capacity of minorities to compete in a society where discrimination remains a significant obstacle.

A second assumption is displayed in the rhetoric utilized by affirmative action supporters to define their opponents. They tend to portray opposition to affirmative action as resistance to the cause of civil rights. If affirmative action is simply the natural extension of the logic embedded in the civil rights movement, opposition to the policy serves the interest of reactionary elements in society. For example, much of the commentary about the Reagan administration's position on civil rights and the reaction to Supreme Court decisions such as *Croson* was advanced in this vein. Liberals suggested that the Rehnquist court had struck a blow against civil rights and had granted a victory to those who desired to "turn back the clock." In Richmond, Virginia, those who had backed the set-aside ordinance maintained that race relations had been harmed by the Court's opinion.

Supporters of affirmative action have constantly reminded Americans that the elimination of legal segregation has not ended discrimination. They have argued that the stubborn persistence of discrimination and its accompanying economic disparities keep the civil rights vision alive and relevant. Those who criticize the standard liberal approach believe that its relevance may actually be exhausted. Critics maintain that the positive effects of affirmative action are at best limited, and they contend that the civil rights paradigm may have increasingly less relevance to the difficulties that face the African American community thirty years after the passage of the Civil Rights Act (1964).

Conservatives and Affirmative Action

Conservative arguments against affirmative action were launched almost from the moment of the policy's inception. Indeed, some observers now believe that opposition to affirmative action enhanced the capacity of the Republican party to wean white voters away from the Democrats in the 1970s and 1980s.[9] The conservative stance holds that affirmative action has undermined our cherished American values, philosophical commitment to equality of opportunity, and political-economic attachment to the free market. The elaboration of the conservative position has taken three main directions. First, a number of philosophers, social theorists, legal scholars, and judges have produced a body of scholarship and judicial opinions which argues that affirmative action policy violates the equal protection clause of the Fourteenth Amendment and actually subverts the meaning of the civil rights movement by substituting racial quotas for the principle of color blindness. Second, conservatives have contended that the economics of affirmative action require interference with the operation of the market that will, in the long run, diminish the material opportunities of African Americans. Finally, many conservatives have asserted that affirmative action is psychologically damaging to the self-image and self-esteem of the individual beneficiaries.

The first argument received its most prominent initial exposition in 1975 with the publication of Nathan Glazer's influential *Affirmative Discrimination*. Glazer argues that the notion of affirmative action underwent an extremely important shift in the seventies: "Until then, affirmative action meant to seek out and prepare members of minority groups for better jobs and educational opportunities. . . . But in the early 1970s affirmative action came to mean much more than advertising opportunities actively, seeking out those who might not know of them, and preparing those who might not yet be qualified. It came to mean the setting of statistical requirements based on race, color, and national origin for employers and educational institutions."[10] Interestingly, Glazer believes that the transformation was occurring in the midst of an avowedly conservative administration. Despite Nixon's public opposition to quotas, the expansive interpretation of affirmative action took root during his administration (37).

Glazer points to three phenomena that contributed to the reinterpretation of affirmative action's meaning. First, he argues that the "civil rights bureaucrats," especially those in the EEOC and at the Civil Rights Commission (CRC), began to maintain that proof of nondiscrimination required the examination of results and not merely the process of admission, hiring, and promotion. Glazer maintains that with this refocusing, bureaucrats redefined the meaning of the Civil Rights Act so that, as one official told the *Harvard Law Review*, "The anti-preferential treatment provisions (of Title VII) are a big zero, a nothing, a nullity. They don't mean anything at all to us" (53). Second, Glazer suggests that the courts were increasingly involved in policy making and that judges themselves began to endorse quotas as an appropriate judicial remedy for discrimination. Glazer argues that the courts, influenced by the "endlessly ingenious" resistance of southern states in voting rights cases, began to apply the same statistical rule in nondiscrimination claims that it had to litigation over access to the ballot (49–50). Finally, he suggests that the civil rights caucus in Congress had acceded to the reinterpretation when it passed a bill on the Equal Employment Opportunity Commission in 1972 that expanded the commission's powers and winked at its activities on the equal opportunity front (40).

Glazer argues that the new meaning of affirmative action was morally bankrupt and practically misguided. He contends that the policy was ethically improper because it redefined the meaning of civil rights in a manner that subverted basic American principles. It "threatens the abandonment of our concern for individual claims to consideration on the basis of justice and equity, now to be replaced with a concern for rights for publicly determined and delimited racial and ethnic groups" (197). In addition, Glazer maintains that its practical implications were questionable, insofar as the policy was both unnecessary and ineffective: it was unnecessary because many blacks had already made significant advances without it, and its effects would be limited because "it is questionable whether they reach in any significant way the remaining and indeed most severe problems involved in the black condition" (69–70).

———

   Free market conservatives such as Thomas Sowell, Walter Williams, and Milton Friedman quickly became important contributors to the burgeoning debate about affirmative action. They concur with Glazer's philosophical stance, though their writings tend to emphasize the policy's presumed economic failures. They believe that affirmative action imposes unwarranted governmental restrictions on voluntary exchange.[11] The core of their position is the contention that governmental support of racial preferment policies attacks the capitalist order itself, the real engine of opportunity in American culture. Free market conservatives maintain that such an attack is misguided because it is grounded in two flawed assumptions: (1) that capitalism is inherently discriminatory and (2) that existing economic disparities among groups in our society can be traced to the persistence of racism.[12]
   For instance, Thomas Sowell and Walter Williams argue that an operating market does not recognize race or gender but works according to economic laws that minimize these factors. They argue that if businesses can succeed by hiring minorities at slightly lower wages, they would certainly do so, if those hired could perform the job adequately. In addition, Sowell and Williams maintain that claims about persistent racism in the United States are vastly overblown. They claim that liberals tend to point to racism as the explanation for economic disparities while ignoring other phenomena such as racial differences in age, geography, and education. Sowell argues, "Statistics have shown that black faculty members earn less than white faculty members, but as these data are broken down by field of specialization, by number of publications, by possession (or non-possession) of a Ph.D. and by ranking of institution that issues it, then the black-white income difference not only shrinks, but disappears, and in some fields reverses with black faculty earning more than whites with the same characteristics."[13]

Free market conservatives agree with Glazer that affirmative action and other policies developed by black leadership are not logical extensions of the original civil rights vision. They are reluctant to grant moral legitimacy to programs that they believe are inherently flawed and self-serving. Sowell, for example, has always rejected the universal claims of affirmative action supporters by raising the issue of class. He argues that affirmative action disproportionately benefits advantaged blacks and creates within the black community an economic division that is greater than the gap between blacks and whites: "Those blacks with less education and less job experience—the truly disadvantaged—have been falling farther and farther behind their white counterparts under affirmative action, during the very same years when blacks with more education and more job experience have been advancing economically, both absolutely and relative to their white counterparts."[14]

Free market conservatives also maintain that the pursuit of affirmative action by black leadership has, in fact, generated a white backlash with serious repercussions for the condition of African Americans. They contend that at times the backlash has taken the form of simply assuming that any black who holds a reputable positions does not really deserve it. On other occasions, conservatives note that the backlash takes a more virulent form. Walter Williams, for example, has gone so far as to argue that some of the recent race-baiting incidents at universities and violence against blacks in American cities are attributable in part to resentment at the policies of racial preferment.

Free market conservatives may acknowledge that the civil rights agenda was a useful tool against overt forms of discrimination such as poll taxes, restrictive housing covenants, and segregated public accommodations, but they suggest that it has limited utility in the 1990s. In fact, some black conservatives such as Sowell and Williams imply that almost all political responses (except those that contribute to further deregulation of the market) are of limited utility. As Walter Williams argues, such reforms will ensure that there will be no need for "second-best" solutions because opportunity will exist for everyone.[15] Much of Sowell's work is intended to demonstrate how minority groups other than African Americans have succeeded in American society by eschewing the political arena and concentrating on achieving economic success.[16]

The final element of conservative attack on affirmative action focuses on psychology and culture. Some African American conservatives have argued that liberal programs such as welfare and affirmative action have promoted cultural pathologies and a mentality of dependency. Indeed, they argue that the traditional virtues of African Americans—self-help, personal tenacity, and community responsibility—have been undermined by well-intentioned liberal policies. In recent years, Shelby Steele's work in this vein has garnered significant attention. In *The Content of Our Character*, Steele argues that one legacy of racial discrimination in America has been the development among blacks of a "disbelieving anti-self" that "believes our wounds are justified by our own unworthiness and that entrenches itself as a lifelong voice of doubt."[17] Steele argues that this anti-self has been so completely internalized that "black Americans today are oppressed more by doubt than by racism" (54). Affirmative action policies may intend to promote black interests but, in Steele's mind, they only succeed in reinforcing an unproductive psychology: "Racial preferences implicitly mark whites with an exaggerated superiority, just as they mark blacks with an exaggerated inferiority. They not only reinforce America's oldest myth, but, for blacks, they have the effect of stigmatizing the already stigmatized" (120).

In the 1980s, the major strains of the conservative attack on affirmative action were institutionalized in the Reagan administration. William Bradford Reynolds, assistant attorney general for civil rights, was the administration's point guard in this respect. During Reagan's first term, Reynolds attempted to influence the manner in which the solicitor general framed the government's argument in various affirmative action cases. He prodded the solicitor general's office to file briefs attacking the entire principle of affirmative action, even in instances where staff lawyers believed the facts of the case could not uphold such a broad-based claim. After the resignation of Solicitor General Rex Lee, the Reagan administration appointed Charles Fried to that position, and Reynolds had no more prodding to do, primarily because Fried shared his belief in the unconstitutionality of most affirmative action programs.[18] When the Supreme Court handed down its decision in *Richmond v. Croson*, Fried described it as the justification for all of his work in the past four years.

Reynolds's argument coincides essentially with Glazer's, but it was articulated in a more politically volatile manner. Reynolds attempted to develop an historical interpretation that portrayed affirmative action as an unfortunate deviation from the original goals of the civil rights movement. He asserts that, contrary to what its critics charged, the Reagan administration was in fact deeply committed to civil rights. Reynolds interprets civil rights as equality under the law operating in a color-blind manner. In his opinion, it was not the Reagan administration but black leadership that had subverted the meaning of civil rights and betrayed the intent behind the historic legislation of the 1960s. In a 1985 article in the *Yale Law Journal*, Reynolds notes that regrettably many of the people in the forefront of the movement advocated practices in direct violation of it. The essence of his argument is that in the 1980s civil rights could be protected by resolute opposition to the policies endorsed (and sometimes practiced) by black leadership.[19]

Besides the public articulation of this position, the Reagan administration attempted to replace the personnel at both the CRC and EEOC with staff who shared the appropriate ideology on civil rights. With the appointment of Clarence Thomas to the EEOC and people such as Clarence Pendleton to the CRC, the Reagan team issued an explicit challenge to black leadership and its definition of civil rights. These personnel decisions resulted in highly visible confrontations with the traditional civil rights leadership and, on numerous occasions, the president not only defended his conception of civil rights but maintained that orthodox civil rights leaders were only a special interest who spoke primarily on behalf of their own interests and not for the good of all African Americans.

The conservative response to affirmative action undoubtedly generated an important challenge to the liberal orthodoxy within intellectual circles, though initially many liberals did not take the challenge as seriously as it warranted. At a minimum, conservatives raised valuable questions about how affirmative action programs actually worked. In some liberal circles there was a tendency to assume that the mere existence of such policies contributed to black progress. In fact, few studies attempted to discern what these programs had accomplished. By focusing on the class bias associated with affirmative action, conservatives questioned whether the emerging black political class was pursuing an agenda that had only limited benefits for the majority of their constituency. Moreover, conservatives demanded that liberals demonstrate that affirmative action was a necessary rung on the ladder of black progress.

Conservative arguments about affirmative action also raised a host of considerations bearing on the more general issue of black progress. By the early 1980s, the limited nature of black advancement was so evident that even if one did not agree with the conservative analyses, it was clear that they raised strategic considerations that had to be addressed. Questions about affirmative action quickly broadened into a host of considerations bearing on the more general issue of black progress. For example, to what extent should black leaders in particular and African Americans in general be concerned about a "white backlash" in formulating their policies, and was it necessary to form interracial political coalitions to push an urban agenda? To what extent would the African American population need to rely on traditions of self-help and community responsibility instead of political activism and governmental policy for future progress? To what extent should education for young black Americans attempt to develop entrepreneurial skills?

There were significant limitations in the capacity of conservatives to answer these questions. Free market arguments contained a curious ahistorical strain. Conservative celebrations of the marketplace and of American capitalism more generally have typically lacked a substantive analysis of structural changes in the national or world economy in recent decades. Readers of Sowell and Williams, for instance, are unlikely to find any attention to the transformation of an industrial society into a postindustrial information economy. Nor is there much discussion of what the increasing internationalization of capitalism means for the citizenry in general and African Americans in particular. We are tempted to suggest that solid historical analysis would simply get in their way, because it might then be more difficult to attribute every problem in contemporary America to liberal programs.

Conservatives also exhibit an almost utopian faith in the free market. They assume that citizens live and prosper best in a situation where a state does not perform functions any more extensive than its responsibility as a police officer. In the world of Sowell and Williams, there is hardly any room for politics besides the necessity of reducing the functions that the state has unfortunately assumed. In none of their major works do they address questions of voter turnout, control of the American state, accountability of elected officials, or what African Americans could possibly accomplish by political action. In an ideal situation, conservatives seem to believe that politics is simply a diversion from the real business of life. Consequently, while conservatives chastise liberals for not attending to the results of affirmative action programs, they themselves fail to consider fully the political context and dilemmas facing black citizens and their political leaders.

The Progressive Critique of Affirmative Action

The debate about affirmative action in the United States has typically been framed in terms of the two perspectives that have just been presented. Liberals claim that the policy is necessary to provide equality of opportunity and conservatives respond by asserting that affirmative action is merely reverse discrimination that undermines the principle it professes to uphold. In recent years, a growing body of scholars have attempted to criticize the standard defense of affirmative action without endorsing the positions articulated by Glazer, Sowell, and Williams. The emerging progressive critique of affirmative action questions the priority that the policy has received in black progress strategies while maintaining that positive governmental action is necessary to remedy market inequities and advance black interests.

This position has been elaborated by a number of scholars and intellectuals, including William Julius Wilson, Adolph Reed Jr.,[20] and the neoliberals associated with the *New Republic*. By placing the analyses of Reed, Wilson, and neoliberal journalists in the same category, we do not mean to minimize the extent to which their analyses diverge on a host of important issues. Reed, for example, has published a harsh criticism of Wilson, claiming that Wilson has inadvertently accepted many of the assumptions about social policy advanced by the Reagan administration.[21] Despite the obvious differences between Wilson and Reed, we believe that our categorization is justified by their common emphasis on the significance of the transformation of the American economy for African American citizens in urban areas, their commitment to the desirability of using government intervention to modify market priorities, and their insistence that the civil rights vision no longer provides an adequate explanation and response to the present dilemma of black Americans. We would emphasize, however, that our categorization refers to a general stance about affirmative action and not to the entire range of social policy issues.

Wilson's controversial book, *The Declining Significance of Race*, is one of the first efforts to describe and explain the growth of the black middle class and the simultaneous expansion of impoverishment and alienation among blacks in inner cities. Densely argued and complicated, the book provoked a heated response in some scholarly circles. Contrary to some critical assessments, Wilson does not argue that racial discrimination has disappeared in American life. His major thesis is that, "in the economic sphere, class has become more important than race in determining black access to privilege and power."[22] In addition, Wilson maintains that many of the policies pursued by black leadership either reflect or sometimes exacerbate the class divisions that have emerged within the African American community.

Although Wilson does not necessarily oppose affirmative action, he contends that its principal benefits were distributed to those blacks who had already escaped the worst conditions of urban America: "Their major impact has been in the higher paying jobs of the expanding service-producing industries in both the corporate and government sectors. The rapid growth of these industries has also contributed to the significant gains that talented and educated blacks have made in white collar positions" (110–11). For the majority of the black poor, affirmative action has been simply irrelevant. "It cannot be overemphasized that liberal programs such as affirmative action, although effective in enhancing job opportunities for more privileged blacks, are not really designed to deal with barriers to desirable jobs that are the result of the use of increasing automation, the relocation of industries, the segmentation of the labor market, and the shift from goods producing to service producing industries" (179).

By pointing to the class-based consequences of affirmative action, Wilson appears to concur with Sowell's analysis. Indeed, Wilson has been roundly criticized as a closet conservative. Yet, unlike Sowell, Wilson is in reality no celebrant of or apologist for the natural outcomes of the market. Indeed, Wilson's work explicitly criticizes the Panglossian outlook on the market advanced by Sowell and Williams. Wilson insists that the transformation of American capitalism from an industrial to a postindustrial economy has impacted most severely on urban blacks. In particular, he points to the decline of high-wage unionized employment, which had not required education beyond the high school level, as a major factor in the decreasing opportunity available to African Americans (144–82).

Wilson's recent work, most prominently *The Truly Disadvantaged*, expands upon this analysis. Drawing upon studies of predominantly black neighborhoods in Chicago, Wilson examines the changing demographics of the inner city. He contends that in the 1940s and 1950s, residential segregation patterns contributed to vertical integration within black neighborhoods—black schoolteachers, physicians, and businesspeople worked and lived among the black working class and poor. Wilson maintains that the economic transformation of urban America has combined with better housing opportunities for middle-class blacks. He describes the result of these trends as the development of "hypersegregated" inner cities that have increasing concentrations of poverty, alienation, crime, and teenage pregnancy. Once again, Wilson argues that affirmative action provides little opportunity for those remaining in these areas. He does not believe, however, that extolling the virtues of the marketplace will do much good if the audience has neither the opportunity nor the skills to enter it.[23]

While Wilson's work emphasizes the structural changes in the American economy that have diminished the life chances of black city dwellers, Adolph Reed Jr.'s work focuses more closely on the actual policies of African American political leaders who constitute what he labels the "new black urban machine."[24] Reed argues that leaders of the new urban machine throughout the United States have embraced the premises of "growth politics." In essence, they have pursued a strategy of economic development that calls for a partnership with corporate enterprise in order to produce the jobs and general economic growth that they believe are indispensable to create and maintain urban prosperity. Unlike Sowell and Williams, Reed does not believe that black leadership has conducted anything resembling an attack on the capitalist order. To the contrary, he contends that key elements of growth politics—tax abatements for business, efforts to attract and retain corporate headquarters, and the construction of convention centers and festival malls—are predicated on very traditional notions of trickle-down economics, now redefined as critical to black progress. In Reed's mind, black mayoral administrations developed a "capacity to displace potential conflict by reinventing development agendas that had potentially disadvantageous outcomes for black constituents as campaigns for the defense of racial self-respect embodied in black officials."[25]

In this vein, Reed suggests that set-asides and other affirmative action programs enable black leadership to portray conservative development strategies as consistent with more general "black interests." Reed criticizes these premises at almost every turn. First, he maintains that there is no evidence to support the assumption that benefits have trickled down to the majority of the population in urban areas. He contends that inner cities are worse off than they were thirty years ago, by whatever index of misery is employed. Second, he does not believe that black leaders were, as they are sometimes portrayed, absolutely compelled to pursue growth politics as the best of the available options. He argues that city leaders have gone on bended knee to corporate leaders when they could have been much more aggressive in exacting revenues from them. Finally, Reed contends (as Wilson does) that set-asides and other affirmative action policies have done little for blacks who are outside of the emerging professional class and that the black urban machine has not addressed the "problem of dispossession among its black constituency."[26]

As proof of his contentions, Reed utilizes the siting and construction of the new Atlanta airport in the 1980s as a case study. During the 1970s, Atlanta underwent a vigorous debate about whether a second airport ought to be built and where it ought to be located. While the Atlanta airport is often called the paradigm example of how black leadership and affirmative action policies can be utilized to shape corporate policies to promote black interests, Reed offers a dissenting analysis. He maintains that there was good reason not to build a new airport (and certainly not to devote public resources to it) and insists that Mayor Maynard Jackson was unwilling to break with the developmental consensus that ruled Atlanta politics. Instead, Jackson went along with the plans and carved out a "black interest" through the use of a "joint venture" affirmative action plan that gave preference in hiring for construction work to majority contractors that had teamed up with minority subcontractors. Although the plan was vigorously criticized and indeed modified and diluted in response to the criticisms of the developmental elite, Reed argues that the plan's focus was on "modifying the allocational dimension of a development policy objective" that was not formulated by Jackson's black governing constituency.[27]

In addition, Reed suggests that the equation of programs such as affirmative action with the "black interest" has, in some important way, contributed to the demobilization of the larger black community and the subsequent neglect of its policy interest. He argues that few black leaders of the new urban regimes have sought to employ the latent political clout of their constituency. Instead, he depicts the new black urban elite as traditional machine apparatchiks, parceling out a few benefits and serving as an internal check on the potential anger and rage of their constituency, while neglecting its most significant problems. Indeed, he maintains that black leaders like Andrew Young have occasionally implemented regressive policies, such as an attempt to create a "vagrant free zone in downtown Atlanta," that are reminiscent of "Great Britain's march into downtown Calcutta."[28]

Both Wilson and Reed argue that the majority of African Americans would be better served if the major political emphasis of their leaders was no longer placed on programs such as affirmative action. Wilson endorses the formation of a national industrial policy agenda that would be directed at alleviating the effects of economic dislocation. He suggests that, while some aspects of this policy might be race specific, its principal emphasis would be on coping with economic dislocation and not on racial compensation.[29] Reed argues that black leaders must become more aggressive in extracting tax revenues from corporations based within their environs and they must be willing to repoliticize their constituency, in order to utilize the potential influence of mobilized masses. Thus, both scholars imply that reliance on affirmative action as a cornerstone of black opportunity will do little to alter the more ominous trends confronting the African American community today.

Wilson's and Reed's arguments help to explain a number of the significant features of the affirmative action policies adopted by black leadership. By situating these programs within the history of policies adopted by black elected officials, they provide a context that is missing in both conservative and liberal perspectives. Sowell and Williams, for example, portray the civil rights vision as one that has become increasingly hostile to capitalist principles. But arguments such as Reed's furnish a much more sophisticated analysis of the relationship of affirmative action to urban development in contemporary America. Reed demonstrates how affirmative action can be linked to development strategies that are in many ways shaped and defined by market priorities. He prompts us to think about affirmative action as part of an accommodationist political stance that does not represent a fundamental assault on market principles.

The perspectives advanced by Reed and Wilson also encourage us to view liberal arguments in a different light. In one sense, Reed's and Wilson's criticisms of liberalism are not very different from those raised by conservatives. They believe that affirmative action has a class bias, that it does not advance the interests of the black majority, and that it may not be the most appropriate policy for black leadership to endorse. But their criticisms of the liberal position attempt to expand the possible options beyond those offered by conservatives. Reed and Wilson emphasize that the choices may not be simply between an unregulated market and affirmative action but between the development of a different orientation about economic development in the city and a different way of combining civil rights activism with economic opportunity.

Yet their perspectives have not been connected to a compelling political alternative. Wilson has suggested that national policy that is not defined in racial terms but that includes features addressing the racial-class dimensions of urban poverty would distribute benefits more widely and reach the "truly disadvantaged." Yet he is curiously silent about the politics that would precede the formation of such a consensus. What kind of political organization would be necessary, within both urban areas and the country at large? Who would define the specific needs and policies that such a program would address? What would be the role of the so-called underclass in its development? How would activists pressure the Democratic Party to adopt such a platform when a significant element in the party is moving in the opposite direction?

Reed shifts the perspective to the local level. Arguing against the fatalism frequently contained in urban politics literature that emphasizes the fiscal constraints on black leadership and the shift of power to the federal government and multinational corporations, Reed maintains that African American leadership could do much more than it has recently accomplished. Reed has performed a valuable service in demonstrating how black leadership can potentially be the subject—not simply the object—of policy. Yet here as well, we cannot discern a well-defined political response. Reed encourages the extraction of more revenues from corporations and outrageous action such as provoking a constitutional crisis that will publicize the plight of marginalized people in urban areas, but these suggestions do not amount to a full-fledged political strategy. No movement or organization is specified, no agenda is formulated, and no timetable is specified. In fact, he appears to recognize this absence when he suggests that his ultimate purpose is merely to reopen debate on the politics of black leadership so that alternative choices may emerge in the future.

Nationalist Perspectives

Although black nationalist thought has been the occasional object of study by white scholars, it is rarely mentioned in white intellectual circles. Periodically, it becomes an object of curiosity and concern for whites because a figure such as Louis Farrakhan or a rap group such as Public Enemy receive media attention. Nonetheless, black nationalist thought has a significant presence within the African American community. Nationalist perspectives exercise considerable influence on many black intellectuals. One could argue that it is the dominant perspective within African American Studies departments in higher education. In recent years, for example, many of the critiques of "Eurocentric" curriculums were rooted in perspectives that emerged from black studies departments and from scholars who have examined the standard texts in American education.

Nationalist arguments are also significant within African American artistic circles and in certain segments of the black press.

Nationalist thinking is, however, quite diverse in its themes and emphases. Its various manifestations include a conservative business-oriented nationalism derived from Booker T. Washington, Farrakhan's fiery brand of religious uplift, the cultural nationalism and Afrocentricity of Malena Karenga, the effort of a scholar such as Manning Marable to combine nationalist perspectives with democratic socialism, and the calculating pragmatism of a scholar such as Harold Cruse. Scholars who have attempted to categorize this element of African American thought have pointed to romantic, revolutionary, and bourgeois variants of nationalist beliefs. Romantic nationalism emphasizes the destruction of African values in the black community by colonialism and Eurocentric education and the elevation of an earlier "African glory." Revolutionary nationalism in the United States has called for overturning the American system and establishing a separate black state. Bourgeois nationalism has presented itself as the best strategy for black advancement within the present configuration of power in the United States.

Nationalist beliefs are compatible with differing stances on the worth of affirmative action. A scholar such as Manning Marable defends affirmative action as a minimum policy for enabling blacks to achieve positions of prominence in American society. In this view, affirmative action is merely a new name for the kind of ethnic politics that most groups in the United States have practiced to advance their interests. The fact that it has become extremely controversial is simply an indication of the persistence of discrimination against African Americans. Other nationalists such as Harold Cruse are apt to be much more ambivalent about the policy. They may find it largely irrelevant to their own agenda. Indeed, they may believe that affirmative action is really an integrationist strategy that cannot be defended as furthering the practice of ethnic pluralism.

Cruse's argument is especially interesting because he relates his criticism of affirmative action to both the strategies advanced by black leaders in recent years and, even more controversially, to the entire strategy of integrationism that he believes was at the heart of the civil rights movement. From Cruse's perspective, the discussion of affirmative action must entail an examination of the manner in which black political officials have represented their constituency over the years. In his two major books, *The Crisis of the Negro Intellectual* and *Plural but Equal*, Cruse argues that

African Americans need to rethink their entire reliance on civil rights rhetoric and the political strategy that has been promulgated by black elected officials. He maintains that although the *Brown v. Board of Education* (1954) decision, which outlawed legal segregation in schools, was an important victory, black leaders have since continually drawn the wrong lessons from it. In particular, he argues that black leaders have regularly employed the rhetoric of civil rights to promote their particular interests instead of turning to what he believes was the more preferable course of black economic and political development. Cruse believes that the emphasis has been misguided because the vagueness of the Fourteenth Amendment's equal protection clause could just as easily be used against blacks as in favor of them.[30]

Cruse suggests that affirmative action should really be viewed in terms of his critique of established black leadership. He does not believe that it is true nationalist policy because black leadership itself, he claims, has lost all its nationalist connections: "Lacking even a clear consensus of a social mission, except more of the vague and evanescent idea of 'civil rights,' the new middle class is *empty*, it is an indulgent 'Me' generation, a class that has growing psychic troubles over portents of an uncertain future" (390). Although black leaders might justify affirmative action in nationalist terms to their own constituencies, Cruse implies that it is a policy that reflects its identity crisis insofar as it fails to establish any independent black economic or political power. He notes that, ironically, affirmative action is considered a liberal policy vehemently opposed by conservatives. From his perspective, it serves as a status quo policy that reflects almost entirely the interests of the new black middle class. In Cruse's words, it is "a *class* phenomenon that reflects *class* interests that are much less 'civil' than they are 'economic' and are similar to those of Booker T. Washington" (388).

Cruse's arguments and recommendations about black economic advancement steer a course between that advanced by Sowell and that endorsed by left-wing academics. Cruse maintains that "in the foreseeable future (let us say until the year 2000), black Americans, with or without civil rights reinforcements, must strive to survive economically within the 'rules of the game' of free enterprise, free market American capitalism. The dominant white American economics ideology will neither foster nor sanction any other form of national economic organization" (341). Unlike Sowell, Cruse advances this position as a recognition of reality and not as a celebration of unlimited opportunity. Moreover, he contends that within this system black economic organization must be nationalist in nature.

In keeping with the intentions of the conservative and progressive critiques, Cruse attempts to open a dialogue about the positions of black leadership on the broader questions of what is needed for African American progress. He strongly believes that the construction of a proper intellectual foundation is essential to the articulation of reasonable policy stances. In *The Crisis of the Negro Intellectual,* Cruse concentrates his criticism on the failure of the intellectual leadership in the black community to distance itself from integrationist perspectives. *Plural but Equal* focuses more centrally on the continuing political consequences of this putative failure. Cruse believes that it is critical to consider affirmative action in the context of policies that the black leadership has developed and defended as crucial elements of African American progress.

Cruse's position is simultaneously perceptive, challenging, and problematic. By raising concerns about the reliance of the civil rights vision on favorable court decisions, he demonstrates the precariousness of its foundations. Before the Supreme Court issued its decisions in *Croson* and other civil rights cases, Cruse had noted the questionableness of reliance on the constitutional interpretation of the Fourteenth Amendment's equal protection clause for black progress. He observed that interpretations had differed considerably throughout American history and that the amendment had been utilized most frequently by those who had little concern for African Americans or, in fact, were in direct opposition to their interests. In Cruse's mind, there was no reason to believe that a conservative Supreme Court would not retreat from the commitment of recent years and once again use the ideology of civil rights to counter black interests.

Cruse's position contains its own particular shortcomings. Most critically, his recommendations for the development of a nationalist economy are not reflective of an analysis of national and international economic trends. He explores the necessity of redeveloping nationalist economic practices in urban America but does not connect this presumed necessity to a broader overview of the urban economic situation or to W. E. B. Du Bois's futile efforts to advance a dual economic strategy in the 1940s. The result is that readers have to wonder about the actual substance of the economic practices that Cruse endorses. Several questions arise about Cruse's belief that blacks should work within the rules of the game but should do so in a nationalist manner. Where in fact will African Americans be working? What will they be producing? What degree of education will be necessary for a nationalist economy? How will these economic practices be connected to a more general economic advance?

Key Themes in the Debate

The debate about the legitimacy and practicality of racial preferment raises a host of important questions about civil rights, economic development, and prospects for black progress in the contemporary United States.

The Meaning and Applicability of Civil Rights

Liberals believe affirmative action to be a natural extension of the civil rights movement. They contend that its principal aims and methods are derived from the vision that animated those who brought an end to legal segregation in the 1960s. In addition, liberals hold that the rhetoric of civil rights remains applicable. In a phrase that they themselves often employ, "there is much work left to accomplish" on this front. The political action necessary to improve the conditions of African Americans can thus properly be called civil rights work. Opposition to affirmative action becomes defined as an effort to "turn the clock back" and limit civil rights.

Critics of the liberal position uniformly find these contentions untenable. Conservative arguments maintain that affirmative action perverts the meaning of civil rights and transforms a concept that was intrinsically connected to individual rights into a theory of group entitlement. Progressive critics do not necessarily contest the inclusion of affirmative action under the rubric of civil rights but question whether the civil rights agenda can adequately address the most pressing needs of the African American community. The nationalist perspective enunciated by Harold Cruse also questions the advisability of relying upon civil rights rhetoric as the principal feature of black economic and political strategy. Cruse suggests that the meaning of civil rights is contestable and that at certain political moments (such as the Reagan era) blacks would (and will) not have the power to advance their own definition. He thus believes it may well be counterproductive to focus on civil rights in this manner.

The Strategy Pursued by Black Leadership

Supporters of affirmative action offer an implicit defense of the strategy pursued by black leadership. This is evidenced in some of the Supreme Court decisions where the justices equate the development of affirmative action policies with the pursuit of equal opportunity for all Americans. It is also manifested by scholars of urban politics who have sometimes evaluated the success of black-governed cities by the capacity, at least in part, to develop affirmative action programs. While most liberals would certainly acknowledge the limitations of these policies in addressing the full range of problems in urban America, they would still endorse their implementation.

Critics of affirmative action do not find the defense entirely convincing. Conservative, progressive, and nationalist arguments maintain that affirmative action has a middle-class bias and does not universally improve the conditions for black Americans, regardless of how the restrictions on black political leadership are viewed. Indeed, in all these perspectives, we cannot avoid the implication that black leadership has failed the black community in significant ways. There is less sympathy for the arguments about restrictions and limitations and a more ruthless analysis of black leadership. At times, black leadership is described as self-serving, as when Sowell attributes the defense of affirmative action to the desire of middle-class blacks to maintain their own perquisites in contemporary American society. On other occasions, affirmative action is merely misguided because it cannot achieve the goals that its rhetoric appears to promise. In any event, critics of affirmative action contend that serious consideration of the faults of black leadership is itself a necessary element of developing better strategies for black progress in contemporary America.

The Most Appropriate Strategy for Black Progress

Ultimately, the debate about affirmative action becomes a discussion of how black progress can be achieved in this nation. Liberals who defend the policy maintain that it is an integral element of any plan to integrate African Americans more fully into the U.S. economy. They suggest that, despite the heated debate over the policy, in many places where affirmative action plans have been initiated, they have significantly aided minorities and, at times, have gained acceptance from whites. Liberals note that many corporations who have instituted affirmative action policies have been content with the results and believe that it has enabled them to recruit talent more widely as well as make their products appeal to audiences that might have gone untapped. Richmond's set-aside plan, though not upheld by the Supreme Court, actually had wide acceptance in the city. Liberals rarely argue that affirmative action by itself is sufficient but insist that the elimination of the policy will make progress more difficult to achieve.

Again, critics from a variety of persuasions question the prominence given to affirmative action in the strategy for black progress. Conservatives argue that it unduly antagonizes white Americans and, in the long run, patronizes black citizens. Moreover, they contend that it restricts the operation of the market in such a manner as to limit opportunities for ordinary African Americans while expanding the possibilities for a narrow segment. Finally, they suggest that it reinforces the ideology of victimization that nurtures dependence on government in the black population instead of building upon the tradition of self-reliance in the black community, a value that has historically been crucial to the capacity of African Americans to survive and flourish as a community in a society that enslaved and still discriminates against them.

Conservatives suggest that black progress can be most easily accomplished by adhering to an ideology of equal opportunity. Since they believe that most forms of officially sponsored discrimination against blacks have been removed, the implication is that political agitation in defense of civil rights has become largely irrelevant. Instead, they maintain that the prospects for black advance require a combination of personal initiative, development of an entrepreneurial spirit, and increased commitment to education within the black community. The political activity that they do endorse is limited primarily to the elimination of liberal restraints on the market (indeed, Sowell favors the legalization of drugs as a way of ending drug-related crime in the black community) and a more assertive use of government as a force to protect the citizenry from crime.

Other critics of liberalism are skeptical about affirmative action but for somewhat different reasons. As we have seen, progressives concur with the class-based critique of the policy and seem to believe that the attention given to affirmative action is, in some sense, a diversion from the real needs of the black community. But they do not believe that deregulation of the market is an adequate answer to the actual dilemmas of urban America. Progressives hold that the market is presently organized under corporate imperatives that have resulted in the diminution of opportunities available to black Americans, especially those in urban America who do not possess a college education. In their minds, social policy must be reorganized to address the needs of these people in a more direct manner than either affirmative action or the ideology of equal opportunity does.

Progressives believe that politics ought to have an integral role in the strategy for black advancement. The implications of Wilson's analysis are that a revived Democratic Party might be able to develop a comprehensive urban economic policy that would funnel resources to the cities with programs that would enable residents of urban areas to obtain and retain jobs. In *The Truly Disadvantaged,* he calls for the development of an interracial class-based politics that will do more good for the real needs of

African Americans than affirmative action has to date. Reed concurs with Wilson's emphasis on political activity but in fact suggests that Wilson's recommendations are excessively tame and elitist. Reed maintains that a genuinely social democratic policy that will eventually help African Americans must be the result of a remobilized urban population in which citizenship is revived in direct confrontation with those who presently control the economic and political resources of urban America.

Harold Cruse's nationalist criticism of affirmative action suggests that, in the long run, the policy is yet another chapter in the failed history of African Americans attempting to integrate into white society. By means of contrast, Cruse believes that blacks need to develop a greater degree of ethnic solidarity, especially in the practical areas of economic and political organization. Cruse's nationalism is grounded in a calculation that progress will be best achieved by the development of this independence. White America, he argues, responds to power and influence, not to simple appeals to morality and the Constitution. Such internal development of the black community will build the kind of power that may enable African Americans to extract more resources from the dominant society. Cruse believes, however, that the majority of African Americans in the late nineties can be helped only by a strategy that emphasizes such internal organization. To a degree, this fits with conservative arguments. But Cruse's recommendations that African Americans work within the capitalist system are entirely unrelated to any celebration of the opportunity that such a system might furnish. He simply sees the recommendation as a recognition of the reality under which Americans are likely to live in the foreseeable future.

Cruse's emphasis on political action and an independent black political party also distinguishes him from both the free market conservatives who eschew politics and social democrats such as Wilson who work within the Democratic party. He asserts that individual initiative must be supplemented by collective organization and the effort by African Americans to determine their own fate politically. Unlike Wilson, however, Cruse avers that the Democrat party has become a political dead end and that blacks must wean themselves from it: "Having pushed civil rights legislation to its outer social limits, the Democratic Party had nothing else to offer blacks but good will and some moral support in memory of Martin Luther King." He adds, "The Democrats are no longer capable of accommodating black social priorities, present or future."[31] In Cruse's mind, African American survival requires the kind of political organization that will continually define and pursue interests that can enable black Americans to cope with the dislocation that has overtaken urban America.

———————

The questions that emerge from the theoretical positions that we have sketched form the backdrop to our examination of black politics and affirmative action in Richmond, Virginia. How did the city's African American leadership define its role? What strategies did they pursue to promote the interests of their constituents? How successful were they in moving the city forward?

TWO

Black Politics in Richmond, 1945–89

The quest for black political power in Richmond has passed through four distinct stages. From the mid-1950s until the mid-1960s, African American leaders, under the rubric of an organization called the Crusade for Voters, pursued a strategy of calculated cooperation, attempting to position black citizens so that in city elections they could exercise the balance of power among competing white groups. The second phase of black politics in Richmond took shape in 1966 when black leaders began to dissolve their relationship with the most prominent white organization, Richmond Forward, and embarked on a journey to achieve independent political power. When African American citizens succeeded in electing a black majority to the city council in 1977 and council members subsequently selected the African American Henry L. Marsh III as mayor, a new era commenced in which blacks exercised direct political power. In 1982, however, the black majority on the council became divided when Roy West, an African American opponent of the Marsh faction, defeated one of its members and not only became mayor but frequently joined with the white council members to thwart the will of the black members. The ensuing years, often dominated by the Marsh-West rivalry, were characterized by an ossification of black politics in which few new ideas and even fewer new people emerged to speak to the condition of black Richmonders.

Richmond's status as the former capital of the Confederacy ensured that the black political struggle would carry important symbolic overtones. In the early 1960s, whites who hoped that race relations in the United States could be significantly improved without disruption and upheaval pointed to Richmond as a model that other southern cities could follow. But when it appeared that blacks might actually gain political control of Jefferson

Davis's capital because of the changing black-white population ratio, many whites in Richmond and in the Virginia General Assembly maneuvered to prevent demography from becoming political destiny. Given Richmond's symbolic stature in the quest for black political power, it is not surprising that the struggle in the city had national reverberations. In the sixties and early seventies, Richmond's school integration strategy, which called for a consolidation of city and county school systems, wound up before the U.S. Supreme Court (where a sitting justice, Lewis Powell, had to recuse himself from the case because of his previous position as chairman of the Richmond School Board). In the early and mid-1970s, the city's proposed annexation of part of Chesterfield County was also litigated in the Supreme Court around the question of whether the annexation impermissibly diluted black voting rights. And, in the eighties, the efforts of Richmond's black majority to promote economic development in the African American community through a set-aside program resulted in the landmark *Richmond v. Croson* decision.

This chapter traces the development of modern black politics in Richmond. We examine its four principal stages and the issues prominent in each phase. We also pay special attention to the manner in which African American leaders attempted to define the purpose of black politics during the last four decades and how these leaders endeavored to educate, mobilize, and enlist the support of the broader black population. For the most part, this requires us to examine the stance adopted by black political figures in regard to the various business and corporate-oriented groups (Richmond Civic Association, Richmond Forward, and the Team of Progress) that figured so prominently in the politics of the white community. But it also demands that we examine how division within the black community was handled by those attempting to shape and define African American political life.

Striving for Influence

In 1948, a business-inspired political reform movement succeeded in changing Richmond's form of governance.[1] During the previous thirty years the city had been governed by a mayor-council system. Thirty-two members were elected to the bicameral council: twelve to a board of aldermen and twenty to the common council. Elections were on a ward basis; there was partisan campaigning; and, as in many southern locales, the Democratic primary was often tantamount to election. The board of aldermen and the common council possessed the power to veto legislation passed by the other chamber. Downtown business interests aligned under the rubric of the Richmond Citizens' Association (RCA) had come to believe that city government was entirely too parochial and cumbersome and ought to be replaced with a more streamlined system. Like other business and middle-class reformers in the South, RCA members believed that Richmond had to adopt a more forward-looking strategy to ensure that it would not be eclipsed by competitor cities throughout the region. In their opinion, a more efficient government would ensure Richmond's continuing regional prominence (176–82). The 1948 charter reform reduced the council members from thirty-two to nine; it abolished the ward system and replaced it with nonpartisan at-large elections; and it reduced the power of the mayor and created the post of city manager as a way of removing essential decision making from parochial and ward-based interests (177–78).

The RCA successfully enlisted local blacks in the charter reform campaign of the 1940s. In light of the voting rights activities of the sixties and seventies in which civil rights groups have worked to replace at-large elections with ward-based systems, black support for charter reform may appear surprising. But the combination of a poll tax and racial gerrymandering made it impossible for Richmond blacks to use the ward system to their advantage in the 1940s. Support for RCA's initiative appeared to be a more promising route to influence. A number of prominent RCA members pledged to implement a merit system in city employment. Others suggested that they would be willing to support a black council member as a means of expressing their desire for harmonious race relations.[2]

African Americans became an organized force during the charter campaign and worked to elect Oliver Hill, a prominent black attorney, to the new council. Hill succeeded in becoming the first African American elected to the city council in the twentieth century by running ninth and gaining the final spot on the nine-person council. Hill's victory can be attributed to two critical factors. First, many black voters cast "solid shot" votes for Hill, marking his name on the ballot but no others. Edward Carter, a black man who had served on the council in 1888, proudly announced that he had cast a "a solid shot" for Oliver Hill.[3] At the same time, Hill's support for the charter reform won him a sufficient number of white votes. Although he had not received the endorsement of the RCA, Hill argued that "as a Negro" his experiences could serve the city well as it instituted charter reform and "promoted a wholesome growth for our city at large."[4]

In his victory statement, Hill observed, "I am fully cognizant of the fact that I have been elected by vote of the citizens of Richmond as a whole and I am grateful to my friends of both races who have worked in the campaign that made my election possible."[5]

The vision of a progressive, racially harmonious city that prompted black support for the charter reform would not be realized in the 1950s. First, the RCA's proposals for a "Greater Richmond" were not necessarily compatible with black interests. The roads and highway proposals contained in a master plan endorsed by the RCA are probably the best example of the manner in which recommendations designed to promote downtown business damaged the African American community. Christopher Silver has noted that the street widening and traffic rerouting resulted in "radical surgery on the city's major black residential area in Jackson Ward."[6] He observes that between January 1955 and 1957 "more than seven thousand persons (or 10 per cent of Richmond's black population) were displaced to make way for the Richmond-Petersburg Expressway and the Belvidere Street Extension" (185).

Second, the defense of racial segregation became the driving force in state and regional politics during the 1950s. As black Virginians applauded the Supreme Court for its decisions on school desegregation and praised the circuit court for asserting that the arguments about schools applied to Virginia's system of state parks and recreational facilities, the state's political elite became tenacious defenders of segregationist policies. Abstract visions of racial harmony gave way to bitter political invective and initiatives designed to forestall black political advancement. When the circuit court ruled in 1954 that the initial *Brown v. Board of Education* decision required the Commonwealth to desegregate its state parks, Virginia Attorney General Lindsay Almond undertook an end run around the decision by proposing to lease the parks to private concerns that would not be subject to the ruling. When black plaintiffs argued in 1955 that the Supreme Court decision required the Prince Edward County school system to develop a plan for immediate desegregation, Almond denounced the NAACP "kleagles" as "drunk with power and hell bent in their orgy to cause chaos."[7]

Almond's fulminations were merely part of a more orchestrated defense of segregation that emanated from the powerful Byrd organization. Arguing that the Supreme Court had instigated "the most serious crisis that had occurred since the War between the States," U.S. Senator Harry Byrd made the "all out defense of white supremacy . . . the dominant theme in Virginia politics."[8] Virginia political debate focused less on whether the Supreme Court decision in *Brown* should be resisted and more on precisely how to oppose it. In August and September 1956, a special session of the Virginia General Assembly passed a series of segregationist measures that enshrined massive resistance as state policy, weakened the NAACP, and prompted a satisfied Senator Byrd to remark, "Once again, Virginia offers peaceful leadership to the South and I believe the offer will be accepted" (114).

Richmond, the former capital of the Confederacy, became not only the political leader but the intellectual center of massive resistance as well. James J. Kilpatrick, then the editorial page editor of the *Richmond News Leader,* gained national prominence—or notoriety—for his columns calling upon the region's leaders to revitalize John Calhoun's doctrine of interposition and to defend state sovereignty against the dictatorial intervention of the federal government. As Numan V. Bartley notes, Kilpatrick's writings provided a "theoretical basis for opposition to desegregation."[9] Kilpatrick argued that the Supreme Court's decision was an unconstitutional usurpation of power and that what Virginia was attempting to do was an "honest and honorable effort to restore to government the constitutional process. We are attempting to restore to all the States that final authority over the Constitution that is their high privilege and solemn responsibility."[10]

Black leaders in Richmond had resisted the latest turn in segregationist politics. They joined with white progressives in 1955–56 to work against a referendum proposal that would have enabled localities to decide whether or not to enact the Supreme Court decrees. In an effort to mobilize voters against the referendum item, they formed an organization called the Richmond Committee to Save Public Schools (RCSPS). Their efforts were to no avail as the Byrd machine shepherded the proposal to victory by a statewide margin of more than 2-1. Black participants on the RCSPS were especially disappointed at the turnout in the African American community when it was reported that only four thousand of the almost twelve thousand eligible black voters actually went to the polls.[11]

The outcome of the referendum prompted a number of the participants on the RCSPS to take a hard look at the state of black political mobilization. There were a number of civic organizations in various black neighborhoods, a group called the People's Political and Civic League that had been associated with the Byrd machine and, most importantly, the Richmond Civic Council, a minister-dominated group that had a presence in most of the black neighborhoods. The Richmond Civic Council had presented itself as the political voice of black Richmonders and had been involved in voter registration efforts and the promotion of black candidates for city and state offices.[12] But their inability to mobilize the black community in the face of a statewide segregationist drive highlighted the organization's inherent weaknesses. Members of the RCSPS saw the defeat as an indication of the need to develop a more effective black political presence to complement the legal activism of the NAACP. They felt that the minister-dominated Richmond Civic Council had proven to be incapable of adequately representing black interests, and they sought, in A. J. Dickinson's words, to construct an "independent organization devoted exclusively to voter registration and politics."[13]

The formation in 1958 of the Crusade for Voters was a watershed in the development of the African American political community. After its inception, Crusade leaders focused first on voter registration and building precinct-level organizations in black neighborhoods. The registration drive initiated by the Crusade, the "Miracle of Richmond," increased the number of eligible black voters from a little less than twelve thousand to more than fifteen thousand. Combined with the efforts of the Richmond Civic Council in the first part of the decade, black voters in Richmond had increased from 9 percent of the eligible voters in 1948 to 22 percent in 1960.[14] The Crusade labored to construct elaborate precinct-level organizations as well. The Crusade founders called block meetings in various neighborhoods, established precinct organizations with their own officers and files, and had the precinct groups choose delegates for the executive committee of the Crusade.[15]

Crusade leaders next turned to changing the manner in which black votes were cast. As we have seen, Oliver Hill's victory in 1950 could be attributed at least in part to the practice of casting "solid shot" ballots. When Hill ran for reelection in 1952, he was defeated despite receiving three thousand more votes than he had two years previously. One reason for his defeat was that many fewer black voters used the "solid shot," and thus the increase in Hill's total from 1950 was insufficient to match the increase in votes that some white candidates received from the black community.[16] To black voters, the "solid shot" appeared to be a perfectly rational way of exercising influence. Its use had enabled them to elect Oliver Hill and its abandonment contributed to his defeat.

The Crusade argued, however, that the solid shot strategy was inadequate as an instrument of exercising long-term influence. Instead, the organization endorsed a slate of candidates and worked to ensure that black voters would cast a relatively united vote that would actually give African Americans influence on the outcome of the entire election. The Crusade's slate was decided in secret deliberations of its "research committee" and not released publicly until the Sunday before election day. Ministers announced the list at church services, and social clubs did the same on Sunday afternoon. Crusade leaders believed that the last minute endorsements maximized the organization's power and prevented white politicians from using the race issue—"the candidate of the Negroes"—against other white candidates.[17]

At first, Crusade endorsements were made almost entirely for the practical purpose of increasing, developing, and maximizing black political influence. In the 1960 election, Crusade leaders sent questionnaires to the various candidates soliciting their views on concerns of interest to the organization. Some candidates did not even bother to return the forms. But such treatment did not prevent the Crusade from endorsing them. The organization's leaders wanted to demonstrate that they could deliver a solid majority of black votes to their chosen candidates and by this demonstration ensure that the black community would be included in the policy agenda of council leadership. For example, in the 1960 election the Crusade endorsed several candidates who were also recommended by the Richmond Citizens' Association (RCA). While most of the victorious candidates certainly did not win solely because of the Crusade's efforts, the election hinted that black voting in Richmond could be influential in electing candidates.

A study of the 1960 councilmanic elections and the returns from selected black majority precincts confirm the impression that the Crusade strategy worked and that its endorsements were influential in the black community. The Crusade had endorsed nine of the twenty-two candidates running in the election. The RCA proposed a slate of nine candidates, seven of whom the Crusade also placed on their endorsement list. Seven candidates from each slate were elected. The six candidates who received the most votes were endorsed by both the RCA and the Crusade. The most important indicator of influence with black voters was that the two RCA candidates not endorsed by the Crusade received only a handful of votes in black precincts while white candidates with the Crusade imprimatur harvested a substantial majority of African American ballots.

Crusade leaders had chosen a propitious time to reorient Richmond's black vote. The Richmond Citizens' Association had not been able to sustain the momentum it had had during the charter reform of the late 1940s, and its effectiveness disappeared due to apathy and internecine squabbling. The ban on partisan competition in the 1948 charter removed the possibility that party organizations could be overtly employed to influence councilmanic elections. Moreover, few existing neighborhood-based organizations and associations could effectively deliver votes. The Crusade's operation quickly became one of if not the most efficient political organizations in the city. The results of the 1960 election, in which seven of the nine Crusade-endorsed candidates were elected, appeared to confirm the perception of the Crusade as an emerging political juggernaut. In Dickinson's words, "Such a well-led, tightly organized group with definite goals and supposed control over a disciplined and loyal segment of the electorate could exert leverage far greater than its numerical strength."[18]

In 1962, the Crusade attempted not only to repeat its success but also to utilize its leverage to promote fair employment policies in Richmond city government. The Crusade research committee conducted an investigation of city employment practices and concluded that "over three-fourths of 1,168 colored persons are disproportionately concentrated in the ranks of menial, unskilled, and semi-skilled employment."[19] On the basis of the study, the Crusade sponsored a petition requesting that city employment and promotion be granted "on the basis of ability, without regard to race or creed."[20] The petition was immediately endorsed by two RCA candidates who had not received the Crusade's backing in th 1960 election and, a few weeks before the elections, the city council adopted a resolution that stipulated that city jobs, applications, and promotions should not be refused on the basis of race, creed, color, or arbitrary maximum age limits.[21]

The Crusade's successes in 1960 and 1962 demonstrated that, even with a poll tax, white politicians could ill afford to neglect African Americans' votes and interests. As evidence of the success generated by the strategy of calculated cooperation, the Crusade pointed not only to its electoral success but to the appointment of blacks to some city boards and commissions as well as the establishment of the first biracial commission on human relations in the South. White politicians did not always believe that they had to cooperate with the Crusade, and they sometimes attempted to handpick their own black "leaders." But they could no longer deny that their own self-interest was becoming increasingly tied to some form of interracial cooperation.

Such a recognition along with moves such as the establishment of the biracial commission appeared to many whites to presage the kind of harmonious race relations that the rhetoric of the charter campaign had evoked in 1948 but that had been destroyed by the campaign for massive resistance. In 1962, the lead article in the *Washington Post's* "Outlook" section declared "Richmond Quietly Leads Way in Race Relations." The reporter Robert E. Baker noted that "the progress that has been made in desegregation and non-discrimination in Richmond is one of the most exciting racial stories in the South."[22] Baker observed that Richmond had both adopted a fair employment policy in municipal jobs that was unique to the South and successfully integrated several restaurants, hotels, and schools. Speaking of the Crusade's political success, Baker remarked: "Perhaps nowhere else in the country, certainly nowhere else in the South, do Negroes use their vote with more sophistication than in Richmond."

In February 1964, Virginius Dabney published an essay in the *Saturday Review* on "Richmond's Quiet Revolution" that concurred with the *Post's* assessment. He asserted that race relations in Richmond were "far more amicable than they are in other places on both sides of the Mason-Dixon line. The race hatreds, the bitter tensions that exist in so many other cities are nowhere to be seen."[23] Dabney attributed Richmond's achievement to a history of interracial cordiality, an "exceptionally able and levelheaded police leadership," a "forward looking and realistically aware business community," and an "uninhibited" use of the ballot by Richmond blacks (18). Stressing the "sane and reasonable character" of Richmond's African American elite, Dabney emphasized that Richmond's leadership—black and white—had been able to reach a mutual accommodation on many of the most troubling racial issues: "The city has given an example of how sane, levelheaded, peaceable, and dedicated white and Negro leadership can achieve impressive results on the interracial front in a short time, without stirring up the ferocious animosities that could rob any apparent gains of all meaning" (28).

The Struggle for Political Control

Baker's and Dabney's odes to race relations in Richmond accurately portrayed the manner in which elite racial accommodation was proceeding in the early 1960s. But their analyses implied that the black community was politically monolithic and thus failed to notice the conflicts and divisions emerging within African American politics. Baker did not describe the manner in which black citizens had protested the urban renewal plans of the downtown business community; Dabney neglected to mention the manner in which support for the candidates of Richmond Forward was causing strain within African American politics. In fact, black politics was about to enter a new stage in Richmond, an era in which the goal would no longer be the exercise of influence but the direct control of political power.

On the surface, the councilmanic election of 1964 appeared to continue the pattern described by Baker and Dabney. A new business-oriented group, Richmond Forward, had organized a slate of candidates for the purpose of placing "progressive" businesspeople in charge of city government. Richmond Forward endorsed a full slate of nine candidates, including one black businessman, B. A. Cephas Jr., who had served on the city planning board and had voted in favor of a downtown redevelopment plan that had included the construction of a coliseum in the area's north core. The Crusade endorsed nine candidates: five members of Richmond Forward's slate and four from the Independent Citizens Ticket.

The 1964 election also witnessed the emergence of Voters' Voice, a new black political organization in Richmond. Although its spokesperson, a young lawyer by the name of L. Douglas Wilder, claimed not to be in competition with the Crusade, observers could hardly think otherwise. Wilder noted that the Voters' Voice wanted "to work in concert with the Crusade" but then implicitly criticized the other group by noting that it was "basically a voter registration group."[24] By contrast, Wilder asserted that Voters' Voice would be the "first Negro organization allowing full voter participation throughout a campaign."[25] The rivalry between Voters' Voice and the Crusade became undeniable when the newly formed organization refused to endorse any of the candidates of Richmond Forward. Voters' Voice threw its support behind seven members of the Independent Citizens Ticket and two black candidates associated with their own organization who did not receive the Crusade endorsement. In an interview conducted more than twenty-five years later (while he was governor of Virginia), Wilder noted that the "Crusade had begun to believe its own press clippings."

The platform of Voters' Voice recommended the construction of a job retraining center, the development of additional recreational facilities, and the transformation of Richmond's biracial commission into a permanent city agency. But its real concerns appeared to be its fear of Richmond Forward and its unease with the Crusade's coziness with the organization. The two black candidates sponsored by Voters' Voice maintained that Richmond Forward furnished "few practical solutions based on a genuine interest in the people of Richmond" and that Richmond Forward's "own special private interests stand to profit most" from its relationship with the Crusade for Voters.[26] They evoked the fear that the creation of Richmond Forward was merely a sophisticated mechanism for giving new life to a failed urban renewal plan that had been vehemently opposed by Richmond blacks: "People in Richmond are well aware that this unslain dragon will rear its ugly head in new 'forward' disguise."[27]

For its part, the Crusade viewed the Voters' Voice campaign as a direct political challenge. The Crusade rejected the two black candidates endorsed by Voters' Voice and did not endorse two independent white candidates that it had previously supported because of their connection to the organization. Crusade leaders emphasized that a unified vote had enabled blacks to make political progress and that fragmentation of the group's vote was politically regressive. A pamphlet distributed by the Crusade defended this position: "In the long run our solid vote is more important to us than any candidate. . . . If we allow misinformed persons or slick politicians to split our solidarity, we will turn the clock back fifty years for the Negroes in Richmond."[28]

The election results were a major victory for Richmond Forward. Six of the nine candidates running under its banner were successful, assuring a council that would be sympathetic to the ideas of the city's most influential business leaders. The election returns also demonstrated that the Crusade held the balance of power in city elections, for eight of the nine candidates that it endorsed were victorious. Kilpatrick echoed the perspective of Dabney and Baker by pointing to the evidence of elite racial accommodation as one of the election's defining features. Kilpatrick claimed that the returns demonstrated that "racial tensions have eased dramatically in Richmond. B. Addison Cephas, Jr., a highly respected Negro real estate and insurance executive, scored a stunning success. . . . His victory resulted from the joint effort of Richmond Forward and the Crusade for Voters; put another way, it resulted from a working coalition of white and Negro business and professional leaders."[29]

Closer analysis of the returns reveals a more confusing picture. In particular, the Crusade's recommendations were not followed unqualifiedly by black voters. Dickinson notes that the "comparatively well-to-do Negroes in Barton Heights and the northside generally followed Crusade recommendations,"[30] but the vast majority of black voters qualified their loyalty. In some precincts, the old habit of the solid shot ballot returned as black voters supported the three African American candidates, Cephas and the two endorsed by Voters' Voice. In other precincts, Cephas did extremely well, but the black candidates of Voters' Voice and a white populist who had criticized the accommodationist tendencies of the Crusade outpolled the other candidates endorsed by both the Crusade and Richmond Forward. While applauding the new dawn of interracial cooperation, Kilpatrick could not refrain from commenting, "It is evident from the returns that the big precincts of Richmond Forward supported Mr. Cephas with far more discipline than the Negro precincts supported Richmond Forward."[31]

During the next two years, three developments altered the manner in which racial accommodation occurred in Richmond. First, Crusade leaders were compelled to reconsider their strategy in light of the 1964 returns. Aware that there were obvious limits to accommodation with the white establishment, the Crusade charted a more independent course. In 1965, the organization refused to endorse Fitzgerald Bemiss, a regular Democrat for the Virginia House of Delegates, because of his connection to the Byrd machine. The Crusade's refusal to endorse Bemiss resulted in the resignation of the organization's president and the departure of some of the more accommodationist-oriented activists. The Crusade did not abandon wholly the policy of calculated cooperation. Indeed, in 1965, black votes helped to elect Mills Godwin—Mr. "Massive Resistance"—as governor of the Commonwealth. But the organization had to recognize the voices that were raised in 1964.

A second development in African American politics was the revitalization of the local black press when Raymond Boone became editor of the *Richmond Afro-American* in 1965. Boone attempted to reduce stories on sensational crimes and social occasions and increase coverage of the movement for social and political freedom. He hired the new president of the Crusade, Milton A. Randolph, as a commentator on local politics and also gave Howard Carwile, a white populist and outspoken critic of Richmond Forward, a regular column. Boone himself adopted a more assertive posture and became an important player in black political circles. Drawing attention to racial inequities and social injustice with front-page editorials, Boone doubled circulation by "articulating a previously muffled voice of outrage and militancy in black Richmond."[32]

A third development that increased the push for an independent black political stance was the elimination of the poll tax in state and local elections. Robert Rankin notes that the poll tax had been part of the Virginia Constitution since the beginning of the twentieth century; to be eligible to vote, a citizen had to pay the poll tax for the three years preceding the election and at least six months prior to the election date.[33] The Twenty-Fourth Amendment eliminated the poll tax in federal elections as of January 1964. In 1966, the Supreme Court used a Virginia challenge (*Harper v. Virginia Board of Elections*) to abolish the poll tax in state and local elections as well (75). Rankin reports that on January 1, 1965, there were 19,177 blacks registered to vote in state and local elections and 29,970 registered for federal elections. Thus, when the Court rendered its decision, 10,793 blacks were immediately added to the rolls for city elections (75).

Richmond Forward responded to the new realities of black politics by attempting to incorporate more elements of the African American elite. The organization placed Wilfred Mundle, another black businessman, on its slate and appointed Alix James, the vice president of Virginia Union University, as its organization's vice chairman. Richmond Forward also contacted a number of the more conservative influences in the Crusade to raise the possibility of greater cooperation.[34] Yet these steps were not enough to counter the African American community's distrust of the organization. Richmond Forward's support for a referendum calling for staggered four-year terms for the city council was seen as a ploy for diluting black influence in councilmanic elections. Moreover, the group's support for a downtown redevelopment package and expressway construction was subject to relentless criticism by Raymond Boone in the *Richmond Afro-American*.

In 1966, Henry L. Marsh III, a young black civil rights lawyer, ran for the city council on an anti-Richmond Forward platform. Labeling himself a candidate from the grass roots, Marsh was the first black candidate to articulate the long-standing concern of the black community that the downtown redevelopment strategy of Richmond Forward—highways, slum clearance, and the construction of a convention center—was incompatible with the broader interests of African Americans. Instead, Marsh called for a government that would "build people not things."[35] Marsh was endorsed by Raymond Boone in a front-page editorial that asserted, "His candidacy symbolizes a chance for us to choose our own representatives. . . . We have no doubt that his voice will be our voice, that he will articulate the views and aspirations of our people who for too long have been enslaved by voicelessness."[36] In addition, Marsh was supported by the Baptist Ministers Conference in a public endorsement prior to the Crusade's last minute recommendations.

The Crusade did not entirely abandon its policy of calculated cooperation in the 1966 election, but it staked out its most independent stance yet. From Richmond Forward's nine-person slate, the Crusade endorsed only three candidates, including two black businessmen, Cephas and Mundle. The only white candidate from the Richmond Forward ticket that the Crusade supported was Phil Bagley. This particular decision revealed the growing distance between the two organizations. Bagley had actually contested Richmond Forward in the 1964 election and was probably the white candidate on the Crusade slate who was least connected to the organization's infrastructure. The Crusade backed seven candidates, including Henry L. Marsh III and the white populist Howard Carwile, who was probably the most vocal opponent of Richmond Forward in the city.

Even before the Crusade's slate was announced, word of the organization's likely estrangement from Richmond Forward was circulated. At this time, the editorial pages of the morning newspaper, the *Richmond Times-Dispatch*, entered the fray on behalf of Richmond Forward. Entitled a "Message to the Negro Voters of Richmond," an editorial claimed that the black people were to be told by the Crusade "not to use their own intelligence in deciding how to vote" and that a "handful of persons" will "direct you how to vote."[37] The editorial went on to suggest that Richmond Forward was the only organization truly committed to interracial cooperation and that it did not practice the "type of political segregation promoted by the organization which will tell you Sunday how to vote on Tuesday."[38] The "sane" and "levelheaded" black leadership that Dabney had effusively praised two years earlier was now condemned on his own editorial page as elitist and separatist.

Richmond Forward retained its council majority in the 1966 election, but the Crusade continued to demonstrate its clout. Bagley, Cephas, and Mundle, the candidates endorsed by both groups, finished first, second, and fifth, respectively. More dramatically, however, the expanded black voting population was the primary force behind the victories of Marsh and Carwile, candidates who explicitly opposed Richmond Forward. To be sure, Marsh and Carwile received white votes that were crucial to their success. Nonetheless, Dickinson's analysis holds true: "This election heralded the arrival of potent black ballot power to Richmond. No longer did the Negro voter hold just the balance of power; he had become a power in his own right, able to choose and elect his own candidates for public office. No longer was an alliance with Richmond Forward a practical political necessity."[39]

Between 1966 and 1968, the battle lines between Richmond Forward and the supporters of independent black political power became even more sharply drawn. For years the city of Richmond had been attempting to expand its boundaries by either merging with or annexing part of one of the adjacent counties. City officials claimed that boundary expansion was imperative to obtain land that could be used for industrial development and thus expand the city's tax base. Observers of city politics believed that there was an economic justification for annexation. But after 1966, the quest for more land and citizens became entwined with racial politics and the desire of white leaders to prevent demographic changes from ushering in a black majority. Secret meetings with Chesterfield County officials held by council members who excluded Marsh and Carwile lent credence to the charge that annexation's driving force was now the political defense of white dominance. One council member is reported to have said at one of the confidential meetings that the city needed "44,000 leadership type of white affluent people."[40]

African American politicians and the black press increasingly condemned Richmond Forward in the same rhetoric that Marsh had employed in his 1966 campaign. In an editorial entitled, "RF Must Go," the *Richmond Afro-American* contended that "Richmond Forward, backed and controlled by the city's big money czars, has been so devoted to pushing its individual and corporate pursuits that it has grossly neglected the needs of the people." The editorial pointed to Richmond Forward's downtown redevelopment projects as the "most horrendous examples of Richmond Forward's concern for profit making over human values" and denounced the coliseum project for "consuming millions that could be spent wisely for human uplift."[41] A black candidate for council, Walter T. Kenney, claimed, "Richmond Forward has not provided the type of leadership in our city which is badly needed; they do not respond to the needs of average citizens in all sections of the city."[42]

The black community's growing antipathy toward Richmond Forward was evidenced in the stance adopted by the Crusade in the 1968 election. Two elements of the Crusade's position illuminate the extent of the split between it and Richmond Forward. First, the Crusade abandoned its own strategy of endorsing a full or nearly full slate of candidates, which had enabled it to exercise the balance of power. Thinking that increased registration might enable it to control councilmanic elections, the Crusade endorsed only five candidates in the 1968 campaign.

Second, the Crusade also entirely abandoned all support for Richmond Forward. Echoing the criticisms of Marsh and the *Richmond Afro-American*, the Crusade's research director Franklin Gayles stated, "Richmond

Forward believes more in multimillion dollar office buildings, city halls, big business interests, coliseums and roads than they do [in] people."[43] Unlike the 1966 election, the Crusade did not even endorse B. A. Cephas and Wilfred Mundle, two black candidates running under the Richmond Forward mantle. From 1966 through 1968, Cephas and Mundle (especially the latter) had been severely chastised in the black press for their inattentiveness to community needs and for their willingness to take cues from their Richmond Forward "masters." As a retrospective in the *Richmond Afro-American* noted, "Cephas and Mundle did not wage their campaigns as black candidates; they ran as members of the Richmond Forward slate, endorsing that group's candidates, programs, and goals. They served on the city council in the same fashion—putting the interests and programs of Richmond Forward before the demands and interests of black people."[44]

Richmond Forward and its supporters on the *Richmond Times-Dispatch* editorial pages vigorously defended the organization's record against criticism from both the black community and white conservatives who believed that the group was not sufficiently interested in maintaining a low tax rate. Richmond Forward countered that it had brought progress to the city and helped to modernize the economy. Its candidates pointed to the civil disturbances that had occurred in the wake of Martin Luther King Jr.'s assassination and affirmed their commitment to law and order. Calling the 1968 contest "Richmond's Most Vital Election in Decades," the editorial page of the *Times-Dispatch* argued that the "choice is a clear one" because under "Richmond Forward's leadership, the city has made impressive and important strides."[45]

The election results maintained Richmond Forward's preeminent position. Six candidates from its ticket were victorious while the Crusade was successful in returning Marsh and Carwile and adding the white liberal James Carpenter to the council. The two defeated Richmond Forward candidates were Cephas and Mundle whose vote totals were reduced from 1966 in both the white and black communities. Some observers have argued that the Crusade made a big mistake in withdrawing their endorsement from Cephas and Mundle. Suggesting that it was equivalent to "cutting off your nose to spite your face," they argued that the Crusade could have had a council that would have included three black members and three people with ideological affinity if it had not abandoned Cephas and Mundle.[46] Crusade leaders defended their decision and argued that the "prime lesson of last week's election is that, first, the colored community is 'sick and tired' of the establishment selecting leadership for them."[47]

In the aftermath of the 1968 election, the council majority quickened its efforts to annex part of Chesterfield County. A Richmond Forward study estimated that blacks had constituted about 44 percent of the electorate in the recent councilmanic contests, and it was apparent that blacks might be an absolute majority by 1970.[48] City officials maintained that the economic justification for annexation was still primary, but a number of remarks by its leaders pointed to the increasing political urgency that was attributed to annexation. One council member accused the minority faction of being "willing to see the city converted into a black ghetto for their own purely political purposes" (98). Chesterfield County officials observed that city negotiators appeared to be much more interested in the number of people that would be annexed than in questions regarding land value and industrial development of the territory. And, according to the recollection of one member of the Virginia House of Delegates, city leaders informed state officials that, "if certain elements of the city of Richmond were to take over the city government, they would tear down all the monuments (to Confederate war heroes) on Monument Avenue" (100).

The city successfully negotiated an annexation that furnished Richmond with more than forty thousand new citizens—the vast majority white—in time for the 1970 council elections. With the addition of the annexed area, the city population was again 42 percent black, approximately the same percentage as in 1960. In the 1970 election, Richmo.1d Forward merged with some of the leaders of the civic associations in the annexed area to form a new organization, the Team of Progress. For its part, the Crusade endorsed a ticket that included the three victors from 1968, two black candidates, and four white candidates from the annexed area who were dissatisfied with the Richmond Forward organization. The results testified to the success of the annexation as the Team of Progress maintained the 6-3 Richmond Forward majority. As John Moeser and Rutledge Dennis observe in their analysis, "The percent of black residents, the percent of black eligible voters, the percent of black registered voters, and the percent of blacks who actually cast a ballot in the 1970 election were all depressed by the annexation."[49]

White city officials soon learned that they were not able to achieve their ends so easily. First, the Supreme Court decided in the 1971 *Perkins v. Matthews* that city annexations are not exempt from the provisions of the Voting Rights Act (1965). Richmond's city attorney wrote to the Justice Department and asked whether the city's annexation of part of Chesterfield County, completed prior to the Court decision, was subject to the ruling

(145–47). Second, a losing black candidate in the councilmanic elections of 1970, the community activist Curtis Holt, filed a class action suit in U.S. District Court, arguing that the annexation diluted the black vote and thus violated the Fifteenth Amendment. Holt called for deannexation and asked that the court throw out the results of the 1970 councilmanic elections (148).

The Justice Department responded to the city attorney's letter by noting that Richmond's annexation did fall under the provisions of the Voting Rights Act and that the annexation "inevitably tends to dilute the voting strength of black voters" (150). In November 1971, U.S. District Court Judge Robert Merhige reached a similar conclusion in the Holt suit and suggested that the city modify its electoral system to select seven at-large council members and two who would run in the annexed area only (158–59). Neither the Justice Department nor Merhige advocated deannexation as the solution. Instead, both argued that a change in the city charter directed at the method of electing council members could be the instrument for enabling compliance with the Voting Rights Act.

In 1971–76, the annexation was the subject of a bewildering array of suits, appeals, countersuits, and negotiations with the Justice Department that involved Holt, the city of Richmond, Chesterfield County, residents of the annexed area, and the Crusade for Voters. Indeed, court orders prevented Richmond from holding councilmanic elections in 1972, 1974, and 1976. City officials asked that the annexation be permitted to stand; Holt and some residents of the annexed area demanded deannexation; and the Crusade for Voters endorsed annexation but only if coupled with a change in the city's electoral system. Barring this, the Crusade preferred deannexation to the new electoral structure. The case eventually reached the Supreme Court in 1975 and the justices agreed that the annexation was motivated by the "impermissible purpose of denying the right to vote on the basis of race" (172). The Court nonetheless returned the case to the district court to determine whether the city obtained legitimate benefits from the annexation that would make it permissible if coupled with a plan for ward-based voting. The Court eventually approved the annexation and instructed the city to hold a special election in 1977 — its first since 1970 — on the basis of the newly designed wards (166–78).

Although elections were not held between 1970 and 1977, politics did not disappear in Richmond. In this period, school integration and busing became critical issues. When it became apparent in the early 1970s that many whites were fleeing to the counties in order to avoid court-mandated busing, city officials filed suit calling for a consolidation of city and county systems. U.S. District Court Judge Merhige ordered the consolidation, but his decision was overturned by the circuit court. The city appealed the case to the U.S. Supreme Court where a 4-4 decision (Judge Lewis Powell did not participate because of his previous position as head of the Richmond School Board) resulted in the confirmation of the circuit court's opinion.

During the first half of the 1970s, resignations from the city council allowed the Team of Progress to add another member to its majority. Marsh and a number of people in the black community continually argued that the city was not making enough progress on equal opportunity issues, particularly the employment of blacks in managerial positions and in certain city agencies that seemed resistant to African Americans. The construction of a downtown expressway and the coliseum kept alive the argument that roads and buildings came before people in the city. There was, nonetheless, some evidence of black-white cooperation during the period. The Team of Progress approved the appointment of a black woman, Willie Dell, to the city council when the liberal minister James Carpenter resigned to perform missionary work in Ecuador. And Marsh was selected as vice mayor as a signal of the Team of Progress's willingness to work with the black community. But as it became apparent that a ward-based system would be instituted, attention in the black community focused on the upcoming elections.

The 1977 special election culminated decades of black struggle for influence and power. Not only were the two incumbent blacks on the city council, Dell and Marsh, reelected, but three other black candidates, Henry "Chuck" Richardson, Walter Kenney, and Claudette Black McDaniel were elected as well, thus giving African Americans majority control of the council for the first time in history. This momentous achievement was then immediately translated into the selection of Marsh as mayor. Many black Richmonders felt they had successfully overcome years of racial gerrymandering, the efforts by Richmond Forward to prevent the emergence of independent leadership, and the perceived attempt by the editorial pages of the daily newspapers to stifle the expression of black political influence.

Exercising Power

Conflict

The emergence of a black majority council immediately raised the question of what stance the new majority would adopt toward the white pow-

er structure. Would it update the old Crusade strategy of calculated cooperation, or would it pursue the kind of boldly independent program that
Marsh had touched upon in the 1966 campaign with his "build people not
things" slogan? In the days directly following the election, Marsh sent out
mixed signals. He served notice that a human rights agenda focusing on
the alleviation of poverty would be a high priority of the new majority. He
also spoke of the necessity of channeling more resources into the school
system. But he took deliberate steps to assure the business community that
a revolution was not coming to the city. He engineered the selection of a
white businessman who was a partner at one of the city's preeminent bro-
kerage houses as vice mayor. He emphasized that the continuation of a
good business climate was critical to the city's future. Indeed, two months
after his election Richmond newspaper reporters thought that Marsh was
running another campaign, a "campaign of reassurance," in which the
business community was informed of his readiness to cooperate. In fact,
during the initial months following the Marsh election, the major com-
plaint voiced by white council members was that he had not developed a
clearly defined agenda.[50]

In 1978, white complaints about the new majority became more pronounced. The discontent no longer focused on the presumed inactivity of
the mayor but on his established priorities and the council's actions. The
most volatile issue centered on the council's dismissal of the white city
manager, William Leidinger, after the 1978 councilmanic elections returned all members of the black majority to office. Marsh claimed that
Leidinger had failed to give proper attention to the stated priorities and
policy concerns of the city council, particularly affirmative action, funding recommendations for the schools, and neighborhood improvement
programs. In addition, Marsh contended that Leidinger had exploited the
city manager's power to "interfere with the council's policy-making role."
In particular, Marsh maintained that Leidinger "estimated revenue projec-
tions consistently low and expenditures consistently high."[51]

The black majority's rationale for Leidinger's removal was not accepted by spokespersons for the white establishment. Members of the white
elite generally believed that Leidinger was an intelligent city manager who
performed his job competently. When Leidinger related a conversation in
which Marsh gave him the opportunity to resign as an alternative to dismissal, a number of business leaders summoned black members of the
council to a meeting in a Main Street office and threatened that "blood
might flow in the streets" if the decision was not revoked. On one level,

the white power structure saw the firing of the city manager as an ugly manifestation of race-based decision making. From this perspective, Leidinger was removed simply because he happened to be white. The editorial pages of the *Richmond Times-Dispatch* argued that "if a white majority were trying to do what council's black majority is doing, the NAACP would be at the courthouse before breakfast to file a suit. And Henry Marsh would be among the first to cry 'racism.'"[52]

What was even more disturbing to the white elite was that the decision to fire Leidinger appeared to be an attack on the role of business in the city. Blacks on the council and others who supported the decision utilized the anti-Main Street rhetoric that had been a recurring feature of black political discourse in the city. Councilwoman Claudette McDaniel, for instance, explained her vote to fire the city manager by observing that "big businesses must take their rightful place" in the new ordering of priorities.[53] Norvell Robinson, president of the Crusade for Voters, expressed his approval of Leidinger's removal with the statement: The decision "is imperative to the agenda of this council in order that it is able to expedite the mandate of all the people and not just a dozen downtown businesses."[54] While Marsh reiterated his belief in a partnership between business and government, he also insisted that "we have to share in the relationship."[55]

The rhetoric in 1978 was much less reassuring to whites than were the statements they had heard in 1977. To some business people, the city council was declaring war on the corporate elite. The white elite believed that the firing of Leidinger might be merely a prelude to a wholesale reordering of policy initiatives. They feared that the council might attempt to extract more revenue in order to finance its newly declared social agenda. The editorial pages of the daily papers voiced these opinions in the sharpest terms, intimating that corporate departures to the counties and white flight would be the likely consequence of such council policies: "Leidinger is to go not because black council members consider him to be an incompetent administrator . . . but primarily because the black council members consider him to be 'pro-business.' They wish to replace him, they say, with someone who is 'pro-people.' This anti-business attitude, if it prevails, could be the ruin of Richmond."[56]

To the black majority, the white establishment had overreacted to what was a perfectly reasonable use of the council's prerogatives. They attributed the establishment's reaction to its reluctance to recognize the reality of black political power in Richmond. In an interview by the reporter and author Margaret Edds, Marsh noted that the council's retention of

Leidinger for fifteen months after the election was a sign of its goodwill: "We went out of our way to accommodate the concerns of whites. The normal thing to have done would have been to change city managers immediately. The city manager that the whites had at the time had led the fight in the courts (on the annexation issue). He had testified against me and the other blacks. He had led the fight to keep us from getting there. We felt it would be a good way of assuring the whites that we weren't trying to castrate them."[57]

Moeser and Dennis's study of Richmond politics notes that commencing with Leidinger's removal as city manager in 1978, Richmond politics became defined by a "series of conflicts that saw council votes sharply divided along racial lines."[58] From 1978 on, votes on a number of important appointments and budget issues were decided by a 5-4 breakdown in which patterns were established by race. The white minority on the council repeatedly claimed that Marsh had decimated the official committee system and that he had excluded the council minority from participation in decision making. The editorial pages were relentless in their criticisms of both the process by which the black majority ruled and the substance of their policies. In essence, white critics of city government viewed Marsh as a racialist intent on balkanizing city politics.

In 1980, the Teams for Progress, the successor to the Team of Progress, backed the campaign of a local white businessman, Andrew Gillespie, who attempted to unseat Claudette McDaniel in the councilmanic elections. Charges made during the campaign further exacerbated racial bitterness in the city. The editorial pages of the afternoon daily, the *Richmond News Leader,* ran a series of columns that accused McDaniel of using city funds to conduct a survey that formed the basis of her master's thesis at Virginia Commonwealth University. The editorial went even further and quoted with apparent approval a charge leveled by a a white councilman that McDaniel probably did not write the thesis herself and was aided by someone at the university. Despite these allegations, McDaniel was returned to office and the black majority remained intact.

The controversy that erupted in 1981 over the council's passage of an ordinance that effectively prohibited the construction of a hotel adjacent to the Main Street business district rivaled the Leidinger removal in its bitterness. Earlier that year, the Hilton Corporation announced its desire to build a $24.5 million hotel in the city just south of the downtown banking center. The black majority on the council worried that the Hilton complex might make it impossible to find funding for the proposed hotel in the city's downtown revitalization plan, Project One, which had been on the drawing board for more than a decade. The council majority re-fused to approve the relocation of sewage lines, which would have permit-ted construction to begin on the Hilton, and then passed an ordinance that required economic development projects to be compatible with the pri-orities of Project One.

The white minority on the council and the editorial pages attacked the council's decision. They argued that it constituted restraint of trade and that the vagueness of the ordinance would mire the city in potentially costly litigation. Former city manager and now council member William Leidinger noted that the "litigation might be far more damaging to Project One than the Hilton competition. . . . We're playing very dangerous and I think that we're going to come out on the short end of the stick." When the city's ordinance became the subject of a *Wall Street Journal* article about Richmond's inhospitable business climate, members of the corpo-rate establishment began to worry that the city would lose its attractiveness to the national business community.

Mayor Marsh and the black majority did not accept the perspective that Leidinger and the editorial pages had used to frame the controversy. Marsh argued that the business community had already agreed that government could be used to promote and guide downtown redevelopment. He did not believe that the ordinance hindering the construction of the Hilton was qualitatively different from any other action the council might take to shape the direction of economic development. He noted that Project One, which the white community largely supported, required that the city put forty to fifty people out of business. Far from being a fight over free enter-prise principles, Marsh believed that the Hilton controversy was inflamed by newspaper editorialists who wanted to "stir up the community against the black leadership." In Marsh's mind, the real objection was to the rec-ognition that black leaders were now making the decisions guiding the development of the city's retail core.

Accommodation

The racial and ideological divisions that emerged with the election of a black majority were genuine, and the personal bitterness that surfaced was palpable. But this does not mean that the black majority had actually abandoned the Crusade strategy of calculated cooperation. Most black council members did not believe that the wishes of the white business community could be entirely ignored, but they wanted to acknowledge these interests in the context of policies that addressed the needs of the black community. As Councilman Chuck Richardson noted in an interview, "We attempted to walk the fine line between appeasement and accomplishment."

Although the Leidinger firing in 1978 provoked speculation among whites that it was the beginning of an antibusiness crusade on the part of the council's black majority, these fears were never fully justified. The antibusiness rhetoric that was voiced during the controversy did not presage a fully developed policy agenda that threatened corporate Richmond or even challenged its notion of the most appropriate economic development strategy for the city. In reality, the antibusiness rhetoric expressed the resentment of the African American population about black exclusion from the process of formulating priorities and from the benefits of growth. Blacks had employed the same language to fight the expressways that were routed through their neighborhoods and the urban renewal plans that uprooted their communities. Such rhetoric did not signify the development of a political philsosophy inherently opposed to the perpetuation of a capitalist economy.

The turmoil that accompanied Leidinger's removal in 1978 obviously lowered the comfort level of corporate Richmond with the black majority council, and it probably permanently scarred Marsh's reputation in the broader white community. But it soon became evident that he did not intend to revolutionize city government. Manuel Deese, the black city manager who was hired to replace Leidinger a few months later, was a professional public administrator who was not actively committed to a definable political ideology. In fact, Deese had been an assistant city manager in Richmond who was originally hired by William Leidinger.

The belief in the necessity of a partnership with business was reflected most visibly in the economic development strategy adopted by the black majority. Despite all the rhetoric about neighborhood improvements and the desirability of combatting business dominance, the new council's plan was remarkably similar to that which had been articulated long before blacks had become politically ascendant. Project One, the proposal endorsed by Marsh and his supporters, was a modified version of a master plan for downtown that had been drawn up in the 1960s when whites firmly controlled city government. The black majority also emphasized downtown redevelopment as the key to the future of Richmond, albeit the reasons for endorsing this effort may have differed from those proffered by the business community. The council thus threw its weigh behind a hotel-convention center complex that it hoped would draw people back to the central city and increase the tax revenues that could then fund educational and social initiatives.[59]

Perhaps it could be argued that the antibusiness ethos of the black majority was demonstrated more through the Hilton controversy than it was in the removal of Leidinger—but such a claim would also be too simplistic. First, the alternative to the Hilton was the Project One development where city funds were being used to subsidize business growth. As we shall see in the next chapter, the city eventually attracted the Marriott Corporation as the linchpin hotel, by offering a substantial buydown on market interest rates for the company. The Richmond City Council never developed the kind of populist orientation that emerged, for example, in Dennis Kucinich's Cleveland. Second, the persistent conflict on the council and the heated exchanges over the Hilton decision did not lead Marsh to reject the possibility of cooperation with the downtown business community. Indeed, in the aftermath of the Hilton controversy, Marsh and T. Justin Moore, CEO of Virginia Power and one of the business community's most respected leaders, engineered a plan for reinvigorating and ultimately formalizing the partnership between the black majority and the white business establishment.

Controversy had not blinded Marsh to the recognition that there were powerful elements in the business community that had an interest in a more cooperative relationship. By the early 1980s, many corporate leaders had come to believe that the highly publicized wars on the council could only undermine Richmond's reputation as a city hospitable to business. A number of these leaders were relatively recent arrivals in the city and had not been part of the long-standing antagonisms between Main Street, the daily newspapers, and the black leadership. They were more committed to preserving and enhancing Richmond's appeal as a location for corporate headquarters than they were in obtaining a Pyrrhic victory in the local political struggle. For this reason, they were able to look beyond the divisiveness on the council and see how their own long-term interests were best served by a less conflictual relationship with the black majority. At the same time, the Richmond arts community (itself substantially tied to corporate leadership) began to view a revitalized downtown as crucial to its plans for preserving the city's architectural distinctiveness and enhancing the visibility of its cultural offerings.[60]

The result was the formation in early 1982 of the public-private partnership called Richmond Renaissance. For its part, the city agreed to put up half of the $2.4 million seed money by using more than 20 percent of its community development block grant funding for the year.[61] Moore, of Virginia Power, observed that the "business community is excited and enthusiastic over entering into partnership with the city in accelerating economic development [and that] it wouldn't have happened without Henry Marsh as the catalyst." City Manager Manuel Deese called it the "greatest damn thing in years" and predicted that it would "make this town explode" with economic development. The editorial page of the *Richmond News Leader* commended the effort, noting that the "formation of Richmond Renaissance for the city's economic revitalization comes as good news. It may even be great news."[62]

By the early 1980s, black-white political relationships were simultaneously cooperative and antagonistic. On the one hand, the public-private partnership for downtown redevelopment—Richmond Renaissance—was hailed everywhere as an example of interracial cooperation that would work for the good of all Richmonders and perhaps serve as a model for other cities. It represented the desire of both the black political elite and white corporate leadership to set aside their traditional distrust and develop a better working relationship. As the newspaper report on its formation mentioned, both "Moore and Marsh emphasized that, besides promoting growth, this is a means of bringing the Richmond community together and of ending the political and racial polarization that has seemed to divide the black governed city and the white dominated business community."[63] At the same time, the racial and ideological divisions that existed on the council and in the city had become exacerbated. Agreement about downtown redevelopment did not dissolve the bitterness that had developed between the two factions, nor did it cause the editorialists to believe that the Marsh faction should be entrusted with the directing the future of the city.

Division and Ossification

The Election of Roy West

Any lingering thoughts about the revolutionary consequences of the new political configuration in Richmond were put to rest in the elections of 1982. Emerging class and ideological divisions in the black community, a long-standing personal feud, and a nearly unanimous white vote in the Third Ward led to the replacement of Willie Dell, a member of the Marsh faction, by the election of Roy West, a relatively conservative black school principal. West had been involved in a running dispute with Marsh from the time Richard Hunter, whom Marsh had helped bring to Richmond as superintendent of schools, had transferred West from a high-school to a middle-school position during a period of consolidation. Perhaps more importantly, West's criticisms of the Marsh faction, his promise to bridge the racial gap on council, and his reputation as a no-nonsense disciplinarian in the schools enabled him to garner about a third of the black vote and almost total support from the 30 percent of his ward that was white.

In the immediate aftermath of West's election, members of the Marsh faction expressed their willingness to work with the new council member, appearing confident that a working arrangement could be achieved. Councilwoman McDaniel also expressed confidence that Dell's defeat was not an indicator of dramatic change: "I think that the team will remain intact. I think that on the tough issues he'll be with us. When we need Dr. West, he'll be with the team."[64] Councilman Richardson also appeared optimistic that West would not undermine the 1977 majority: "Dr. West is from a similar background to other members of council, the majority members. . . . The rhetoric of independent thinking was in a campaign. I also have thought independently, but it happens that my thinking has coincided with four other members of council."[65] West conceded that he would be willing to work with the Marsh coalition but continued to maintain that he would be in nobody's pocket: "I can be counted upon to vote on any issue in a positive way that will benefit people. . . . I'm not going to vote in a vacuum; my vote will be based on an analysis of the facts, my study of the facts. When I vote, I will have done my homework. I'm not going to be a knee jerk politician."[66]

It soon became evident that West's election did not mean the continuation of business as usual in city politics. Richmond's council-manager form of government provides for the mayor to be selected by city council members. As the day neared for the council to choose the mayor in 1982, it was apparent that the job was West's for the taking, if he voted for himself. Prior to the election, West was known by almost no one in the business community. But after his upset victory, a number of white business people, who had been impressed by his rhetoric of independence, asked him to consider becoming the mayor by adding his own ballot to those of the four white council members. As Henry L. Valentine, former vice mayor and president of the Main Street investment firm Davenport and Company, noted in an interview with Margaret Edds, "I never heard of Roy West, until people around town said, 'I think that you ought to look at him.' I went to see Roy West after he was elected with five or six other people. We told him, 'Look, you'll never hear from us about how you vote. All we want from you is to treat the white citizens with respect and civility.' "[67]

West did not indicate his decision to Valentine's group. But he consulted with a number of his black allies and they concluded that his role on the council "would be lessened a great deal if I did not take the leadership role."[68] One of the people with whom he consulted was L. Douglas Wilder, then a state senator. Indeed, some stories suggest that Wilder helped to engineer West's selection as mayor in order to eliminate Marsh as a potential rival for the unofficial role of the state's most powerful African American politician. Both Wilder and West have always denied this description of the former's role. But Wilder admitted that he met with West and told him that he "should not come away from this situation with nothing" if he decided to take the offer.[69] In any event, the selection of Roy West as mayor was an unexpected and stunning turn in Richmond politics.

On the day of West's selection, Marsh was gracious in defeat, extending his "sincere congratulations to our new mayor" and expressing his desire to "pledge to him my support and urge all of those who support me to work with Roy."[70] Most black members on the council publicly adopted what was described as a "wait and see" attitude about West's mayoralty. McDaniel reiterated her belief that West would "vote on the crucial issues the same way we have voted on crucial issues. He was raised in the same system we were raised in. He understands that."[71] Only Kenney publicly expressed the fears of the 1977 majority: "I think that you're going to have 80 to 90 percent of the black community very distrustful again of the type of government leadership."[72] West observed that his decision was based on the assumption that he could do a better job as a bridge builder between council factions if he was sitting in the mayor's chair: "There was a feeling that the mayor, the former mayor, was so strong, so smooth, had some smarts about him, that he could neutralize anything that I could do and would create the impression of Roy West as an obstructionist. So that's it. It boiled down to whether I wanted to be a bridge as a council person and be trampled over or whether I wanted to be the bridge as mayor and let them tiptoe across."[73]

Change and Continuity

West had been mayor for barely a year before the newspapers reported that the council was as "deeply divided as it has been at any time since ward elections brought blacks to power in 1977."[74] West's criticism of Richard Hunter, the school superintendent supported by Marsh, his stated intention to appoint school board members who shared his concern about the direction in which Hunter was taking the schools, and his willingness to form a majority on council appointments by voting with the four white members angered the 1977 majority. Marsh portrayed West in very much the same terms that black activists had used for the black council members supported by Richmond Forward, B. A. Cephas and Wilfred Mundle: "I think that the city's situation is very similar to what it's always been—a struggle between the white political forces and the black political forces. The black political forces had control for five years. Prior to that time, the white political forces had control and now the white political forces have control again by virtue of the election of West in the 3rd District."[75] Reflecting on West in 1990, Richardson noted that West repeatedly undermined black interests even though he sincerely believed that he was doing the right thing.[76]

West responded to these sorts of accusations by accusing Marsh and others of character assassination simply because he did not embrace Marsh's style of "messianic leadership." West argued that there was a "deliberate effort to discredit me, and they have nothing in my record to base that discrediting process on. I don't intend to be deflected by that kind of thing. I intend to forge ahead."[77] West contended that his refusal to be pigeonholed into a faction and Marsh's continued pursuit of power were really at the root of the criticism. He maintained that he certainly had not betrayed black interests and that his capacity to get along with white council members was in the interest of all Richmond residents, black and white.[78]

The focus of the city council in 1984 quickly became Willie Dell's effort to win back the seat that West had wrested from her in 1982. In Marsh's opinion, the future of black power in the city was at stake in the contest.[79] Dell echoed Marsh's assessment in her own explanation of the campaign's meaning. She maintained that the result would be pivotal in determining "who's going to set the priority for the city and who gets to set the direction for the city—whether it's going to be Main Street folks or whether it's going to be grassroots leadership or whether the leadership is going to be back in the hands of black people."[80] West countered Dell's argument by maintaining that, in bringing dignity to the city and fair representation to all, he had done more for African Americans than the Marsh faction had ever delivered.[81] In the election, West won even more easily than in 1982, garnering 56 percent of the total vote. He held his own in the predominantly black precincts that constituted 69 percent of the ward's voting population. He swept the three predominantly white precincts, 2,636 to 148.[82]

West's 1984 victory left no doubt that the shape of Richmond politics had been permanently reconfigured. It demonstrated that the 1977 majority was now history and that Marsh would not return as mayor. West's success in 1984 led to further slippage in the group that composed the 1977 majority. McDaniel decided to endorse West for mayor in order to promote her own selection as vice mayor and enhance her capacity to channel city funds into her ward when the council apportioned the budgetary pie. West's victory and McDaniel's endorsement did not necessarily reduce the animosity between the mayor and groups, such as the Crusade for Voters, that were associated with Marsh. In fact, by 1986 West was sufficiently powerful and confident that he unleashed a blistering attack on the Crusade for Voters when it failed to endorse his candidacy. Claiming that he deserved the endorsement because he had "performed far beyond the expectations of any reasonable, logical and fair minded person or organization," West contended that the relationship between Marsh and the Crusade's research committee was plainly analogous to the "computer programmer checking all of the circuits to ensure proper programming."[83] West went on to argue that the Crusade had lost its clout in the black community and that "it had run its course because of its ineptness. It has not really kept track of the time. It has not kept track of the sophistication of the voters, and, as such, it is still dealing in 1986 with 1946 approaches."

The bitterness between West and Marsh defined Richmond political life for most of the eighties. Yet the two rivals did not disagree on all political issues. Significantly, West did not depart visibly from the path that Marsh had staked out in downtown redevelopment. Moreover, West's conservatism did not extend to the kind of free market approach to the role of government advocated by scholars such as Thomas Sowell and Walter Williams. At no time did West argue against the priority that had been accorded to downtown revitalization. On the contrary, he maintained that his selection as mayor would lubricate the process inasmuch as he would be less contentious than Marsh in his relations with the business community. West suggested, in essence, that he would be better able to implement the plans that Marsh had helped develop.

West's position on the various set-aside programs developed by the Marsh faction as an element of the downtown revitalization programs is also instructive in this regard. Here again, West did not exhibit the ideological opposition to these policies that conservative intellectuals have expressed. He regularly expressed his commitment to minority economic development as a means of demonstrating that he had not sold out African Americans in order to garner Main Street support. He suggested that his relationship with the white council members enabled him to persuade them of the importance of this issue to African Americans. Councilwoman Carolyn Wake, owner of a small hardware store, expressed her admiration for West's approach: "Set-asides to me are just abominable. I was a little person. We started out alone, had to work and claw our way up. Since nobody set aside for Carolyn, I can't understand why there should be set-asides for anyone else. Roy talked to me and I began to see, 'No, Carolyn, you didn't do it all on your own.' Father knew someone at the bank to talk to, etc. etc. Henry [Marsh]'s attitude was I don't have to talk with you. Roy takes the time to make you see; at the same time, he tries to see and understand the businessman's point of view."[84] In fact, West often chided members of the 1977 majority for not doing enough on affirmative action. He argued that they were more talk than substance. When the set-aside program that was the basis of Croson's challenge was established, West wondered why such a policy had not been implemented sooner.

A good case could be made that West did not exhibit anywhere near the attention that Marsh had to the substance of economic development. West's major areas of interest appeared to be discipline in the schools, crime, and publicizing the shortcomings of traditional black leadership. The business community was probably not familiar with West in 1982 because he had simply not developed an interest, position, or record on matters germane to economic development. Main Street support for West rested not on a detailed understanding of his positions but on the claim that he would be independent from Marsh. West did not obstruct any of the plans that had been developed but, at the same, he was not a leader and innovator. In this sense, the rivalry obscured the deeper level of agreement that existed between the two.

To some extent, the anti–Main Street rhetoric of those who had been associated with the Marsh-led majority was misleading. It was true that West often traded upon his good relationship with whites—his "bridge building" credentials—to score political points against his rivals in the black community. But as we have seen, the black majority on the council had made its peace with downtown redevelopment and had promoted it as a policy advantageous for the black community. By the mid-1980s, it was much less clear what it meant to be against the "Main Street folks" and what the alternative black position really was, except for a few more dollars for social services and community action programs. A different city council probably would have had a different distribution of city funds for neighborhood projects. But it was not easy to point to principles about major city economic problems that would have been differently articulated.

Inertia and Stagnancy

After the 1984 election in which West successfully withstood the challenge of Dell, black politics in Richmond entered a period of stagnancy. The West-Marsh rivalry continued to be the defining feature of African American politics, but no one seriously believed that Marsh might recapture power. McDaniel's defection from the Marsh faction in 1984 became even more pronounced during the rest of the decade. Attempting to position herself to become the next mayor, McDaniel began to vote frequently with the West majority. Richardson remained a political ally of Marsh in council voting but also made it clear that he believed Marsh had made both political mistakes and a misstep in attempting to monopolize black power in the city. But McDaniel's and Richardson's personal dilemmas often overshadowed the political approach they had begun to take: McDaniel was the subject of a police investigation regarding allegations of conflict of interest; Richardson was arrested for possession of drug paraphernalia. He was acquitted by a jury of the felony charge and allowed to remain on the council, but his trial and the admission that he had been an addict since his service in Vietnam surely reduced his effectiveness on the council.

By the late 1980s, West's luster had also dimmed. Having come to council as a self-professed bridge builder, his behavior increasingly belied this image. West launched tirade after tirade at the school system and was extremely critical of its leadership. His own performance as a middle-school principal was subject to both complaints and litigation. While West attempted to portray himself as a Joe Clark disciplinarian bringing order and good manners to an unruly school, others began to question whether he was simply a petty, obsessive man who placed his own rules before student learning. In the mid-1980s, West literally shot himself in the hand and was then compelled to provide an explanation of why he was carrying a gun. By 1988, West's allies in the business community had virtually abandoned him, believing that he had taken on an imperial air and was more interested in serving as de facto superintendent for the school system than he was in performing the traditional mayoral duties.

By 1988, black politics in Richmond (of whatever form) had lost most of its momentum. The 1977 black majority had been fatally weakened and effectively dissolved. Two black council members were fending off legal charges in the courts. And, while Roy West was still valued in the white community as a countervailing force to Marsh, disenchantment with his activities was evident. Perhaps most disturbing was that no new leaders had emerged to redefine the situation and reorient black politics. Indeed, throughout the 1980s, it was difficult to point to one black political leader (with the exception of West) who had emerged during the decade. The cast remained the same. The disputes sounded depressingly familiar. And the answers to the city's problems advanced by the various factions did not seem very different from those articulated at the beginning of the decade. In 1990, the Crusade for Voters, Marsh, and a powerful minister, Dwight Jones, succeeded in punishing McDaniel and replacing her with Adolphus Prince, an associate pastor at Jones's church. But Prince soon proved to be a weak council member who regularly voted on Marsh's side but provided little new vitality for the council.

The inertia in black politics cannot be attributed to a general level of satisfaction in the African American community. Richmond had a substantial black middle class and, in some national studies, was ranked as a relatively appealing location for black professionals. But the city had not been able to avoid most of the problems that confronted other urban areas in the country. Domestic and drug violence had reached an all-time high in the city. In the latter part of the 1980s, Richmond was consistently ranked in the top ten murder capitals in the country on a per capita basis and occasionally in the top five. Dropout rates in high schools and poverty rates in inner-city neighborhoods were unacceptably high. In any case, no one in the late 1980s looked to Richmond as a model of what black leadership could accomplish. City leaders rarely talked about what they had achieved but instead spoke of the woes they had fended off as the most notable examples of accomplishment.

THREE

Set-Aside Politics

The city of Richmond officially committed itself to affirmative action in 1974 when it adopted an employment program intended to ensure that qualified minorities would be sought out for positions in the municipal workforce. In part, the plan was a response to a directive from the federal government that municipalities provide evidence of their intent to implement equal opportunity policies. It was also a result of pressure applied by the black community for a number of years. Distressed by the lack of African Americans in senior management positions and by the paucity of representation in departments such as fire and police, black leaders had demanded that the city make a more determined effort to diversify its workforce. At the time of the plan's adoption, William Leidinger, the city manager, asserted that the performance of department heads would be judged, in part, by their success in meeting affirmative action objectives.

The first explicit use of economic set-asides, however, did not occur until the election of a black majority to the city council in 1977. Set-aside programs were instituted initially on a project-by-project basis. The city council established specific provisions for minority involvement in development undertakings when city funds were utilized. The council required that certain aspects of these projects involve a specified percentage of minority workers, managers, and businessowners. In 1983, the Richmond City Council expanded the use of set-asides from specific projects to all municipal construction contracts by requiring that minority subcontractors receive 30 percent of the dollar value of the total contract whenever the prime contractor was white. The subject of the historic *Croson* challenge, this ordinance was premised on the joint venture provisions included in the construction of the new Atlanta airport and on the legislation upheld by the U.S. Supreme Court in the 1980 *Fullilove v. Klutznick* decision.

The commitment to affirmative action in the form of economic set-asides is best understood in the context of black politics in Richmond (see chap. 2). Set-asides emerged shortly after a black majority was elected to the Richmond City Council and succeeded in installing Henry L. Marsh III as the city's first African American mayor. Set-asides were an instrument with which the new black majority attempted to demonstrate that it could shape economic development policy to benefit African Americans. As set-asides became a routine feature of the city's revitalization initiatives and were ultimately institutionalized in all city construction contracts, they took on even greater political importance. Set-asides eventually became the glue that allowed black and white Richmonders to agree on development initiatives, as well as a symbol of the city's capacity to transcend racial differences and move forward in harmony to realize the vision of a greater Richmond.

This chapter begins by analyzing the manner in which the African American community responded to various proposals for downtown revitalization in Richmond during the past fifty years. We indicate how the development of set-aside policies served to reconcile black leaders to projects that they had once opposed or had only grudgingly accepted. The second part of the chapter examines the institutionalization of set-asides in the city ordinance that provoked the *Croson* challenge. We demonstrate that the city's effort to promote minority economic development through the set-aside policy achieved, at best, limited economic success. The final section describes the evolving functions of affirmative action in Richmond and how it was transformed from a black political demand to an instrument of elite racial reconciliation. Indeed, we argue that its political and symbolic significance became more important than its capacity (or incapacity) to rectify the economic conditions it was originally designed to address.

African Americans and Downtown Revitalization

Three Responses

From the mid-1940s to the beginning of the 1990s, proposals to move Richmond forward economically contained inevitably some recommendations for downtown revitalization. Proponents of such plans typically argued that they were necessary (1) to save a declining retail core from extinction, thus ensuring that even more businesses did not leave the center city for the outlying counties and (2) to guarantee that Richmond could remain competitive with its regional rivals in the Southeast. In many reports, locally based study groups and external consultants pointed to Richmond's "untapped potential" that could be realized through downtown regeneration. At various times, the reports endorsed the development of roads and highways for easy access to downtown, the construction of a coliseum/civic center complex, the development of a major marketplace, the restoration of Second Street (the traditional hub of black business), the creation of a downtown mall, and the recovery of a canal system next to the James River.[1]

Proposals for revitalizing downtown were not universally applauded by Richmond's white citizenry. Neighborhood groups and small businessowners organized in the late forties and again in the early sixties to block projects that were premised on the vision of a "Greater Richmond." At times, opponents of the downtown revitalization plans were motivated by a direct self-interest. Neighborhood-based organizations worried that the corporate-oriented visions would deflect resources from their community's needs. Small businessowners often discovered that their shops would be sacrificed to the buildings and highways planned as the concrete manifestations of Richmond's progress. But there was a philosophical dimension to this opposition as well. In Richmond—the capital of Harry Byrd's "pay as you go" Virginia—fiscal conservatives did not believe that city government should spend taxpayer money for projects that should be undertaken, if at all, by the private sector. This was a primary reason why Richmond entered urban renewal relatively late compared to other cities and why groups such as the Richmond Citizens' Association (RCA) and Richmond Forward felt it necessary to enter the political arena so directly.[2]

The reaction of black Richmonders to proposals for downtown revitalization has run the gamut from outright opposition through grudging accommodation to, more recently, enthusiastic support for redevelopment initiatives. Historically, the African American community has been skeptical of the more grandiose visions sometimes advanced by supporters of downtown redevelopment. Black citizens recognized that dreams of revitalization rarely mentioned the human price that often accompanies such projects, a cost usually borne by minority and poor communities. As Christopher Silver writes, black Richmonders were often compelled to shoulder more than their fair share of the burdens of "progress." For example, the Richmond-Petersburg turnpike started in the 1950s not only physically bisected Jackson Ward, it also reduced the amount of affordable housing available to black citizens throughout the city. The official alternative—relocation to a government housing project—was no alternative at all to those who valued their independence and wished to avoid the social stigma of living in the "courts."[3] In the 1960s, criticisms of downtown revitalization were leveled again as spokespersons for the black community denounced Richmond Forward for its inclination to build "things" instead of "people." Concern about the costs of "progress" sometimes led black citizens to make common cause with conservative whites who wished to restrict the role of government in general.[4]

But African Americans have not adopted a uniformly intransigent stance on downtown revitalization. During the past forty years, a number of prominent black citizens have spoken about the need for the African American community to recognize their self-interest in Richmond's economic progress and see how various projects might be contoured to their advantage. In the late 1940s, Councilman Oliver Hill joined with the Richmond Citizens' Association in supporting the construction of an expressway. Hill maintained that "progressive thinking Negroes" recognized that the city had to grow and move forward, though he called upon the city to use its "ingenuity and financial resources" to get more "public and private housing."[5] In the early 1970s, the Crusade for Voters echoed Hill's words when it recommended that Richmond proceed with the development of a downtown expressway, even though its primary users would be commuters from the suburbs.[6] Although the African American community was wary of and often opposed to downtown redevelopment plans, a number of its leaders felt that revitalization was necessary if Jackson Ward, the traditional hub of black business and culture, was to regain any of its tarnished luster.

In the 1980s, some black leaders identified black interests in the city even more closely with the downtown revitalization agenda. Unlike the arguments advanced against Richmond Forward in the 1960s, such leaders contended that black political influence could be utilized to shape revitalization projects so that they could advance African American interests. From this perspective, downtown revitalization served two major purposes. First, the projects themselves became a means of promoting black entrepreneurship, because of the city's various set-aside guidelines that had to be followed when city funds were involved. Second, black leaders argued that these projects were instrumental in enabling them to support the social agenda that was in the interest of the entire African American community.[7] Opponents of downtown revitalization were described as people who had psychically abandoned the city and did not care if the whole community failed.

Henry L. Marsh III and Downtown Renewal

The career of Marsh, Richmond's first black mayor, is probably the best example of how the perspective of African American leaders has evolved in the past thirty years. At one time or another, Marsh has exhibited each of the tendencies that has characterized the black response to downtown redevelopment initiatives. In 1966 he was elected to the city council as a vocal opponent of Richmond Forward. More than any other political figure in Richmond at the time (with the possible exception of the white populist Howard Carwile), Marsh was the focal point for the anti–Richmond Forward sentiment emerging in the black community. He helped to push the Crusade for Voters away from both its endorsement of Richmond Forward candidates and its implicit support for downtown revitalization. Marsh did this by drawing a stark contrast between what he labeled as his own "human rights" agenda and Richmond Forward's growth-oriented agenda. This position was embodied in his campaign slogan, "Build people not things."[8]

During Marsh's first ten years on the council, he also demonstrated a willingness to accommodate to some measure of center city redevelopment. The evolution of his position on the downtown expressway provides a good example of this tendency. Throughout the 1960s, Marsh was an opponent of the construction of the downtown expressway. While some businesspeople called the expressway "the most important downtown development of our generation" and the *Richmond Times-Dispatch* editorialized that, "with the Expressway, the prospect for downtown Richmond is splendid revitalization; without it, the prospect is misery and decay . . . the death of downtown," Marsh contended that the project was too expensive for the benefits that would accrue.[9] Yet as matters progressed, he adopted a much more conciliatory stance toward the project. In January 1973, Marsh reversed his position on the construction of the downtown expressway and persuaded the Crusade for Voters to abandon its opposition as well. He argued that the expressway should be built because delaying it would cost the city money and make the city less capable of providing social services to the black poor. In response to a question from a black Crusade member ("What is in this for us?"), Marsh noted that there would be $300 million in new downtown development, 25,000 new jobs, and up to $6 million in additional city revenues.[10]

By the early 1980s, Marsh's position on downtown redevelopment had turned almost 180 degrees. Redevelopment was no longer the antithesis of a human needs program. Nor was Marsh's change simply a pragmatic maneuver designed to raise money for an explicit social agenda; in fact, downtown revitalization was now the principal expression of a black political interest in the city. Marsh argued that the construction of the hotel-convention center complex and (later) the festival marketplace would be one of the principal means by which black officials could funnel money into the African American community. The key was to use the emergent black political clout to shape the development so that it contained an explicitly black component. When city money was used to support development projects, Marsh attempted to ensure that the black community would not be excluded from its benefits, either in terms of high-paying construction jobs or ownership of businesses and involvement in management.[11]

Marsh's support of downtown revitalization as essential to the promotion of black interests does not mean that the black civic elite and the Main Street business community agreed on all city policies. What happened, however, was that the structure of the conflict was transformed. It no longer centered on the issue of whether downtown revitalization should be promoted. Instead, the conflict increasingly focused on precisely where it should occur and how it should be shaped. We have previously mentioned Mayor Marsh's support for Project One and the controversy that erupted in 1981 over the construction of a Hilton Hotel outside the area designated for the city-assisted undertaking. A more detailed examination of the controversy illustrates this shift in focus.

The origins of Project One can be traced back to the 1950s and 1960s when business leaders recommended that a convention center complex be constructed to enhance downtown development. In 1973, the idea was resuscitated when the city council engaged the Booz-Allen and Hamilton firm to prepare a report on whether Richmond should build a center and, if so, what kind of facility it should be. When the firm reported that neglecting the opportunity would cost Richmond considerably in lost tourist business, momentum increased for its construction. In 1975, Mayor Tom Bliley argued, "If we don't build the center, we're talking about a loss of 7 million dollars per year." And one city council member defended the plan by remarking, "I know of no cleaner money that can come to a city than convention money. A conventioneer comes to town and we don't have to educate his [sic] children or give him welfare and he doesn't use the public library. If he gets arrested, he even pays for that." In 1976, the city council approved the construction of a "highly visible, multiuse development project downtown" that would include a "convention exhibition center, a convention-oriented hotel, construction of a mall and plaza along Sixth Street, as well as development of retail space and other entertainment facilities."

Yet the proposal for a convention center had foundered under continual opposition. At first, there was extended debate about whether the site for the center was appropriate or whether it should be located elsewhere in the downtown area. Later, a number of small downtown businessowners actively lobbied against the plan. Those who would be displaced by the project were especially vocal, while others contended that it would result in higher taxes that would be burdensome to taxpayers and jeopardize their own financial solvency. The merchants took the city to court in an effort to force it to hold a referendum on the issuance of the bonds to be used to finance the city's contribution to the project.[12] When the legal proceedings were finally settled in the city's favor, the project stalled once again, this time because of the difficulty in obtaining financing during the interest rate spiral of Jimmy Carter's administration.

The funding difficulties in Project One were most visible in the city's difficulty in attracting a major hotel chain as the linchpin of the undertaking. On at least two separate occasions, developers made a commitment to build a hotel but were then stopped by economic reasons. For a time, it appeared that the market might succeed in accomplishing what the opponents of Project One could not achieve in the courts.

In 1981, this difficulty threatened to turn the entire plan to ashes. In August of that year, the Hilton chain announced that it wanted to come to Richmond and build a 350-room hotel in the downtown area just south of the Main Street banking district. A luncheon was held at a major Richmond bank to announce the planned hotel. Conspicuously missing from the meeting was Mayor Marsh. The reason for his absence soon became evident. The city had hired a major national hotel consulting firm, Laventhol and Horwath, to evaluate the market and analyze how Richmond should position itself. The firm's report asserted that in 1981 the city could support only one major new hotel of over four hundred rooms.[13] Viewed from this perspective, construction of the Hilton might render it difficult to attract a hotel chain for Project One and to obtain financing for the venture. In Marsh's opinion, construction of the Hilton might well undermine the revitalization of Broad Street in favor of a Main Street to the James River strategy that would offer no direct help to the African American community.

Marsh thus engineered a city council ordinance stating that all downtown development projects with city approval must be compatible with

Project One. When the Hilton proposal came before the city planning commission (because the hotel needed an easement in order to connect its sewer line to the city utility system), it was rejected on the grounds of ordinance number 81-200.[14] The Hilton Corporation sued the city for $250 million.[15] The editorial pages of the local papers claimed that the ordinance was a disgrace; former city manager and now Councilman Leidinger argued that the black majority was "playing very dangerous"; some observers argued that this was confirmation of Marsh's antibusiness tendency. The controversy received national attention when the *Wall Street Journal* published a story on the inhospitable business environment in Richmond.

For Marsh, however, this way of framing the controversy was incorrect. He contended that he wasn't antibusiness. In fact, speaking of the Main Street business community, he told the reporter and author Margaret Edds, "We adopted most of their plans."[16] In essence, Marsh believed that the delay in the construction of the Hilton would enable Project One to get off the ground. If the Hilton had been built first, it would have meant the end of Project One because it would have been impossible to attract a hotel chain that could have obtained financing for construction on Broad Street. Thus, the Hilton controversy was not about whether Marsh was in favor or opposed to downtown revitalization, or even whether he was pro-business or antibusiness; it was about whether Project One could be salvaged. Marsh concluded that it was the obligation of the black majority to shape market forces away from the Main Street to the James River strategy and direct development toward the sites more accessible to places where black citizens lived, worked, and did business.[17]

Affirmative Action and Downtown Revitalization

Affirmative action programs, especially in the form of economic set-asides, were crucial to black Richmonders' support for downtown revitalization initiatives. Affirmative action was the principal means by which the black political elite attempted to demonstrate that (1) they could successfully extract political concessions from Main Street and (2) redevelopment policies could be shaped to benefit directly the African American community. Indeed, any serious discussion of set-aside programs has to recognize both their context and their political purposes.

The black majority made a conscious effort to write set-aside goals into the legislation when the city government committed public funds to economic development projects. During the initial phase of Project One, the city council passed a set-aside ordinance calling for 25 percent of the construction jobs to go to black Richmonders. The set-aside provision enabled black leaders to argue that downtown revitalization would no longer occur simply at the expense of black citizens. In Marsh's opinion, these projects could be utilized to procure relatively high-paid construction jobs for working-class blacks. In addition to good wages, these jobs would enable blacks to gain both entry to an industry from which they had been excluded and the kind of experience that might, at a future date, permit them to become entrepreneurs.

One of the most notable economic development initiatives of the 1980s was the plan developed by Marsh and T. Justin Moore, CEO of Virginia Power, to formalize the partnership called Richmond Renaissance. The city agreed to put up its half of the $2.4 million seed money by using more than 20 percent of its community block grant money for 1982. Richmond Renaissance had a board of directors that included the city manager and selected members of the council, the black civic elite, and the major corporations headquartered in the city. It also hired a full-time staff director to organize its ongoing projects.

Richmond Renaissance was instrumental in bringing to fruition Sixth Street Marketplace, the centerpiece of the convention center complex. The marketplace became another example of how siting decisions and set-aside provisions were employed to unite the pursuit of black interests with downtown revitalization. For example, site considerations focused on the decision to place the festival mall on Broad Street adjacent to Project One rather than on the James River south of the business district, isolated from the traditional avenues of black commerce. When the idea for the marketplace was initially floated, James Rouse recommended that it be placed along the river, largely because of the success that waterside malls had experienced in Baltimore and Norfolk. The black majority on the council resisted the idea and eventually persuaded Rouse and the local business community that the marketplace should be accessible to black neighborhoods and that it could serve as a potent symbol of interracial cooperation. The final decision sited the festival mall, Sixth Street Marketplace, on either side of Broad Street, the traditional dividing line between black and white Richmond, and the walkway over Broad that would connect the principal sections of the marketplace was called the "Bridge."

When Sixth Street Marketplace was approved for construction, the city manager negotiated a series of agreements on minority participation in the project. Although Marsh was unable to obtain support for an ordinance requiring 33 percent minority ownership and was compelled ultimately to accept a 15 percent ownership quota, substantial provisions for minority involvement remained. According to the city's agreement negotiated with the developer, 20 percent of all architectural and engineering services, 30 percent of all construction contracts, 30 percent of all construction workers, 30 percent of professionals employed by the partnership, and 20 percent of all service contracts would be reserved for minorities. The 1977 black city council majority believed that such policies ensured that the African American community would no longer be excluded from the benefits of growth.

The Richmond Set-Aside Program

The specific set-aside policy that formed the basis for the *Croson* challenge emerged from an effort by black city council members to institutionalize the provisions that had been used in the various redevelopment projects, applying them to city policy more generally. Drawing on the experience of Maynard Jackson's Atlanta, black leaders believed that city government could become a vehicle of economic opportunity for at least some black entrepreneurs. Objections to the set-aside proposal were swept aside and legislation was passed easily by the city council.

Origins of the Set-Aside Program

After Maynard Jackson was elected mayor of Atlanta in 1973, he became a strong advocate for building a new Atlanta airport. When the debate turned to a location for the new facility, Jackson endorsed a proposed site in Henry County south of the city. He maintained that this location, adjacent to Atlanta's black neighborhoods, would "stimulate development on the city's south side and would thereby yield material benefits for Atlanta's black community."[18] In the ensuing political struggle, Jackson's choice for the site was ultimately rejected. When a decision was finally made to build a new terminal adjacent to the existing one in south Atlanta, Jackson could still claim victory because he said that the chosen site would contribute to black development.

Jackson attempted to ensure that economic benefits would be channeled to the black population by applying Atlanta's minority participation in municipal contracts ordinance to "all contractual phases of the airport construction project." "The plan quickly became known by one of its components—the 'joint venture' provision—that called for non-minority contractors to form limited joint-venture partnerships with minority owned firms in order to receive special consideration in the competitive bidding process."[19] Jackson's decision to apply the city's affirmative action provisions to all phases of the airport construction provoked a heated response from the business community and the local media worried about the effects that such a large "social experiment" might have on business efficiency. Jackson ultimately modified his stance on the joint ventures to mollify some of the business opposition and ensure his own reelection. Nonetheless, the joint-venture provisions left in the Atlanta airport plan became a model for many black officials across urban America.

The Atlanta airport was hailed in urban political circles as an example of how black leadership could direct the benefits of economic growth to the African American community. This was critically important because many black elected officials had realized that guarantees of legal equality and the achievement of political power did not necessarily improve the economic condition of their constituents. Having obtained political office, black leaders increasingly began to participate in coalitions with relatively conservative business interests in order to generate the economic growth that might enable them to promote their social agenda. Black officials around the nation were impressed by the manner in which Jackson had succeeded in playing the politics of calculated cooperation. To elected officials struggling, as one Richmond councilman phrased it, to "walk the thin line between accomplishment and appeasement," Maynard Jackson had shown how the politics of growth endorsed by a city's corporate establishment could be used to enhance the economic opportunities of African Americans.[20]

One of Richmond's city council members, Henry "Chuck" Richardson, was very familiar with the Atlanta program. Richardson's sister had married Maynard Jackson, and on a number of occasions Richardson had spoken with his brother-in-law about the establishment and implementation of Atlanta's set-aside policy. Impressed with what Jackson had accomplished, Richardson hoped that some of the lessons in Atlanta could be applied to Richmond. Richardson was aware that the city council had written set-aside provisions into its support for Project One, but he felt that it was necessary to move beyond the strategy of establishing set-asides on an ad hoc basis and embed them into city contracting as a routine policy. Concerned about the apparent lack of minority businesspeople in the bidding of city construction contracts, Richardson approached the city manager and requested a study of minority participation in city construction. At the same time, he approached the city attorney and requested that he begin the process of determining whether a set-aside policy could be established that would be consistent with the congressional program established in 1977 and endorsed by the Supreme Court in its 1980 *Fullilove v. Klutznick* decision.

In response to Richardson's requests, a committee was formed in 1982 headed jointly by the city attorney and chief of purchases and stores to study the situation in Richmond. The committee spent several months reviewing records to determine the extent of participation by minority firms in city construction projects. It also interviewed owners of minority businesses to identify specific areas where they had been excluded from participation. The committee found that in 1978–83 minority businesses received only 0.7 percent of the more than $124 million in city construction contracts. When this statistic was viewed in the light of the historic exclusion of African Americans from Richmond's political and economic life and with knowledge of discrimination in the construction trades, it was apparent that the city had a moral and political responsibility to address the inequity.

The committee then shifted its focus to framing a set-aside program. At the time, participants in the process believed that a policy could rest on a firm legal basis. They were aware that other cities had also formulated programs. Perhaps more importantly, committee members concurred with Richardson's belief that the Supreme Court's 1980 decision in *Fullilove v. Klutznick* furnished a legal justification for their effort. *Fullilove* had upheld the minority business provision of the 1977 Public Works Employment Act that, in essence, required at least 10 percent of federal funds granted for local public works projects be used by the state or local grantee to procure services or supplies from businesses owned by minority group members.

The city council members who supported the set-aside proposal believed that they were simply applying the principles of *Fullilove* to the local level. The key part of the ordinance developed in Richmond was that, absent a waiver, "all contractors awarded construction contracts by the city shall subcontract at least thirty percent of the contract to minority business enterprises."[21] In fact, in almost all of its significant features, the city attorneys tailored the set-aside proposal to what they believed that *Fullilove* permitted. In other words, they felt that the legality of the set-aside provision had been established in the case. Their definition of minorities, which extended beyond the African American community to include "Spanish speaking, Orientals, Eskimos, and Aleuts" (and which returned to haunt the city in the *Croson* challenge), was arrived at simply by replicating the language of the congressional law. Further, in the selection of 30 percent as the set-aside target, the city chose a point about midway between the percentage of contracts awarded to minorities in 1983 and the percentage of minorities in the city's general population, precisely what Congress had done on the national level in 1977.

When Richardson introduced the set-aside bill, the city council passed it on a 6-2 vote with one member abstaining. All five black members of council, including Mayor Roy West, supported the bill; former city manager Leidinger also joined the majority. Debate about the ordinance consumed approximately two hours at the culmination of a five-hour meeting. In the council discussion, Richardson mentioned that the purpose of the bill was to "have those dollars recycled back to minority businesses." Seven members of the public testified at the meeting, two in favor and five opposed to the proposal. Those in favor noted that Richmond was simply enacting a plan similar to those established by other cities—and it was about time for the council to take action on the issue. Five representatives from the local construction industry spoke against the ordinance. They argued that there were not enough minority subcontractors available, even though local trade associations were actively seeking to recruit minority members.

In the Supreme Court decision that upheld the circuit court's overturning of the set-aside ordinance, Justice Sandra Day O'Connor noted that Richmond had not furnished adequate proof of discrimination in the local construction industry. In other words, the Court maintained that the city never established a factual predicate of discrimination that warranted such an extensive program of racial remediation. Councilman Richardson noted in an interview, however, that the council majority simply felt that it was exercising legitimate legislative power and that it did not occur to them that this bill required more extensive proof than any other piece of legislation they might pass. The city adopted this position as well in its various court appearances about the ordinance, suggesting that the gross statistical disparity in the pattern of distributing construction monies was a sufficient rationale for a legislative body to pass such an ordinance.[22]

Operation of the Program

The city's edict resulted in an immediate and dramatic increase in the percentage of city construction money earned by minority businesses.

White firms had to seek out minority subcontractors if they were to remain players in public sector construction. In the first full fiscal year after the plan went into effect, minority participation in city construction contracts increased to 40 percent. In fiscal year 1985–86, minority participation dipped slightly to 37.8 percent and then increased again in 1986–87 to 39.3 percent. Charles Taylor, chief of purchases and stores, acknowledged in an interview with us that the figures for the first eighteen months of the plan could be misleading because the city had not yet instituted a compliance procedure to ensure that the official minority subcontractor was a legitimate minority business. By 1985, however, the city had developed a compliance instrument by which firms had to be certifiably 51 percent minority-owned to be eligible for set-aside approval. City officials believed that in 1985–87 they did a much better job of checking on the legitimacy of minority contractors, though Taylor admitted that occasional complaints were registered throughout the course of the program.[23]

City leaders often pointed to these aggregate figures as evidence for the success of the set-aside program: it was mentioned in their brief to the Supreme Court and noted in testimony before a U.S. House of Representatives subcommittee on government operations that held hearings on the effects of the *Croson* decision. In this study, however, we wanted to go beyond these aggregate figures and gather data on the distribution of the set-aside monies within the minority business community. This data would enable us to both sketch a distribution pattern and identify and further examine the companies that had benefited from the policy. We obtained a list of minority contractors and the dollar amounts that each had received from the city from the time that the certification procedure was instituted in 1985 to the elimination of the set-aside program by the circuit court in 1987.[24]

Forty-seven companies received construction monies for an average of $248,786 per company in the two-year period—but these funds were not evenly distributed. Perhaps the most interesting feature of the distribution was that in 1985 and again in 1986, two contractors received a majority of the money that went to minority firms. In 1985, Dwight Snead's company earned $1,971,000 and Quail Oak Company received $828,000, out of a total of $5,446,291 earned by minority firms. In 1986, Quail Oak received $1,731,297 and Snead earned $1,529,833 out of the $6,246,667 that went to minority contractors.

The dominance of these two companies, after a relatively workable practice for certifying minority businesses was instituted, could be attributed to three factors. First, both businesses were uniquely situated to take advantage of the set-aside opportunity. Dwight Snead had been operating his own company in Richmond for a number of years. Snead's father had owned a small landscaping firm in the city and, on the urging of some of his father's affluent clients, Dwight Snead had attended the University of Massachusetts and obtained a degree in landscape architecture. He initially started a business on Long Island but then returned to Richmond and established his own contracting firm. Snead's business was modest but profitable. When the set-aside program commenced, he had already developed the name recognition and business reputation that made him a logical choice for nonminority firms looking to comply with the ordinance. As Snead remarked, "During the set-aside program my phone was ringing off the hook."[25]

The Quail Oak Company was also well situated but for slightly different reasons than Snead. Quail Oak was a family-owned firm run by two siblings. After graduating from high school and working in a grocery store, the Harris brothers decided to strike out on their own; they established a small landscaping business, cutting lawns, planting trees, and working on the grounds for new homes. But what allowed the Harris brothers to take advantage of the set-aside opportunity was their connection with the Minority Business League, an organization devoted to developing minority entrepreneurship and partially funded by the city. The Minority Business League was established at the turn of the century by Booker T. Washington as part of his effort to enhance the economic position of African Americans. The Harris brothers had utilized its programs along with those of a local community college to learn about business techniques. The director of the Minority Business League sat on the city committee that helped to develop the set-aside program, and she was able to inform the Harris brothers of the opportunity created by the ordinance.[26]

A second feature that contributed to the dominance of these two companies was the nature of the local construction industry. According to most accounts, the Richmond construction business is heavily dependent on reputation and skillful networking. Indeed, the set-aside program was intended by city officials to limit the effects of the old boy system, a framework that many black leaders felt served to exclude black-owned companies from obtaining work that they were competent to perform. The development of a set-aside program did not eliminate the importance of reputation in obtaining contracts but merely ensured that minority businesses would be included. Once the Snead and Harris companies were perceived as competent and reliable, white contractors approached them with increasing frequency. It was not surprising that they received so much business because the principal interest of the prime contractors was getting the work done on time, not with increasing the number of black entrepreneurs in the city.

Third, both the Harris brothers and Dwight Snead used the set-aside program as an instrument for diversifying and expanding their companies. Indeed, the paths followed by their companies are exemplars of what the defenders of affirmative action said should happen. Critics of set-aside policies have sometimes argued that such policies simply help business-people who are already affluent. This was not the case in Richmond. Snead had a small business that underwent a substantial expansion as a result of the set-aside program. The Harris brothers had a fledgling operation that became a major success during the course of the program. By 1987, when the program was eliminated by the circuit court's decision, both firms had become less dependent on the set-asides for business and more competitive in private bidding for prime contractor jobs. Curtis Harris noted, "I didn't know when and if the set-aside program was going to end, but I knew that it made good business sense to diversify so that I wouldn't be lost without it."[27] Speaking in 1989, both Snead and Harris suggested that the gross receipts of their companies had not been significantly diminished since the end of the program. But they also mentioned that they are called much less frequently by white contractors and that they would have never reached their current level without the opportunity furnished by the set-aside ordinance.

Perceptions of the Set-Aside Program

Besides examining the distribution of set-aside funds, we were also interested in learning how people involved with the program perceived the policy. In particular, we were concerned with the structure of perceptions by race. Our conversations with some of the participants, developers, and observers of the program illuminated the manner in which people viewed a number of the larger theoretical issues concerning affirmative action. By focusing on the operation of the set-aside program, we eventually elicited statements about people's view of the construction industry and American capitalism more generally as well as the extent of the influence that they believed race continued to exercise in American society.

Most whites who were involved with the set-aside program as contractors or who viewed it from a vantage point within the construction business (as an official of a trade association or a bonding company representative) tended to be critical of the ordinance. First, they argued that the program was a giveaway, that it granted favors on a racial basis and thus undermined the basic principle of competitiveness upon which they had normally operated. Second, they contended that the set-aside program had allowed more fraud and abuse to seep into the system. They generally conceded that at the outset of the program, the city did not have adequate controls to ensure that minorities were actually doing the work on contracts and that so-called minority firms were not fronts for white businesses. Even in later years, complaints surfaced that minority contractors were given special treatment in obtaining contracts only to farm the work out to non-minority firms.

Whites also tended to suggest that racial bias had been eliminated in the construction industry. They claimed that by 1985 contractors were judged strictly according to performance. For instance, one interviewee said that, at least in Richmond, there is so much construction work available that anyone with a reputation for performing a job in a skillful and timely manner will be certain to obtain other jobs because there is a shortage of responsible and skilled contractors in every part of the business: "No one cares about race anymore. There isn't one iota of discrimination in the construction industry. You get a reputation for doing a good job and the telephone calls will keep coming."[28]

Interviewees traced problems, such as the availability of bonding (which is a significant obstacle to minority firms and other small contractors), not to discrimination but to the lack of experience on the part of minority entrepreneurs, which was common to all small businesses, black or white. From this perspective, contractors who were accustomed to operating, in the lingo of the trade, "out of the back of their pickups" had rarely utilized the financial accounting practices that would make them acceptable risks to the insurance companies that provided bonding. Sometimes this was attributed simply to a lack of knowledge about the requirements, but some bonding agents believed that it was due to a conscious decision to remain in the underground economy and accrue the tax advantages of not keeping complete financial records.[29] Whites in the industry suggested that the answer to such dilemmas was in the kind of business education that trade groups might provide to *all* small businesses, rather than in the establishment of racial set-aside programs that might simply generate abuse and resentment.

Black interviewees in both the construction industry and the political arena held widely divergent perspectives on these issues. In their minds, the construction industry had long been an almost impenetrable bastion of racial discrimination. They believed that company owners, trade associations, and unions had prevented African Americans from entering the business and had conspired to keep them from gaining a foothold. Perhaps more importantly, blacks did not believe that the industry had significantly changed over the years. While black contractors acknowledged that reputation was important, they certainly did not believe that there no longer remained an "iota" of discrimination in the construction trades. They pointed to the informal networks that dominated the local industry and that had deliberately excluded black contractors. Some noted that Richmond's Association of General Contractors had very few minorities and certainly did not actively solicit their membership in the organization.

Set-aside programs were thus perceived as a necessary policy for promoting black competitiveness insofar as they guaranteed access to a market with discrimination embedded in informal practices but denied by the bonding industry. Black political leaders believed that the use of government to correct market deficiencies was absolutely necessary because of the nature of the industry in which friendship and social relationships had irrevocably altered whatever meritocratic component had existed. From this perspective, the residue of resentment that accompanied the programs was inevitable inasmuch as the policy represented a challenge to normal operating procedures.

The division of opinion about the merits of the set-aside program in Richmond is consistent with national findings about racial attitudes concerning affirmative action. Yet it is important to understand that the beliefs of whites in the construction industry were never really politicized in Richmond. Other white businesspeople did not join the contractors in opposing the policy, nor did the white population turn the set-aside program into an issue during council elections. Thus, the program that provoked a landmark Supreme Court decision made scarcely a blip on the Richmond political terrain. To understand why this was so requires an examination of the broader function that affirmative action served in the city.

Affirmative Action and Elite Racial Reconciliation
The Political Uses of Set-Asides

Affirmative action was initially pursued by the black majority on the city council as a means of ensuring that city policies furthered African American interests. The comments of black political officials who supported the city programs sound very much like liberal scholars' defense of affirmative action. On the one hand, black council members believed that affirmative action was a logical continuation of the goals of the civil rights movement and a sensible instrument for remedying past injustice. As Marsh was fond of saying, the point had been reached in American life when it was "time to integrate the money." In addition to addressing historic discrimination, black political leaders viewed affirmative action as a forward-looking policy. Councilman Richardson maintained that it provided "access to opportunity," enabling African Americans to participate more fully in American life, both economically and politically.[30] Black leaders in Richmond portrayed their support of affirmative action policies as proof of their commitment to the community that had nurtured them. For example, when Roy West was criticized by the Marsh faction for insufficient vigor in the pursuit of black interests, he rejected the charge by pointing to his support for the set-aside program.

Yet the evidence presented here on the institutionalization of set-asides in city construction contracts suggests that the policy did not achieve anything resembling the effect on African American economic development that its supporters publicly claimed it would. The kind of evidence we have highlighted would not have been particularly difficult to obtain, but no political official ever sought to do so. Even in the aftermath of the Court's decision to overturn the set-aside program, set-asides merited little discussion. A thorough analysis of whether and how the program worked was simply never an issue. No one really addressed how well "the money was integrated" or what kind of opportunities really existed.

What accounts for the silence on this matter? Maybe the city intended a review at the five-year mark and the Court's decision short-circuited the plan. Or perhaps city officials simply did not want to provide any ammunition to the legion of litigants willing to haul Richmond into court for its set-aside policy. Both of these explanations may contain a measure of truth, but it seems to us that something else was occurring as well: namely, affirmative action policies in Richmond served political goals much more than they did the economic development of the black constituency. Understanding the lack of scrutiny received by the programs requires us to grasp the political goals that were served.

Set-Asides as a Means by which Black Officials Could Demonstrate Accomplishment.   In city after city during the 1970s and 1980s, studies highlighted the deterioration of conditions and the difficulties that newly elected black leaders faced in pursuing their goals. Scholars contend that the restructuring of the federal budget after years of Republican control of the executive branch, combined with the recession of the early eighties, residential housing patterns that continued the exodus to suburbia, and the increased willingness of business to abandon the central city, had put unbearable strain on municipal governments. Some researchers have gone so far as to suggest that we have witnessed the "end of urban politics" as cities lost their autonomy and became mere pawns in the larger game of American politics. Buffeted by these apparently inexorable forces, set-asides became a means of indicating that African American politicians could accomplish something and had not lost their souls while they did so. This is why in Richmond, when West was criticized for insufficient attachment to the cause of black uplift, he rejected the charge by pointing to his support for the set-aside program.

Set-Asides as a Crucial Feature of the Unofficial Theory of Black Progress that Animated the City's African American Leadership.   We have seen that affirmative action was often defended in terms of providing benefits to the entire black community, either in the same way that the civil rights movement ended legal segregation or in the manner that nationalist community organizations benefit the majority of people who participate. Yet black leaders in the city of Richmond would hardly be surprised by the results of our examination of the set-aside program. In fact, a number of them provided us with "not for attribution" statements that amounted to an explicit confirmation of our findings. One high-ranking city official noted that the real purpose of the various set-aside programs was to "create a few black millionaires." Another mentioned that the program was very successful for "the chosen few," and one former council member speculated that a "small handful of people" were probably aided by the set-aside policies.

The reluctance to provide these statements for attribution may stem simply from the desire not to provide any further ammunition for the mounting number of affirmative action critics that have emerged in American society. But there may also be more subtle factors operating. In essence, the official rhetoric employed to justify these programs may not cohere with the actual theory of black advancement practiced by African American officials in Richmond. The official rhetoric about set-asides typically points to the democratic and egalitarian consequences of the policy. By saying that it is time to "integrate the money," one evokes the struggle for civil rights in the sixties when the movement attempted to integrate all public facilities. By noting that affirmative action is essential for black economic development, officials appeal to a quasi-nationalist sentiment that suggests that the community as a whole will advance.

Yet by admitting that the programs may in fact help to create a "few black millionaires" and aid only "the chosen few," a very different perspective on black progress is implied. According to this outlook, city government could be used to create (or perhaps reestablish) a black economic elite that might eventually become a countervailing power to the Main Street establishment in city politics. Black officials in Richmond have never really believed that control of the city council provided effective black power in the city. They have always spoken about the continuing influence of the Main Street establishment. Set-aside provisions for ownership, contracts, and management positions were the instrument by which a new black elite might be created. Thus, "integrating the money" was not quite the same as integrating the lunch counter. It is a kind of trickle-down theory of political influence, namely, that creating millionaires would eventually help to create the kind of black influence in the city that could rival traditional white power.

Set-Asides as an Instrument of Elite Racial Reconciliation.   In the early 1960s, Richmond had received national attention as a southern city that was far ahead of the rest of the region in terms of race relations. We indicated in the previous chapter how the *Washington Post, Saturday Review,* and *New York Times* carried articles and columns from this perspective. But Richmond's reputation as a model for racial harmony was soon shattered. In the last half of the decade, the black civic elite and Richmond Forward, the political voice of the Main Street establishment, became increasingly alienated. This estrangement continued throughout the seventies and early eighties as the election of a black majority on the city council, the subsequent firing of Leidinger, the controversy over the Hilton Hotel, and a series of highly charged negative editorials in Richmond's daily press about the new leadership pointed to persistent divisions in the city.

None of the major players in city politics had an interest in having Richmond's reputation permanently besmirched. Marsh remarked that he certainly did not want Richmond to turn into another Newark. The city's business leaders did not want to be perceived nationally as tenacious defenders of white privilege, nor did they want the city government to pursue policies that were inhospitable to business development. In fact, they had hoped to use the city's architectural distinctiveness and diverse cultural offerings to attract other companies to the city.

The one highly visible effort to remedy this division occurred in 1982 with the formation of Richmond Renaissance, the public-private organization dedicated to the revitalization of downtown and adjacent areas in the city. The inclusion of affirmative action provisions in downtown revitalization projects became, as Clarence Stone noted in his study of Atlanta politics, the glue that held this precarious coalition together. It allowed the black civic elite to identify downtown regeneration with broader African American interests. Further, it was the concession that the predominantly white Main Street establishment agreed to make in order to guarantee that its agenda for preserving and revitalizing downtown would be pursued by the black leadership.[31] In this situation, neither of the two powerful groups in the city had any serious interest in studying how well or poorly set-asides functioned economically, because the real goal that these helped to accomplish was the maintenance of racial peace in the city. Support for set-asides was a public demonstration by the city's large corporations—a number of which were under attack regionally or nationally—that they had the best interests of the entire community at heart.[32]

Affirmative Action and Social Theory

Understanding the political uses of set-asides helps to explain why we are dissatisfied with much of the conventional debate about affirmative action policies. Scholars such as Thomas Sowell and Walter Williams correctly note that these programs may modify the operation of the market and that the results of the policies can exhibit a troubling class bias. But conservative critics often ignore the historical genesis of affirmative action, the specific ways in which it has evolved, and the social and political forces that have supported such policies. They continually portray affirmative action as a liberal ploy for mandating equality of result, which is then presented in the rhetoric of equal opportunity. To the extent that businesses adopt such policies, conservatives typically maintain that the fear of litigation is the primary motivation. But this analysis is too simplistic as an explanation of why the programs have arisen, what they are intended to accomplish, and why they are supported.

In Richmond, affirmative action began as a method by which a liberal council majority attempted to redirect benefits to the minority community. It eventually became an instrument to serve other political purposes. Indeed, the threat of legal sanctions became increasingly less important in corporate acceptance of affirmative action. While we discuss the corporate embrace of a form of affirmative action in more depth in chapter 5, at this point, we can say that support for affirmative action served as a concrete sign that the business leaders were willing to work with African American political leaders. Moreover, if corporations originally agreed to set-aside provisions in order to keep the political peace, by the end of the 1980s they discovered that affirmative action could be beneficial to their own interests. Indeed, a number of major corporations in Richmond pointed proudly to their own affirmative action programs as examples of their commitment to the broader community.

The free market conservative critique of affirmative action fails to consider the subtle divisions of opinion that may exist among the business community and conservatives about the worth of affirmative action. While all businesses endorse the continued existence of capitalism and believe that a market economy is essential to human prosperity, they may have very different ideas about the appropriateness of government efforts to shape the marketplace in order to promote particular social policies. In Richmond, the challenge to the set-aside program came from the construction industry, a business sector that was not part of the Main Street establishment. The construction industry saw the set-aside program as an inefficient, unnecessary, and perhaps unconstitutional infringement on its freedom. The Main Street establishment welcomed the policy as a means of transcending racial division and getting on with the revitalization of downtown.

Our study of the set-aside program in Richmond offers little consolation to liberal defenders of affirmative action. Liberals typically argue that affirmative action helps to rectify past injustices and provides access to opportunities. While our examination of the set-aside program demonstrates that the ordinance helped to funnel money to black entrepreneurs and may have even improved the psychological climate for minority businesses, it is also true that the extent of the program's benefits were limited. Just two contractors received the majority of the money spent on the entire set-aside program. Moreover, the program could not guarantee that blacks would be more widely employed in the construction industry or that the money would be distributed more evenly. The program worked to the extent that it took two companies—one small and one just starting—and enabled them to become competitive in the private sector. But it was a program in which the aggregate total (more than 35 percent of city construction dollars being received by minority companies) was much more impressive than the specific distributional pattern.

In addition, we have argued that some of the liberal rhetoric associated with these programs cannot always be taken as indicative of the actual intentions. The rhetoric endorsing these programs may have deliberately obscured the manner in which black leadership expected it to function. Prior to the formation of the policy, there was a debate within the African American community about the extent to which set-asides could actually foster black economic development. The position of those who were skeptical of the program and believed that its benefits would not extend beyond a handful of entrepreneurs was not taken as seriously as it could have been. Thus, civil rights rhetoric is sometimes used to disguise what might be called a trickle-down approach to black economic development.

It might be argued that the role of affirmative action in fostering a black economic elite and improving relations in a racially divided city is justifiably more important than the limited economic advantages of the programs. We do not want to disparage this assertion completely, though we do want to express reservations about the extent of its validity. Clearly, Richmond was a divided city, and the capacity of its elites, both black and white, to reach an accommodation was not an insignificant achievement. Richmond has been able to attract more convention business, and it has managed to ensure that its national reputation is not that of a cauldron of racial conflict. Given the situation that existed in 1981–82, we could point out that Richmond has avoided the worst catastrophes that have befallen some other metropolitan areas.

Black leaders might also maintain that generating downtown revitalization has provided the opportunity to improve the lives of the masses of black Richmonders, even if the particular set-aside programs had limited relevance. In fact, they often argue that Richmond would be much worse off if the downtown revitalization projects had not occurred at all. They tend to argue that affirmative action policies are accompanied by the kind of agenda that will be able to offer more opportunities and advantages for African Americans. They contend that such initiatives have enabled them to enhance employment opportunities, alter budgetary priorities, and improve schools.

Such claims of progress are, of course, subject to analysis. Precisely what kind of politics has accompanied the affirmative action agenda in Rich-

mond? Did it help to produce black political and economic empowerment? Or could a contrary case be made that it has produced little progress
and needs reconsideration? Should we look at affirmative action politics
as an approach that has characteristic benefits as well as liabilities? In the
next chapter, we turn to these questions regarding the relationship of set-
aside politics to the broader strategy for African American advancement.

FOUR

Set-Asides and the Broader Strategy for Black Progress

In the previous chapter we maintain that Richmond's set-aside programs served political purposes that were, in some sense, separate from the official justification of promoting minority economic opportunity. We contend that set-aside policies were a critical element of the broader political strategy adopted by black leadership in Richmond.[1] Our analysis indicates that the set-aside programs resulted in limited gains for the African American community inasmuch as only a handful of companies were able to take advantage of the city policy. If, as supporters of these policies contend, set-aside programs were merely part of a more general strategy—a link in a larger political chain—then we must examine the consequences of this broader approach to black progress. In other words, did the political framework established by the city's black leadership advance the general interest of the African American community, even if the set-aside policies were not very successful in a direct economic sense?

This chapter probes this question in more depth. We begin by assessing the claims that black leadership has made about its own success. We examine four areas that are commonly referred to as examples of substantial accomplishment: (1) the level of black employment in municipal government, (2) the council's redirection of budgetary priorities since the ascendancy of an African American majority to power in the 1970s, (3) the decision by Richmond Renaissance in recent years to devote a portion of its resources to revitalizing Jackson Ward, the traditional hub of African American commerce and culture, and (4) the promotion of black political participation and the recruitment of new black political leadership. In each of these areas, black elected officials point to accomplishments that they believe serve to justify their approach during the 1980s. In essence, black leaders argue that they have enhanced economic opportunity, buttressed the educational structure, channeled resources into black neighborhoods, and promoted African American political development.

There is a measure of validity to these arguments. At the same time, like most assertions of political accomplishments, the claims are often too casually made, inflating the magnitude of the progress attained and ignoring countervailing trends in the broader African American community. These omissions have consequences, of course, for the manner in which we evaluate the set-aside programs implemented in cities such as Richmond. Rather than a link in a broader chain of black progress, set-asides may be a defining feature of a *particular strategy* for African American advance that has both characteristic strengths and predictable weaknesses.

Black Leadership and City Employment

Besides attacking legal segregation, the civil rights movement worked to reduce the extent of racial discrimination in employment. Movement leaders pointed to discriminatory practices that limited job opportunities for African Americans and worked to pass legislation that would make such procedures illegal. During the Montgomery bus boycott, the city's civil rights leadership advocated the hiring of more African Americans as bus drivers. In the 1963 March on Washington best remembered for Martin Luther King Jr.'s "I Have a Dream" speech, other talks by Roy Wilkins and A. Philip Randolph focused on the importance of increasing job opportunities for black Americans. One of the key provisions of the Civil Rights Act passed by Congress in 1964 was the section prohibiting discrimination in employment. Given the movement's emphasis on this theme, it is not surprising that the evaluation of black political leadership often focuses on its record in opening up government employment to African Americans.

In the decade prior to the election of a black majority to the Richmond City Council, black political leaders regularly mentioned discrimination in city employment as an important problem. Indeed, it was viewed as a prototypical example of the white establishment's insensitivity to African American needs. This issue was perhaps most visible in the periodic controversies that emerged about police conduct. During this time, black citizens became increasingly concerned about their treatment at the hands of city police. A number of highly publicized incidents occurred in which black citizens claimed that they had been subjected to police brutality.[2] Discussions of these incidents in black political circles and in the African American press often referred to the paucity of blacks employed by the police force. Although Richmond was approximately 50 percent black in 1971, only 12 percent of the police was African American and no black held a rank higher than sergeant. Citizens invariably pointed to this racial imbalance as a significant factor in the brutality suffered by the black population. As Preston Yancy, a columnist for the *Richmond Afro-American*, observed, "There is the need for more black policemen. Cities with a large black population must have more black policemen if crime rates are to be checked and if hostility against the police is to be checked."[3]

The African American community believed that the police force was simply the most egregious example of a problem that permeated city employment practices. Starting in the late 1960s, there was a continual stream of complaints about city hiring. African American leaders noted that not only had the construction of the downtown coliseum displaced poor blacks from their homes, it had also failed to provide significant employment opportunities for African Americans. As Raymond Boone, editor of the *Richmond Afro-American*, remarked, "The Richmond Coliseum uprooted countless black families in a tight, Jim Crow housing market to furnish new highpaying jobs for whites (not a single black is hired in a top money making position) to entertain the well heeled and to create more profits for downtown merchants."[4] African American leaders also referred to the absence of blacks from administrative posts in city government, observing in 1971 that no city agency was headed by an African American.

The pressure applied by the black community helped to reorient the city's employment policy. Between 1971 and 1973, two African Americans were appointed to head city departments and Elijah Rogers was selected as the first black assistant city manager. Moreover, the city responded to the 1970 congressional modifications of the Civil Rights Act by developing the Richmond Affirmative Action Plan to ensure that there was equal opportunity in municipal employment. This was the first time that Richmond officially committed itself to a form of affirmative action. The city promised to prepare quarterly reports of Richmond's employment practices with respect to race and gender; it spelled out specific nondiscriminatory hiring practices; and the city manager asserted that he would hold department heads responsible for implementing the program as part of their job performance review.[5]

Thus, the initial report in 1973 confirmed what many black leaders had been saying for years. The report demonstrated that total black employment was only 31 percent of the workforce, and most of these workers were concentrated in unskilled, low-paying jobs. Besides their relative absence in administrative level positions, blacks held few of the jobs in the skilled craftsman category and very few of the foreman and supervisory positions and were severely underrepresented in departments such as public works, planning, data processing, and general services and finance. No black woman earned more than $16,000 in any city position. As Assistant City Manager Rogers noted, "Up to now we have only been able to speculate on the employment picture in city government, but we now have concrete evidence of the situation and it will be up to us to move to change it."[6] City Manager William Leidinger averred that he would use future affirmative action reports to determine "if any department showed a pattern of discrimination in future hirings."[7]

The members of the black majority council who were elected in 1977 frequently point to the progress made in city employment as a principal indicator of the difference they have made in Richmond. They speak of the hiring of African Americans as city managers and department heads. They point to the fact that African American citizens can enter city hall and feel that Richmond is their city as well. And they maintain that their efforts have enabled more black Americans to view municipal employment as a possible source of opportunity and mobility.[8]

These claims certainly have some validity. The progress in black city employment between 1973 and 1988 was considerable. But the interpretation of the causes of this progress and how far-reaching its effects have been must take into account several factors that qualify the rhetoric. For example, African American opportunities for city employment developed in a period when population loss and budget cutbacks were making fewer government jobs available to the black population. The total workforce in Richmond peaked about 1978 and then declined. Efficient city operations demanded that officials cut back the city workforce at the very time that blacks were becoming politically ascendant. Two city managers, African Americans Manuel Deese and Robert Bobb, mentioned in their budget messages that reductions in the city workforce were examples of their commitment to fiscally responsible management. As early as 1979, Deese argued, "This budget can and must project workforce reductions. The times and the nature of our departments and agencies dictate that we find ways to do more with fewer people and operating dollars."[9]

This effect can be illustrated by examining both percentage increases and the absolute number of people employed in various job classifications used by the city's personnel department. For example, the percentage of blacks holding service and maintenance positions increased from 50 percent in 1973 to 86 percent in 1988. Despite this sizeable increase, the total number of African Americans employed in these positions actually declined in the same time period.[10] Between 1973 and 1978, almost three hundred African Americans were hired in the service and maintenance classification. Yet between 1978 and 1988 more than three hundred jobs were lost as economic policy dictated a leaner workforce.

It was only in the two highest job classifications—administrative and professional—where a percentage increase in black employment was accompanied by an increase in the absolute number of African Americans employed. Between 1973 and 1988, black employment rose from about 14 percent in these categories to 43 percent of the workforce.[11] For example, at the highest administrative level, the number of African Americans employed rose from ten in 1973 to forty-three in 1982. Thus, black opportunity increased at all levels of city employment when measured by percentage of employees. But population shifts in the county and broader economic trends also imposed a fiscal discipline on Richmond that differentially improved the opportunities for African Americans who were highly educated and skilled.[12]

A second critical factor in the interpretation of black employment gains in Richmond is the timeline of the progress. We have indicated that there were substantial increases in black employment by the city between 1973 and 1988, but the progress in the five years prior to the election of the black majority—a period when there were no councilmanic contests because of litigation over a controversial annexation plan designed by white councilmembers—was equally substantial. This was, in fact, the take-off period in which African Americans went from being substantially underrepresented at every level to a point where some representation was effected in all aspects of city employment.

This factor can be easily illustrated. In the very top administrative classification, the percentage of black representation increased from 5.7 in 1973 to 14.8 in 1978 to 21 percent in 1982. There were ten African American administrators in the top category in 1973, thirty-two in 1978, and forty-three in 1982. The biggest jump was made prior to the 1977 election of the black majority council. The same point holds true for service and maintenance workers at the bottom of the job classification structure. Black representation in this category went from 50.3 percent in 1973, to 66.9 percent in 1978, to 69.8 percent in 1982. Again, the largest advance occurred in the years immediately preceding the election of the black majority council and black mayor.[13]

In *Civil Rights: Rhetoric or Reality*, Thomas Sowell uses a timeline analysis to compare the economic gains made by African Americans before and after the passage of civil rights legislation. Sowell points out that the advances made in the decade preceding the passage of the Civil Rights Act were as substantial as the progress in the ten years following its passage. Sowell argues that blacks actually did better when they concentrated on advancing through individual initiative than when they focused on political action. Indeed, this argument is an integral feature of his free market attack on the strategy of utilizing the state as an instrument for bettering economic conditions. Sowell contends that politics is largely irrelevant to black progress, except when liberal policies regulate markets so as to inhibit the kind of individual initiative that could result in long-term advance.[14]

The results of our timeline analysis of employment gains in city government bear some resemblance to Sowell's description of black progress. While we suggest that African American advancement in municipal employment began prior to the time that a black majority obtained control of the city council, our interpretation of why this happened is substantially different from Sowell's. First, employment opportunities for blacks were enhanced in Richmond by the application of national civil rights legislation to local government policies. In fact, national legislation was clearly the impetus for the formulation of the city's first affirmative action program in 1973. This is a vivid example of a case where politics mattered.

It is also important to note the *kind* of politics that were effective in Richmond. Members of the black majority city council are fond of suggesting that their work enhanced employment opportunities. This is partially true. But it is our contention that it was to the extent that they contributed to the pressure placed on elected officials *prior* to their election as council members that achieved very substantial gains. If we recognize that employment gains preceding the election of a black majority were as significant as those that followed, we can see that a relatively mobilized African American citizenry accomplished as much in this area as did the election of officials designed to represent the will of the constituency. In effect, black elected officials consolidated the gains that pressure politics achieved prior to their election.[15]

Budgetary Priorities of Black Leadership

African American leaders in the 1960s and 1970s extended their critique of the Richmond city government's hiring practices to the more general budgetary priorities of the council. It was a common practice for representatives of the black community to highlight the necessity for replacing a budget based on the desires of corporate Richmond with one that addressed human needs. This slogan ("Build people not things") undergirded Henry L. Marsh's original campaign for city council in 1966, was repeated throughout the early 1970s by the Crusade for Voters, and was an integral feature in the agitation about the public school system in this period. Moreover, it was used by the newly elected black majority as a justification for the removal of Leidinger as city manager in 1978 (see chap. 2).

One method for measuring the influence of black elected officials is to check whether they were able to redirect city spending in keeping with their stated priorities from the time they assumed power up to the *Croson* decision. There are, of course, a number of objections that can be raised to the appropriateness of examining budgets to illuminate the priorities of black leadership. Studies demonstrate that budgets are typically fashioned in an incremental manner, and the existing base tends to be more influential than the ideological disposition of elected officials. In addition, Richmond's council-manager form of government leaves the creation of the budgetary framework to the city manager who may be guided by concerns other than council's ideological leaning. Finally, the black majority on the council has been seriously divided since 1982, and this fragmentation has given more influence to white council members than most would have envisioned in 1978. Although these objections should make us cautious about the conclusions to be drawn, they are insufficiently compelling to deter the analysis.

The Richmond City Council hires and fires the city's managers, and in 1978 the majority demonstrated that it was willing to exercise this power. Moreover, there was considerable black influence on the city council during 1978–90, which provided time for black leaders to put a distinctive stamp on the budget, even if the black majority was torn by internal division.

Analysis of the budgetary priorities of the 1980s indicates that there was a noticeable shift in at least one element of city spending priorities. This can be discerned in the share of the city's general funding that goes to the school system. In the fiscal year 1980–81, 22.3 percent of the city's general fund budget went to support the school system. (This figure understates by about 3 percent the actual amount because it did not include employees' fringe benefits that are contained in later figures.) By fiscal year 1988–89, 31 percent of the city's general fund spending was allocated to the educational system.[16] In addition, throughout the 1980s, the city schools received a budgetary appropriation that was significantly larger than the percentage increase in the total general fund. In fact, by the end of the 1980s, comparative data with the predominantly white surrounding counties showed that Richmond exceeded the counties in dollars spent per pupil, though city leaders argued that the special populations that had to be serviced in poorer areas rendered this comparison extremely misleading.

Other than education, spending on recreation and culture was the only area of the budget where spending significantly increased in the 1980s. By the end of the decade, recreation and culture was receiving about 5.7 percent of the city's general fund expenditures, an increase from about 3 percent at the beginning of the decade. While the city increased its spending on recreation and culture, its funding for health and welfare declined during the 1980s. Although the percentage of Richmond's revenues that came from the state and federal governments remained relatively constant during the period, funds available for health and social services were reduced. At first, the city attempted to compensate for the shortfall, but other choices and demands on its funds made this unworkable. The general fund budget allocated 13.3 percent for health and social services in 1980, a figure that declined to 12 percent by the end of the decade.

The black majority on the city council probably made a difference in reorienting Richmond's priorities, but the change was not as substantial as the rhetoric often claimed. Through sound fiscal management, they were able to reduce the amount of money the city spent on servicing its debt and shift those funds to education. Yet this was the only major difference in the budgetary politics of the black-dominated city council. For the most part, the 1989–90 budget looked very much like the 1980–81 budget. Thus, the establishment of a "human rights" economic agenda that differed substantially from previous councils was not evident in the budget. Nor was there a substantial shift in the sources of revenue. Individual property tax increased modestly, and the tax burden on corporate Richmond decreased modestly in the decade during which a black majority sat on the council. But cautious incrementalism remained the order of the day.

Indeed, we would argue that even the shift of funds to education must be critically analyzed. The impetus for this change was the popular mobilization in the black community that had occurred while Leidinger was city manager in the year preceding the 1977 elections. In addition, the infusion of funds did not prevent or reduce the bitter controversies that raged in the 1980s about the school system. Various factions on the council quarreled over the job performance of Richard Hunter, the superintendent appointed by the original black majority. When he judiciously left town within a year after Roy West's election as mayor, the superintendent's position was subjected to a politically motivated game of musical chairs for the rest of the 1980s. School board appointments were often made in keeping with the factional divisions on the council. And schoolteachers continually voiced their belief that money was not being spent on the classroom but was instead diverted to a bloated central bureaucracy isolated from the concerns of those in the classroom. Most teachers believed that, at best, the city was doing an average job of educating the city's youth. Dropout rates remained unenviably high, incidents of school violence increased, and test scores did not appreciably increase despite the expenditure of additional funds.

In addition, some observers believed that the city was developing a two-tiered educational system, based more on class than simply racial differences. The creation of magnet schools at the elementary level and the development of a separate high school for the gifted enabled Richmond's better students to receive a quality education, though even this was insufficient to stop the exodus of a portion of the black middle class to suburbia. Nonetheless, students from particular Richmond high schools were accepted each year at the most elite institutions in the state and the nation. At the same time, the inner-city schools appeared to be engaged in what was at best a holding action, as these attempted to provide basic educational services to a clientele that, in William Julius Wilson's phrase, was increasingly concentrated in areas of social isolation. It was an open question whether the schools could overcome the problems with which they were confronted.

Redevelopment with a Human Face

In the early 1980s, civic and business leaders established a public-private partnership called Richmond Renaissance. Emerging from a conflict between black political leaders and the white business establishment, Renaissance was an organization designed to promote downtown revitalization and serve as a concrete example of a new spirit of interracial cooperation. Renaissance enticed the Marriott Hotel chain to serve as the anchor of a downtown convention center and brought James Rouse to the city to launch a festival mall, the Sixth Street Marketplace. By the mid-1980s, however, an undertone of discontent rumbled in the black community about Richmond Renaissance. Despite the organization's public image as the city's most notable example of black-white economic cooperation, the African American civic elite's private assessment was much less positive. As it became evident that the positive spinoffs from the Sixth Street Marketplace would have a limited impact in the black community, sentiment grew among the African American elite for pushing Richmond Renaissance to commit to a major project that would benefit black residents. This sentiment was not politicized in a highly visible manner but was conveyed in a series of meetings of the Richmond Renaissance Board of Directors, although one black council member observed publicly that it was time for the organization to demonstrate its concern for the entire community. This remark was echoed by the group's outgoing chairperson, a white businessman, in a speech given to the Richmond First Club, a corporate-oriented good government group.[17]

Christopher Silver notes that Richmond's economic development plans in the post–World War II era had either ignored or actually harmed Jackson Ward, the city's most historically significant black neighborhood.[18] Located in the north quadrant of the downtown business district, Jackson Ward's history reaches back nearly two hundred years when free blacks built cottages and established churches and businesses to serve the community. In the early twentieth century, Jackson Ward became a hub of black commerce, establishing a reputation that extended well beyond Richmond and the state's boundaries. The neighborhood was home to Maggie Walker who was both the first woman and the first black bank president in the United States. The ward's Hippodrome Theatre regularly hosted luminaries of the jazz world, including Fats Waller and Billie Holiday. Yet the neighborhood was ravaged by the racist decision making that characterized Richmond's politics. The ward's residents were victimized by the city's unwillingness to provide needed services, by the encroachment of what Silver calls "objectionable" nonresidential land use, and by a highway and turnpike that bisected the neighborhood and displaced a significant proportion of its residents (185).

In 1996, the significantly smaller Jackson Ward is bounded by an interstate highway to the north, two local streets to the south and east, and a four-lane city thruway to the west. Although reduced in size, the ward still includes nearly 20 percent of the land area in downtown Richmond. Only 16 percent of the homes in the neighborhood are owner-occupied, and close to 25 percent of the housing units are vacant, though a gentrification process is underway in one section. The population of Jackson Ward has decreased to 1,500 and a substantial proportion of those are elderly. Only

20 percent of the dwelling units have a resident under age eighteen, while 30 percent of the households include someone age sixty-five or older. Further, only 50 percent of the area's population works full-time.[19]

Given its significance in the historical memory of black Richmonders, its proximity to existing downtown revitalization programs, and the fact that 81 percent of its population is African American, Jackson Ward's rehabilitation became the top priority of the black civic elite concerned about the necessity of modifying the programs of Richmond Renaissance. This plan, developed by Renaissance and the city and popularly known as Jackson Ward Vision 2000, was formally announced as a forthcoming initiative in December 1987 and brought to the public arena for discussion. In the spring of 1989, the city council announced a step-by-step process that it hoped to implement during the nineties. From the council's perspective, Jackson Ward's revitalization would be a concrete manifestation of its ability to make Richmond Renaissance work for black Richmonders.

The planning strategy for the revitalization process consisted of two interrelated steps undertaken from January to May 1989. The first part was a community development process intended to ensure that the design for Jackson Ward was not simply imposed upon the residents as had occurred so frequently in the past. Public meetings were held, and planners solicited citizens' input into the vision for a revitalized Jackson Ward. The second part of the process consisted of consulting economic development professionals on the possibilities for improving the neighborhood. The two tracks were eventually brought together in an incremental and stage-specific plan that will take twelve years to complete. To facilitate its implementation, the city manager earmarked $1 million in capital improvement funds to be used from 1989–94 for streetscaping and other aesthetic improvements. In addition, in 1988 Richmond Renaissance announced the formation of a bank-sponsored community development program that would contribute seed money and identify specific projects to improve the community.

The revitalization of Jackson Ward is typically portrayed in official pronouncements as a project that will have almost universal benefits for both the city and its African American community.[20] On the one hand, the ward will supposedly become an upscale restaurant and entertainment district that both Richmonders and visitors will patronize. David Lee, a Boston architect hired as a consultant for the project, presented the following vision to a group of revitalization supporters: "Imagine brick walkways bordered by decorative shrubbery leading from the convention center at

Fifth and Marshall Streets into the heart of the historic, once bustling black neighborhood. Picture . . . an attractive sidewalk café to tempt passers-by. Then turn onto Second Street. There, you are greeted by a renovated Hippodrome, once again a showpiece for talented performers. Alongside are a myriad of places to eat and drink." In addition to the restaurant-entertainment complex, planners envision a minority business institute, a museum of African American culture, and a revitalized black commercial hub. Overall, supporters of Vision 2000 believe that it will enable Jackson Ward to regain its regional and perhaps national prominence.

At the same time, the revitalization process is intended to improve the quality of life for the neighborhood's current residents. The housing stock will be rehabilitated; new residences will be created for low- and moderate-income citizens; the elderly will be given an opportunity to move to a complex specially constructed for their needs; and the neighborhood will become safer and have better services for its residents. Thus, Jackson Ward is envisioned as a neighborhood that will be simultaneously upscale, racially diverse, a model of class integration, and architecturally distinct by the year 2000. Its supporters believe that the plan is an exemplar of reconciling commercial progress with social concern—upscale development with a human face.

To date, there has not been much movement on the general revitalization of Jackson Ward as the hub of the black business community, and there are serious questions about the extent to which it will ever occur. Private money in Richmond is moving toward commercial development near the riverfront, which borders the Main Street business community, rather than into the downtown section adjacent to Jackson Ward. Yet a few modest steps have been taken on a few elements of the Vision 2000 package. The state has agreed to rent a significant portion of one of the office buildings that is being constructed, and it appears that a housing complex for the elderly will reach fruition.

Even if the project is infused with more energy (and money), we remain skeptical of how fully the various impulses which animate it can be reconciled. Admittedly, there is a consensus in the city that Jackson Ward should be revitalized. But a consensus about a general goal can obscure tensions about its meaning and implementation. Ideas about what revitalization should accomplish may not be shared by residents and by those who represent commercial interests. A survey commissioned by Richmond Renaissance and conducted by the Survey Research Laboratory of Virginia Commonwealth University illustrates this point. For instance, of the twenty-five projects slated as goals for 1995–2005, the five that attracted the most interest from residents were either housing or public service. While 52 percent of the people who live in the neighborhood thought that what the elite perceive as the linchpin of the project—the development of an African American business institute—was a good idea, more than 80 percent of the residents felt that the introduction of a grocery store in the area was more important. In addition, the residents expressed a desire for such basics as better lighting and low-interest rehabilitation loans. They have considerably less interest in hotels, new office development, or Lee's proposed sidewalk cafés.[21]

We might ask how Lee's vision of an upscale entertainment district could be implemented without displacing Jackson Ward's current residents and existing businesses. Perhaps it is possible to restore a luster to Jackson Ward that has been tarnished, but can this be accomplished and still maintain housing for people in which 27 percent are sixty years of age and older, in which 31 percent have less than a high school education, and where 28 percent presently earn less that $10,000 annually? We can imagine the pressure on rents, on taxes for home owners, and on the general desire of people who have moved in to "protect" their investment by recruiting people with similar class backgrounds as neighbors. At best, the revitalization of Jackson Ward is more a testimony to the good intentions of black leadership than it is evidence of their capacity to shape downtown revitalization to benefit black neighborhoods.

Political Struggle and Popular Demobilization

Richmond's black leaders often refer to how they have opened up the political process as evidence of the difference they have made. Occasionally, they suggest that African Americans now recognize that they can exercise influence and are more likely to use the available political avenues. Other times, black leaders refer specifically to individuals that they have identified and brought into the process by appointment to city boards and commissions or by encouragement to become candidates for office. In other words, black elected officials suggest that they have been instrumental in building a stronger African American attachment to the political order.

Yet an analysis of events in Richmond complicates this story considerably. During the late 1970s and 1980s, public life in Richmond was characterized by two seemingly contradictory trends. On the one hand, the period was marked by a series of highly charged political confrontations. To many people, Richmond was fast becoming an example of excessive politicization. In the late 1970s, the Marsh faction and corporate Richmond struggled to define the terms of accommodation between Main Street and the new black civic elite. From 1982 through 1988, city politics was defined by a series of bitter disputes between Marsh and West, who replaced Marsh as mayor. West was a conservative, black middle-school principal who unseated a liberal member of the Marsh faction in the 1982 councilmanic elections and became mayor when he accepted the support of the four white council members. The Marsh faction charged that West was simply an instrument of white control, while the new mayor denounced the Marsh faction for its useless and counterproductive politics (see chap. 2).

While political contention during the 1980s among various elite groups remained at a level that struck many observers as unhealthy, ordinary African Americans were becoming politically demobilized. This demobilization took three principal forms. First, the momentum built from 1956–77 in terms of African American voter registration stalled. After a black majority was elected to the Richmond City Council, organized efforts to maintain and enhance voter registration diminished. The ratio of black registered voters was dramatically unaltered by the struggle in the Third Ward over West's election, Jesse Jackson's two presidential campaigns, and the two historic campaigns of Richmond native L. Douglas Wilder. Virginia has a policy of purging voters from the rolls if they have not cast a ballot in four years. Figures indicate that during the 1980s, voter registration declined in three of the black majority wards in the city.[22]

Second, African American political officials did not attempt to increase the level of participation by their constituents. Although elected officials attempted to draw some individuals into politics through the appointment process, they rarely encouraged greater political participation by organized groups. Given the ongoing delicate negotiations with the white elite over economic development, black leaders did not wish to introduce uncontrollable extraneous factors into the process. In addition, like most political officials, black leaders operated to maximize their own reelection chances. They saw little advantage to bringing into the political arena a new group of participants who may or may not have felt that their interests were served by the current order.

The one time when black leadership took definite steps to mobilize African American voters came in response to West's election. Throughout the mid-1980s, Marsh and the Crusade for Voters—the preeminent African American political organization in the city—worked to defeat the new mayor. Two points are worth noting about their effort. First, the effort was undertaken as a means for the 1977 majority to regain the power it had lost because of West's election, not to promote new initiatives or innovative perspectives on city policy. Second, the absolute failure of their efforts indicated, at least in part, the extent to which mobilization politics had become foreign to black elected officials by 1984. On a number of occasions, some black leaders mentioned that they might have to "go back to the streets," but it was becoming increasingly apparent that they would not be particularly comfortable there.

The third form that demobilization took was that neighborhood groups did not organize on a relatively enduring basis to address problems neglected by the city leadership. Unlike a number of other cities where neighborhood groups arose to voice discontent with elected officials' priorities (e.g., in Houston, Chicago, and Atlanta), Richmond had little street-level activism. Community groups occasionally visited city council meetings to voice their discontent with a proposed policy, and a modest degree of activism arose from a concern with "black on black" crime. But Richmond did not have a set of black leaders who became prominent due to their work with community organizations. In fact, not a single individual emerged out of neighborhood groups to have an impact on African American electoral politics in the 1980s.[23]

A number of factors help to explain the popular demobilization that occurred in the city. First, neighborhood groups rarely had the resources in terms of time, staff, and funding to maintain an enduring presence. Given the effort in Richmond that went into building a black majority on the council, it is not surprising that most citizens were not especially active in trying to ensure that their needs were met by the new black elected officials. They had achieved what they had struggled for two decades to accomplish and did not see any need to mobilize against the very people whom they had elected as their representatives.

A second possible explanation for the demobilization in the broader black community is related to the manner in which its historical mobilization had occurred. The major black political organization in the city, the Crusade for Voters, originated in an effort to maximize black voter registration and unify black votes. Initially, it did a superb job in using precinct organizations as a registration tool. The Crusade maximized black voting strength in the 1950s and 1960s by designing a process that enabled African Americans to wield the balance of power in city elections. The group announced its endorsements on the Sunday prior to elections and stressed that unity was critical to successful black political influence. In the early sixties, the Crusade's success in promoting a relatively unified black vote soon gained it a reputation as one of the most formidable political organizations in Virginia and the nation (see chap. 2).

The Crusade's emphasis on black unity made good political sense for the two decades after its inception. Indeed, one observer has claimed that the Crusade's model was, in reality, the Byrd organization that had served white Virginians so well for more than three decades.[24] We believe that the black church served as a model rather than the Byrd organization. In any case, the intensity and extent of white opposition to black political advancement required a political strategy that could make the most effective use of what little power African Americans possessed. The Crusade originated in a campaign against massive resistance and operated for almost a decade, at a time in which the poll tax was in effect.

The Crusade's call for unity also made sense during these years because the group was working on behalf of issues that appeared to benefit all African Americans. In his discussion of the civil rights movement, Charles Hamilton uses the concept of indivisible benefits to describe policies that benefit an entire constituency. Hamilton contrasts this with the notion of divisible benefits that accrue to selected members of a group. In Richmond, the opposition to massive resistance, the effort to establish a human relations commission, proposals to end discrimination in city employment, the movement to ensure that annexation did not entirely dilute emerging black political power, and the campaign to elect a black majority to the city council were all actions that could result in indivisible benefits. To the extent that the Crusade promoted these goals, the group could be defined as the voice of black Richmond.

There was a down side to the manner in which the Crusade came to dominate black politics in Richmond, which became evident in the years following the emergence of the black majority on the council. The Crusade's top-down style of politics ultimately reduced the pressure placed on black leaders by their constituents and prevented publicly airing political criticisms. Given the efforts of the white establishment to regain power and the factionalism that fragmented the black community after West's election, a case could be made that the Crusade's prescription was fully warranted. Nonetheless, it resulted in the virtual abandonment of efforts to discover innovative responses to the most perplexing dilemmas that confronted African American citizens in the 1980s.

The concerns expressed by the Crusade in the 1980s were no longer obviously addressed to the principal needs of ordinary African Americans. While the organization continued to speak as the legitimate voice of black interests, its justification for doing so was less clear. The self-professed "revolutionaries" of the 1950s had not shifted allegiance in the 1980s. They still defended allocations to the Richmond Community Action Program; they continued to be involved in voter registration drives; and they verbally protested against federal cutbacks in social programs and Supreme Court decisions that overturned the policies of black leaders. But the issues with which they were preoccupied—set-asides, the revitalization of Jackson Ward, and increasing black representation in administrative levels of government—were not matters that ordinary African Americans placed at the top of their political agenda.

A third explanation for demobilization is rooted in the political events of the late 1970s and 1980s. The political crises that followed the election of the black majority made it difficult for many African Americans to question the wisdom of their leaders' policies. As the new black leadership fought with the Main Street establishment and were the subject of continual criticism in the city's two daily newspapers, the tendency to view criticism of the newly elected officials as playing into the enemy's hand became more pronounced.

Perhaps no one expressed this dilemma better than Preston Yancy, a columnist for the *Richmond Afro-American*. Yancy's columns in the years after the 1977 election eloquently articulated the dilemmas of black progressives. He criticized the continuing efforts of the white establishment to denigrate the capabilities of black politicians. In particular, he was unrelenting in his attack on the divisiveness that he felt was engendered by the editorial pages of the local dailies. At the same time, Yancy attempted to call black leadership to account. He was skeptical of the rush to embrace downtown revitalization and to redefine it as a black cause. He suggested that the firing of a white city manager could have been handled more adroitly. And he speculated that the long-term economic crisis in the black community would require more creative solutions than those offered by the black council members.

In a number of columns, Yancy wrote of the personal anguish that he had experienced in staking out his position. He noted that it was essential for

African Americans to hold their politicians to high standards of performance, but he also recognized that racial strife between the black civic elite and the white business establishment placed critics like himself in a precarious position. He was aware that his criticism might be used not as a prod for better government but as a means for discrediting black leadership.[25]

Given the narrow margin of the black majority on the council, Yancy's concern was legitimate. To many black leaders, the 1982 election of West to the city council and his subsequent elevation to mayor was an object lesson in what could happen when fragmentation replaced unity. But black leaders also pointed to their slim majority as a way of both insulating themselves from the legitimate criticisms that people such as Yancy offered and avoiding public discussion of their priorities. In a sense, the choice was not simply unity versus fragmentation but whether ordinary African Americans would be encouraged to participate in defining the direction that the city would pursue.[26]

The structure of the city's electoral process may be a fourth element contributing to the demobilization of African American citizens. In 1977, the at-large system of councilmanic elections was replaced with a ward-based system. The change was part of the compromise endorsed by the U.S. Supreme Court in the litigation that allowed the annexation of part of Chesterfield County to stand. The switch to a ward-based system was consistent with a pattern that had developed throughout the American South in the wake of the Voting Rights Act. The NAACP, the American Civil Liberties Union, and other civil rights groups had campaigned to replace at-large systems with ward-based ones, asserting that the former had been employed to dilute black voting rights and maintain white hegemony. The campaign was successful in Virginia and elsewhere.

In Richmond, the immediate result of the new electoral system was dramatic as a black majority was elected to the city council for the first time. The racial composition of the council remained the same for the next thirteen years, although the unity of the black majority disintegrated with West's election and Claudette Black McDaniel's defection to the West camp a few years later. In 1977, blacks probably would not have obtained political power if the at-large election system had continued. The evidence overwhelmingly indicates that the shift to ward-based elections has improved the electoral chances of black candidates. Indeed, since the inception of the ward-based system, white business leaders and political conservatives have repeatedly called for a return to some version of at-large elections. Normally presented as an instrument for improving the quality of government, black leaders (with some justification) have occasionally regarded such plans with suspicion and as a subterfuge for the reassertion of white political control.

Yet looking back at 1977–90, the evidence suggests that there are costs as well as advantages to the manner in which the system operated in Richmond. With the exception of a few constitutional offices, such as sheriff and commonwealth attorney, there are no citywide elected officials in Richmond. Since the council selects the mayor, there is really no opportunity in the campaign to debate the major decisions made by the council in establishing priorities. At no point, for instance, has the entire city discussed and voted on downtown revitalization. In addition, there is no necessity for candidates to build broad-based or issues-oriented coalitions. Put simply, there is no system of electoral accountability for decisions that affect the vast majority of Richmond's citizens. Consequently, there is no incentive for electoral mobilization in the traditional sense.

Affirmative Action, Black Leaders, and the Question of Politics

The themes covered in this chapter are ostensibly unrelated to the affirmative action program that led to the *Croson* case and other manifestations of set-aside politics in Richmond. We suggest, however, that the connection is genuine and substantial. First, the role of set-aside programs can only be understood within the broader context of the economic development strategies followed by the African American leadership in urban areas.[27] Examining affirmative action requires us to investigate the extent to which related policies have been successful. Second, we have attempted to expand the criteria typically employed to evaluate both affirmative action programs and the effectiveness of African American political officials. In particular, we have contended that evaluations should move beyond narrow economic categories and examine the manner in which policies advance or limit the opportunity for the political development of the community. Do leaders promote the use of democracy by the citizens? Do they help to develop the capacity of the community for self-governance? Do they promote or retard the emergence of new leaders with fresh ideas?

We have suggested that the strategy pursued by Richmond's black leadership has resulted in some gains for the broader African American community, but we have also noted that it has contributed to a political demobilization that has made it more difficult to question the leadership's priorities. We do not mean to say that this has been a conscious strategy developed by individual officials or that they have entirely abandoned their constituents. Examples abound where elected officials have stood up for the interests of ordinary black citizens. But we have argued that the nature of political conflict in Richmond, the structure of its system, and the alliances built presumably to further black interests have worked cumulatively to inhibit the political development of ordinary African American citizens.

This argument leads us once more to question the conventional liberal and conservative perspectives on affirmative action. The standard defense of the policy typically ignores the questions that have occupied this chapter. Liberal defenses of affirmative action normally treat the policy in pristine isolation and rarely ask what place these policies occupy in the economic development strategy of urban leadership or in the political development of the black community. This may permit philosophical arguments to be more precise and parsimonious, but it comes at the expense of understanding the subtleties involved in the actual pursuit of affirmative action.

The conservative critique of affirmative action normally evades this issue as well. Thomas Sowell, for example, is primarily concerned with proving that political action is irrelevant to black economic advancement, other than to the extent that it removes governmental impediments to the operation of the free market. Sowell thus refuses to entertain the possibility that there may be a connection between political success and economic progress or that a different kind of politics (other than deregulation) might advance the interests of African Americans.

An increasing number of scholars, however, are coming to understand the importance of politics to the discussion of affirmative action policies. They recognize that these programs cannot be discussed in isolation from questions about the effectiveness of black leadership, the prospects for interracial cooperation, the nature of choices facing urban leaders, and the effects of particular policies on national elections. The discussion in the next two chapters underscores the centrality of these issues.

FIVE

White Responses to Affirmative Action

The conventional wisdom about the political consequences of affirmative action points to the advantage that has accrued to the Republican party. Many commentators have observed that the Democratic party's defense of gender and racial preferences is at odds with the beliefs of the vast majority of Americans. Despite many Democrats' claims that the concern about quotas is a "phony issue," affirmative action has become a powerful instrument employed by Republicans to tap white Americans' resentment toward the nation's liberal elite. Observers point to U.S. Senator Jesse Helms's resuscitation of his flagging reelection campaign in North Carolina in 1990 by raising the issue and to the gubernatorial contest during the same year in California where Republican Pete Wilson successfully undermined the campaign of Dianne Feinstein by raising the prospect of ethnic quotas in the state workforce. The latter example demonstrates that the issue has salience outside the South. By 1995, Republican presidential hopefuls were using their opposition to affirmative action as a means of demonstrating their conservative credentials.

The conventional wisdom captures an important truth about the manner in which white response to affirmative action has influenced significant electoral contests. The picture becomes more complicated when affirmative action is viewed in other political settings. There are three contextual considerations that complicate the conventional wisdom. First, white responses to affirmative action may not be univocal. In Richmond, some white elites did not voice any objections to the affirmative action policies pursued by the black leadership. Second, white support for particular kinds of affirmative action policies may cross ideological lines. In Richmond, major corporate actors not only refrained from objecting to the city's affirmative action plans but boasted of their own affirmative action programs. Finally, since local affirmative action policies may be part of a broader development strategy, it is important to examine how whites have responded to the more general strategy as well as to specific affirmative action initiatives.

This chapter examines white responses to affirmative action in the context of Richmond politics. We begin by summarizing the major findings in public opinion surveys on white beliefs about affirmative action. We analyze the strengths and weaknesses of these surveys as tools for explaining white political behavior. We then describe the diversity of white responses to both the city's particular affirmative action programs and the general strategy for African American progress enunciated in the aftermath of the 1977 elections. We conclude by analyzing the manner in which these responses have shaped the nature of politics in the city, simultaneously expanding and limiting the options available to Richmond's African American leadership.

White Racial Attitudes and Affirmative Action

Scholars who have examined public opinion about race in the United States typically point to four prominent features of white public opinion. First, white Americans have become increasingly supportive of equal legal rights for black citizens and of the goals embodied in the civil rights legislation of the 1960s. Questions that fall under the general heading of "racial tolerance" indicate that whites are more willing to support equal legal rights now than at any previous time since data has been collected. Albert Karnig and Susan Welch report that "some previously quite controversial issues—for example, segregation in public transportation—are not now even salient. Even on issues that are still controversial, such as school and residential integration, the increase in pro-integrationist response by whites has been steady."[1]

Reports also observe that negative stereotypes about African Americans are held by fewer white Americans. Although a substantial minority still hold these stereotypes, the percentage has been steadily declining. In addition, whites are much more willing to express a receptiveness for social interaction with blacks than they did thirty years ago. A *Washington Post* poll notes that more whites attest to social relationships with blacks and to their children's interracial friendships than previously. Some scholars also believe that racial incidents on campus, murders in Howard Beach and Bensonhurst, and the Rodney King decision may not be reliable indicators of broader social trends. Speaking prior to the King decision, Guy Smith, director of the General Social Survey at the University of Chicago, maintained that, despite incidents such as Howard Beach and Bensonhurst, the level of tolerance expressed by the general population remains as high as it has ever been.[2]

A second feature that frequently appears in studies of white public opinion is the recognition by whites that some actions should be undertaken to improve the conditions of minorities who have been victims of discrimination. If the discussion is kept at a sufficiently general level (i.e., whether there should be "programs" to help African Americans get jobs or have better access to housing and education), support in the white community remains relatively strong. Indeed, when whites are asked questions about affirmative action that eschew mandatory quotas, a large majority support such programs.[3] James R. Kluegel and Eliot R. Smith observe that such programs are supported by about 70 percent of whites, and other findings confirm their assertion.[4] This evidence has, at times, led analysts, such as the pollster Louis Harris, to assert that whites in fact approve of affirmative action.

When the discussion turns to specific policies that governments have actually employed or proposed, a third element in the structure of white public opinion is highlighted. Support for the principle of improving conditions is accompanied by widespread disapproval of policies that contain provisions for preferential treatment. As W. Richard Merriman and Edward G. Carmines write, "Even when whites pass the test of racial tolerance . . . this in itself does not mean that they will support compensatory efforts on behalf of blacks."[5] Affirmative action is obviously the most vivid example of this feature of white public opinion. The *Washington Post* survey demonstrates that whites think that much remains to be done to achieve equality for blacks, but when the notion of preferential treatment is raised, the level of white support drops precipitously. Less than 30 percent agree that minorities and women should be granted special preferences in hiring and promotion in order to compensate for past discrimination. Moreover, there is now evidence that a minority of whites believe that the pursuit of equality has gone too far.[6]

The distinction between white and black public opinion on this issue is striking. Although support among African Americans also drops considerably as questions move from a philosophical commitment to more equality to attitudes toward particular programs, the percentage of blacks that support affirmative action is twenty to thirty points higher than for whites.[7]

Recent polls suggest that the "perception gap" about what is needed to improve conditions for racial minorities among black and white Americans increased significantly in the 1980s. The *Washington Post* poll discovered that the percentage of whites who believe that things are improving for African Americans is much higher than the percentage of blacks who share this opinion.[8]

The fourth relevant element of white opinion focuses on the reasons that more blacks than whites experience higher levels of poverty and social distress. Polls indicate that a substantial percentage of white Americans believe that poverty results from the lack of personal responsibility exercised by the impoverished. Most whites simply do not believe that racial discrimination in contemporary America is sufficiently onerous to prevent blacks who want to get ahead from doing so. On the other hand, African Americans, Sigelman and Welch maintain, "inhabit a world characterized by perceptions of discrimination against themselves personally and, even more commonly, against blacks in general. . . . Not only do most blacks perceive widespread discrimination. They also believe that such discrimination is the major reason why blacks continue to have trouble finding good jobs, adequate housing and other forms of social and economic security."[9] Taken together, these public opinion data suggest, as Linda Williams, an African American political scientist, has observed, that whites have come to believe in the principles of legal equality, antidiscrimination, and equal treatment under the law but that they have a very different perspective than blacks on how to implement these principles.[10]

This description of white racial attitudes illuminates important political developments within the last twenty years. A number of commentators have evoked these sentiments as at least a partial explanation for the difficulties of the Democratic party in recent decades. For example, in *Politics and Society in the South*, Merle Black and Earl Black rely on data about white attitudes to explain the difficulty that Democratic presidential candidates have experienced in the region. They suggest that white middle-class southerners simply do not share the beliefs that leaders of the Democratic party have advanced about appropriate strategies for black progress.[11] Writing about a different region of the country, Jonathan Rieder contends that white ethnics have abandoned liberalism in part because its meaning has been transformed from support of equal opportunity to approval of preferential treatment. One of his interviewees remarked, "I was pro-civil rights. I supported the Selma march and the civil rights movement in its early phase. But when someone tries to take something from me to benefit others, I'll fight it. I'm against compensation. That's reverse discrimination. It's a gut reaction for me."[12]

The high profile campaigns of Wilson and Helms point to the political explosiveness of the preferential treatment issue. In North Carolina, many believe that Jesse Helms's successful appeal to fears of racial quotas was a decisive factor in the last week of the campaign against the African American challenger Harvey Gantt. The Helms campaign used a television commercial that showed a working-class white male receiving a job rejection letter that explained that the position was offered to another worker because of a need to meet a racial quota. In California, Dianne Feinstein's remark that she wanted the ethnic composition of the state workforce to mirror the ethnic composition of the state as a whole led to a successful attack by her gubernatorial foe, Pete Wilson, on her support for unjustified quotas.

On the other hand, the data that point to increasing racial tolerance explain why a black candidate such as L. Douglas Wilder can be a successful contender for statewide office in Virginia. In his victorious quest for lieutenant governor in 1985, Wilder obtained about 44 percent of the white vote, and in 1989 Wilder became the first elected black governor in the nation, receiving about 41 percent of the white vote. In both elections, he received a higher percentage of the white vote than any other Democratic presidential contender in Virginia since Lyndon B. Johnson. In both campaigns, Wilder not only distanced himself from the Rainbow Coalition politics of Jesse Jackson but also studiously avoided endorsing any policies that appeared to require preferential treatment. In his gubernatorial campaign, he deflected a question about affirmative action in one of the debates by responding that he believed that economic growth would ultimately rescue the people who were not making it in the wider society. Labeling himself as the governor of "all Virginians" and refraining from group-based appeals, Wilder campaigned as a serious contender because of the increased racial tolerance that the polls have illustrated.

White Response to Affirmative Action in Richmond

Any attempt to understand racial dilemmas in the United States in the late nineties cannot ignore the implications of white racial attitudes. But we must also acknowledge that the conventional description of these attitudes fails to tell us everything we need to know about the politics of affirmative action. Attitudes may influence behavior, but the relationship is not always linear. If we simply focus on attitudes and sentiments, we may ignore the historical development of affirmative action policies and the trade offs embedded in their formulation. We know, for example, that many white businesspeople—the supposed guardians of the equal opportunity ideology in the culture—have often seen fit to accept, maintain, and offer public support to affirmative action policies. Why does this happen, and what does it mean? In addition, the discussion of attitudes and sentiments does not necessarily explain why affirmative action policies are sometimes politicized and sometimes ignored. In short, to understand affirmative action policies, we have to examine a range of political variables as well as white sentiments.

Business Acceptance of Affirmative Action

In previous chapters, we describe how some of the most prominent members of the group that opposed the election of a black majority council were associated with the Richmond business community. The "Main Street establishment" included bankers, stockbrokers, and lawyers whose vision for the future had long defined the city's economic development strategy. In the heated atmosphere of the 1970s, white businesspeople often warned Richmonders that a majority black presence might result in a commercial ghost town in which residential property taxes would skyrocket. Some observers believed that the city was headed for a titanic collision between the new political leaders and the Main Street establishment.

Although the distrust between the two groups has never completely dissolved, the level of overt antagonism has been significantly reduced. Concerned about a declining population base, an increased demand for services, and threats by local corporations to flee to the counties, black city officials sought to enhance the city's tax base by embracing a modified version of an old master plan for downtown revitalization. Key members of the Main Street establishment recognized that the growth politics embraced by black leadership did not threaten their interests, and thus Main Street joined with black leaders in support for downtown redevelopment projects. As we have seen, the terms of accommodation required corporate leaders to agree to plans developed by the African American leadership to carve out a black interest within the revitalization strategy. Further, we have argued that affirmative action policies were the manner in which the "African American interest" in revitalization strategies was typically defined.

The Main Street establishment found the terms of the compromise acceptable. Richmond corporate leaders never objected to city-sponsored affirmative action plans connected with downtown redevelopment. Indeed, they often referred to the "new spirit of compromise" that animated the Richmond community. In addition, many corporations had begun their own affirmative action programs and publicized such efforts to increase minority employment and the use of minority suppliers.

Nationally, the roots of corporate-initiated affirmative action can be traced to the 1970s. On the one hand, these programs resulted from external pressure and the threat of discrimination suits that could be extremely costly in terms of time, money, and reputation. In the 1970s, Supreme Court decisions on "disparate impact" cases and congressional laws requiring companies that receive federal funds to have a plan for minority business development prompted corporations to take steps that they might not have made on their own. In his 1975 *Affirmative Discrimination*, Nathan Glazer contends that American business decided to implement affirmative action programs on the basis of a decision that it was less onerous to comply with government-encouraged employment quotas than to assume the legal risks of adopting a principled stand against affirmative action.[13]

Corporate affirmative action has also been rooted in voluntary decisions made by the private sector. This tendency can be traced to President Richard Nixon's "black capitalism campaign" of the early 1970s. In his first term and prior to the full implementation of the "southern strategy," Nixon made some overtures to segments of the black community. In particular, he wanted to promote black business as a stable alternative to the social revolution that he feared was the ultimate goal of ongoing community activism in the black community.[14] In 1972, Nixon convened a White House meeting with a number of the nation's major corporate leaders to discuss the development of a plan to bring minorities into the economic mainstream. One initiative that resulted from the conference was the effort to form a network of Minority Supplier Development Councils. According to the original plan, the government would contribute 85 percent of the national organization's start-up costs and the corporate sector would pick up the rest. The national organization would in turn fund local councils that would work with private companies in their own communities.

For the most part, discussions of corporate-initiated affirmative action have focused on the legal compulsions to which business has reacted. However, these discussions omit the manner in which portions of the private sector have voluntarily accepted (and promoted) affirmative action as an instrument of achieving broader business goals. A curious irony marked the middle and late 1980s. The U.S. Supreme Court, under the leadership of William Rehnquist and the influence of Reagan-appointed judges, became much less tolerant of affirmative action plans designed by local governmental bodies and less demanding of affirmative action from the private sector. But corporate leaders themselves were rarely open about this issue. In fact, their rhetoric was typically much more conciliatory. Under attack for heartlessly abandoning their communities, business leaders spoke proudly of their socially responsible efforts. They pointed to statistics about the changing nature of the American workforce, noting that more than half of it is composed of minorities, immigrants, and women. And they admitted that their executives would have to learn to affirm and manage diversity. As James R. Houghton, CEO of Corning Corporation, describes his company's commitment to diversity, "It simply makes good business sense."[15]

In Richmond, the Virginia Regional Minority Supplier Development Council (VRMSDC) has been one of the most visible examples of voluntary corporate commitment to affirmative action. The organization consists of approximately seventy corporate members, including Virginia Power, C&P Telephone, and Wheat First Securities, as well as AT&T, Sprint International, and Philip Morris. The council's main work is to facilitate a professional and business interchange between its members and minority suppliers. It sponsors the annual Virginia Business Opportunity Fair, a corporate awards banquet, a series of forums and workshops designed to offer business information to minority entrepreneurs, and an annual directory of minority businesses in Virginia.[16]

When the Reagan administration curtailed funding for the National Minority Suppliers Development Council in 1986, the VRMSDC operated with only an executive director and secretary. In recent years, an increase in the funding commitment of local companies has enabled the Virginia organization to undertake a modest expansion. The VRMSDC has since added a third full-time staff person. It no longer operates on a month-to-month budget but presents a yearly plan for which it is funded. Its current annual budget is $133,000, which includes salaries, benefits, and operating expenses.[17] Further, a number of CEOs have been more willing in recent years to commit their personal time to help the council pursue its goals more effectively.

In addition to support for the VRMSDC, Richmond corporations undertook a number of affirmative action programs on their own. Our interviews with officials of some major Richmond-based corporations that are members of the VRMSDC—Crestar Bank, Signet Bank, Philip Morris, and Virginia Power—highlighted three principal directions that corporate-initiated affirmative action took.

First, several corporations had initiated or supported training programs for minority entrepreneurs. Crestar Bank Corporation, for instance, had previously operated its minority development program on the basis of what was described as an "open door policy" that was not "doing the job." Crestar decided that minority firms needed special assistance and initiated training sessions with minority entrepreneurs on conducting business with large corporations. For example, one aspect of Crestar's training focused on how to prepare the special invoicing required in contracts with large corporations.[18] Philip Morris Corporation also referred to the training programs that it maintains for minority entrepreneurs and pointed to its in-house management development training program, a free service to selected minority entrepreneurs to facilitate their acquisition of business knowledge and technical skills. The company also sponsors three full tuition scholarships for minority businesspeople to attend an institute at Dartmouth College each summer.[19]

Second, corporations frequently highlighted their actual purchases from minority suppliers as an example of their commitment to affirmative action and black economic development. Virginia Power, for example, does not have a percentage set-aside requirement but has developed well-defined dollar goals. Its 1980 goal of $2 million was revised upward considerably throughout the decade. The goals for 1989, 1990, and 1991 were set at $7.4 million, $8.9 million, and $9.4 million, respectively. The company's minority business administrator emphasized that these "goals are carried out from the executive level to the lowest level buyer."[20] Crestar Bank has a definite set-aside figure, earmarking 10 percent of its supplies to be purchased from minority firms. Philip Morris did not keep specific figures for its Richmond operations but mentioned in 1984 that the number of minority suppliers for the company had increased in less than three years from 40 to more than 120.

Third, corporations sometimes noted support for historically black institutions as an example of commitment to minority economic development. For example, Philip Morris's promotional literature emphasizes its work with minority institutions. One brochure notes that the company "has deposit, line of credit, payroll and other relationships with approximately sixty banks nationwide." In 1986 the vice chairman remarked that Philip Morris had $2.4 million on deposit in African American–owned banks as well as a $24.5 million line of credit at these institutions. In addition, the corporation has contributed to Richmond's predominantly black university, Virginia Union. The company donated funds when the school was faced with a threatening fiscal crisis in the 1980s. It has also provided a $250,000 five-year grant (for continued support) and maintains a company scholarship program for females over age twenty-five who want to pursue higher education in order to further their career.[21]

Corporate-initiated affirmative action programs in Richmond serve several positive functions. For the companies involved, these programs can help to develop a loyal base of suppliers and to recruit talented African American personnel. In addition, the policies can help to establish a better image for the company in the African American community. This was extremely important for corporations such as Philip Morris. The largest private employer in the city, it was under increasing attack in the 1980s by antismoking groups in Virginia and around the nation. One method for parrying the assault was to become a model corporate citizen. The company became a patron of the arts, and it utilized minority suppliers, in part, to remind Richmonders of the company's contribution to the area's well-being.

During the 1970s, Virginia Power (or VEPCO, as it is called) gained an unfavorable statewide reputation for what were perceived as arbitrary rate hikes. In fact, Henry Howell, a populist candidate for governor, defined the company as the state's principal villain with his campaign slogan, "Keep the big boys honest." Launched in the 1980s, VEPCO's affirmative action program was part of a larger strategy to refashion its image both in Richmond and throughout the Commonwealth.

Company-sponsored affirmative action programs were also related to the changing nature of Richmond business. Many local corporations were increasingly developing a national and international presence. They hoped that other corporate headquarters could be attracted to the city, and thus they did not want their home base to be identified as a cauldron of racial conflict. Participation in Richmond Renaissance was one way to meet this goal. Initiating and publicizing their own affirmative action programs reinforced this commitment. Moreover, it was a relatively inexpensive way of doing so. The programs were not sufficiently extensive to generate a significant white backlash, nor were they subject to the kind of court challenge that ended the city's set-aside policy.

It is not going too far to say that corporate Richmond provided the most significant and extensive white support for affirmative action in the area. Corporations wholeheartedly endorsed the compromise that made downtown revitalization possible; they initiated and publicized their own affirmative action programs; and they provided financial support for the VRMSDC. With respect to affirmative action, ideological considerations were clearly subordinated to decisions based on long-term corporate self-interest.

Business Opposition to Affirmative Action

The city's set-aside program and other affirmative action initiatives were not accepted by all segments of the business community. Objections were raised by the predominantly white construction companies that were affected by the policy and by a few other white-owned small businesses. To these businesses, the city's policy was simply reverse discrimination that utilized the political power of a black majority city council to penalize white businesses. The construction companies that were affected by the program complained bitterly from its inception to its conclusion. At the council meeting the evening the ordinance was passed, they argued that the policy was illegal. They complained in the early years of the program about fraudulent practices, and they maintained that their own organizations had been singled out for unfair treatment.

The national trade organization to which these companies belonged, the Association of General Contractors (AGC), organized national opposition to policies such as Richmond's set-aside program. During the 1980s, the AGC's literature kept members informed of various court challenges to the set-aside ordinances in cities throughout the country. Moreover, the organization provided assistance to companies desiring to challenge the policies. It also developed an extensive public relations program to explain why these set-asides were misguided and ineffective.

None of the companies that opposed the set-aside program exercised much influence within the broader Richmond business community. They were not part of Richmond Renaissance; their offices were not on Main Street; they were not included among the power brokers when reporters discussed the major players in the city's business community; and they carried absolutely no weight during city council deliberations. In short, they were simply not part of the political accommodation reached between the black civic elite and the Main Street establishment during the early 1980s. Given this lack of informal and formal political influence as well as their opposition to the program that was central to the political compromise between the dominant elite groups, it is not surprising that construction companies saw the courts as the only place to which they could turn for relief.

Citizen Indifference

We have shown that politics in Richmond was highly contentious for most of the period 1967–82. Yet the set-aside program formulated in 1983 registered hardly a blip on the Richmond political landscape. While the city council's discussion prior to passage occupied the better part of two hours, the set-aside policy received little attention compared to that paid to school integration in the late 1960s and 1970s, the annexation struggle, the firing of the city manager, Roy West's 1982 election, or the decision to prevent the Hilton Corporation from building in the city. In no city council campaign was the set-aside program an issue, and no one in Richmond politics utilized opposition to the program as a springboard to political influence.

The lack of citizen opposition to the program did not necessarily mean that white voters approved of the city's policy direction. A 1990 poll conducted by Virginia Commonwealth University probed the extent of support for the set-aside ordinance. While 59 percent of blacks in Richmond believed that the city should be allowed to set aside 30 percent of its construction work for minority-owned business, only 24 percent of whites supported such a policy—a finding consistent with national poll data on preferential treatment programs.[22] But this may have been the only time that most Richmond whites really had the opportunity to comment directly upon the policy. It could be argued that the structure of city council elections, in which candidates ran in wards and the mayor was selected from and by the council, precluded discussion of citywide issues. In this respect, it is impossible to determine white voters' attitudes toward the program.[23]

White Response to the Emergence of Black Political Power

On the other hand, it is easy to see how white voters felt about the general direction of the city because the election results in the various wards, the levels of attendance in city schools, and other factors provide a good indication of emerging sentiments. We have previously summarized the manner in which the Main Street establishment responded to the emergence of black political power in Richmond, moving from opposition to at least a grudging acceptance of political reality. The responses of ordinary citizens in Richmond were not uniform, ranging from accommodation to outright opposition.

Accommodation

For some white Richmonders, the compromise settlement on political power embodied in the formation of Richmond Renaissance was a model for how the entire community ought to respond to the emergence of black political power. They felt it was time for white Richmonders to recognize that African Americans would likely exercise political power for the foreseeable future. Yet it was also incumbent upon African Americans to recognize that the future of the city was dependent on harmonious race relations in which the attractions and advantages of the city were not subordinated to a narrow, racialized conception of politics, culture, and economic development. Put simply, it was time for well-intentioned people of both races to put aside differences and work for the benefit of a greater Richmond.

These sentiments were expressed most visibly in the various civic groups that were organized for the purpose of promoting the downtown area or spotlighting the arts. Summer street fairs, music festivals, and other cultural events in Richmond were organized to ensure that the entertainment would appeal to all segments of the community. Organizers often developed imaginative agendas for entertainment, where the same weekend festival might include appearances by a southern rock group such as the Marshall Tucker Band as well as by a Chicago blues player such as Buddy Guy or a rhythm and blues group such as Kool and the Gang. These events were inevitably accompanied by a raft of publicity attesting to the manner in which the entire community had come together to have fun and celebrate.

The push for accommodation was also seen in the work of public task forces commissioned to address specific problems such as education, crime, or economic development. Typically, citizen commissions noted that it was imperative for all Richmonders to work together to address the city's problems. Such groups frequently called for more partnerships along the lines modeled by Richmond Renaissance as the appropriate response to the problem at hand, whether it was business involvement with the schools, efforts to promote job training programs for at-risk youth, or methods for "selling" the city to outside companies looking for a new location.

The accommodation effort did not, however, permeate all areas of the city or all segments of the culture. The attempt to promote a cultural revival was closely tied to the desire of major businesses to improve the attractiveness of the city as a locale for corporate headquarters—it was not a grassroots effort supported by the entire community. And citizen commissions were typically much more influential at the elite level than with ordinary citizens. Most residents were probably unaware that such commissions existed and did not take their recommendations very seriously.

Resistance

Most white citizens did not reach a harmonious accommodation with the black majority council immediately following its election in 1977. Watching the emerging conflict with the Main Street establishment and reading the critical editorials in the daily newspapers, many whites began to view the new black majority in negative terms. Much of their antipathy was directed at the new mayor, Henry L. Marsh III. Whites increasingly came to believe that Marsh was utilizing his newfound power simply to reverse the table. In many parts of the white community, Marsh was perceived as a racialist who utilized his control over the other members of the council to impose his agenda upon the rest of the community. Although some whites discounted the newspapers' label of "King Henry," even some whites who had originally supported Marsh began to view his actions with more skepticism.

The breakup of the at-large system and the introduction of ward-based voting left whites with a majority in four of the nine councilmanic districts. These wards elected white council members. The five black majority wards had elected African Americans. But in 1982, one of the members of the original Marsh faction, Willie Dell, was challenged by another black candidate, Roy West. West had been a high school principal who had been reassigned to a middle school as a result of a consolidation developed by a superintendent who had been chosen by the Marsh faction. West was a vocal critic of Marsh, arguing that he had divided the city along racial lines and that it was time to elect a council member who might bridge rather than exacerbate existing racial divisions.

White voters comprised about 30 percent of the northside ward in which Dell and West ran for election. For the mostly middle-class white voters, the election became a referendum on the five years of the Marsh majority. West received extensive backing from segments of the business community that had been annoyed with Marsh's policies. A local organization with ties to the Main Street establishment, the Teams for Progress, worked hard to defeat Dell. White voters gave their near unanimous support to West and he received enough black votes to oust Dell. Following the election, West was installed as mayor when he agreed to accept the four white votes on council and vote for himself as well. This election was especially significant in Richmond because it effectively destroyed the Marsh coalition that had run the city since the special election of 1977.

West quickly became the white community's most popular black politician. His no-nonsense approach to discipline in the schools won him considerable black support as well. Extolled as the man who had defeated Marsh, many whites applauded West's willingness to cross racial lines when considering matters before council. In this context, West's support for the set-aside policy received no public criticism because most whites felt that he made decisions on the merits of a policy. Indeed, Carolyn Wake, a white councilperson who had vigorously opposed the Marsh majority, observed that West's support for the set-aside program was instrumental in making her rethink why it might be reasonable for the city to implement such a policy. By the end of the 1980s, West's volatile personality had alienated many of his original supporters, but it could not be denied that support for him had served, at least for a time, as the means by which white Richmonders had expressed their uneasiness with the Marsh faction.

White resistance to the Marsh majority and the new city council in 1977 was also evident in south Richmond. Throughout the 1980s, election returns in the middle-class neighborhoods of Westover Hills, the transitional neighborhoods around Hull Street, and the area annexed from Chesterfield County in 1970 gave increasing evidence that whites in these areas did not believe that they were adequately represented.

White discontent was expressed in three main ways. First, the rhetoric voiced in councilmanic elections continually appealed to the sentiment that the concerns of south Richmond were not taken seriously in the city council. Images of neglect, inattention, and indifference dominated the campaigns of the 1980s. The tendency was so pervasive that candidates who successfully used the rhetoric of neglect in one election were frequently attacked by their challengers in the next election with the exact same charges. In 1988, Joyce Riddell won election on the promise that she would be a spokesperson for south Richmond. Riddell was defeated two years later in a challenge by Charles Perkins on the grounds that she did not stand up for the neighborhood. In the same year, Councilwoman Geline Williams, whose seat spanned neighborhoods in south Richmond and the West End, lost every precinct in south Richmond to a write-in candidate. She held on to her seat only because of big majorities that she piled up in the West End.

The rhetoric of neglect voiced in the white precincts of south Richmond was related to a second cause of discontent: a belief that south Richmond neighborhoods had been sacrificed to the downtown revitalization agenda. Whites in south Richmond were never enthusiastic about the downtown renewal plans and were frequently vocal in their criticism. As it became evident that Sixth Street Marketplace was draining city coffers to the tune of $4 million per year, the criticism became more pronounced. William Golding, an eccentric councilperson elected in 1990 from a predominantly white precinct, recommended that the city deal with its marketplace dilemma by "blowing it up." While other responses were less provocative, south Richmond support for downtown revitalization was clearly shallow at best.

A third concern that animated white citizens in south Richmond centered on the real estate tax rate. Richmond's real estate tax rate was significantly higher than in the surrounding counties. In 1987–90, it fluctuated between $1.49 and $1.46 per $100 of assessed value while the tax rates of the three adjacent counties went from a low of $.70 to a high of $1.09.[24] Many white property owners in south Richmond believed that their taxes were out of line. They felt that they received minimal services and that the city provided substandard schools. White residents of the annexed area were especially irritated because many of them would have preferred to be located in Chesterfield County where the tax rates were lower and the schools better.

White residents in south Richmond were limited in what they could accomplish politically. They did not have the electoral votes to control the city council. Their objections to downtown revitalization plans were effectually minimized because the coalition between the black civic elite and the Main Street business establishment was too powerful to break. Indeed, a number of city council representatives from south Richmond quickly discovered that joining this coalition was the price of getting things done. Given their historical inability to form political coalitions with black organizations, they were unable to develop an alliance that would combine everyone concerned about the downtown agenda. Their complaints about the tax rate did have an effect, if only to convince the city manager and elected officials that Richmond could not finance its services by depending on an ever increasing real estate tax rate.

The final locus of white resistance to the Marsh majority was the editorial pages of the daily newspapers. Some black officials still blame the editorial writers for kindling racial tensions in the aftermath of the 1977 election of the black majority. They believe that the editorials engaged in a vicious brand of racial stereotyping, culminating with an editorial that described the behavior of the new city council as "monkey see, monkey do." For their part, the editorial writers believe that considered judgments about policy were interpreted as racially motivated when no such intention existed.

The editorial writers directed several lines of attack on the Marsh majority. They accused the new black council members of pursuing policies that were antibusiness, observing that the firing of City Manager Leidinger would damage Richmond's reputation and dim the possibility of attracting taxpaying companies. They argued that Marsh was acting like an old-fashioned machine politician, excluding any potential rivals from policy discussions. They contended that Marsh was a racialist who endorsed policies that would have been widely perceived as racist if the power lines had been reversed. And they argued that the new majority was profligate in its use of taxpayer funds, spending money without sufficient attention to the disincentives that accompanied its policy decisions.

It is difficult to gauge the editorials' effect on policy and political culture. In some more liberal circles, the dailies became known as the "Times-Disgrace" and the "Richmond Misleader." When the black civic elite joined Richmond Renaissance, a perhaps unintended result was to loosen the coalition between Main Street and the editorial writers. Certain policies—such as the set-aside program—to which the editorials objected on principle were accepted by the Main Street community as the price of doing business. But, at a minimum, the editorials reinforced the beliefs of many whites that the Marsh majority was racialist in purpose and that it was best for them to depend on the city for nothing but the bare minimum of essential services.

White Flight and Psychic Emigration

Perhaps the white response that had the most telling effect on Richmond was simply flight from the city. As in many other urban areas, the population of Richmond has remained stagnant, while that of the adjacent counties has burgeoned. In fact, the two largest adjacent counties now have more people than the city proper. The population of Henrico County grew by more than 20 percent in 1980–90, from 180,000 to 217,000 people. In the same decade, Chesterfield County grew by almost 50 percent, from 141,000 to 209,000. At the same time, the city's population declined by 8 percent, decreasing from 219,000 to 203,000.[25] Many factors have spurred the growth of the counties, including migration from other sections of the state, the North, and the Midwest, the amenities that suburban communities offer, the size of the house that purchasers can obtain for their money, tax rates, and the tendency of businesses to relocate where their workers reside. But it is undeniable that part of the growth of the counties can also be attributed to people who have moved out of the city and do not want to live in it, either from the fear of crime, concern about the quality of the school system, or unwillingness to pay the substantially higher tax rates.

White exodus from the city became especially notable in the late sixties and early seventies when Richmond had to implement a court-ordered busing plan. The percentage of white children in the city schools dropped precipitously as many families moved to the counties. These trends continued throughout the 1970s. Preliminary figures from the 1990 census indicate that, although Richmond's black population has increased, the city is now losing African Americans to the counties as well as whites. Many of the same reasons that prompted whites to move to Henrico and Chesterfield—crime, open space, and schools—now motivate a portion of black Richmond to make a similar move.

For the whites who have remained in Richmond, a partial withdrawal from the public realm has become the preferred mode of response. These citizens still maintain a modest level of civic participation: they vote in elections and pay taxes without excessive grumbling. But they do not see their identity and life chances directly related to the future of the city. And they have taken steps to insulate themselves from the more egregious problems that afflict Richmond. One of the most visible elements of this psychic if not physical flight from the city is the reluctance of Richmond whites to send their children to the city schools. In one large predominantly white section of the city west of the Boulevard, there are only slightly more than one hundred families who send their children to city high schools. These citizens may well lament the state of the city school system, but they have found that paying for private alternatives is preferable to becoming involved in political activity designed to remedy the problem.

White Response and Black Progress

How have the responses of white Richmonders to the emergence of African American political power influenced the potential for black progress? In some ways, their responses have expanded the range of action available to African American leaders. Undeniably, black politicians hold more important positions and make more significant decisions than they did twenty years ago. At the same time, white responses have also limited the choices available to black leaders. Compromise with the Main Street establishment compelled African American officials to eschew certain lines of action. For example, white resistance to higher taxes has made certain policies unthinkable. And, more subtly, white secession from the political arena has made it difficult to develop a consensus for addressing some of the city's more critical problems.

The accommodation that black leaders reached with the Main Street establishment expanded the range of action that was open to them. It accomplished this in two principal ways. First, the compromise was a public ratification of the political change that had occurred: white business leaders agreed that the black civic leaders were critical in discussions about the city's future economic development. Second, as we have described, accommodation enabled black officials to demand that economic development projects contain features with benefits for the African American community. This was the origin of the affirmative action elements in many of the city's construction programs. Finally, the rapprochement with the business elite enabled African American politicians to develop a program for the revitalization of Jackson Ward, the traditional hub of black commerce in the city.

The partial secession that was a feature of the white response could also be said to have expanded the range of action open to black political leaders. To the extent that whites no longer believed that Richmond was *their* city or that they ought to exercise a veto on development plans, African American officials were free to establish their own strategies. To be sure, there were limits on what could be accomplished—the antitax sentiment, the need to retain business confidence, and the impact of national economic trends were the most notable limitations—but it was evident that ordinary whites did not have the same proprietary interest in the city that was present in the mid-1960s when they controlled political power and sent their children to Richmond schools. They had accepted black political control of the city as the likely reality for the foreseeable future.

By 1990, the white business elite and ordinary citizens had come to understand that the majority of the city council would remain black, that the major appointments in the city (e.g., city manager, police chief, and school superintendent) would probably be African American, and that major projects in the city would have to include features that clearly benefited at least a segment of the black community. This did not mean that white Richmonders would support any policy that black leaders might propose. It did, however, mean that city officials knew that their positions were relatively secure, that whites were unlikely to initiate citywide campaigns of racial division, and that black political officials had to be consulted about activities that would utilize the public purse.

It is also obvious that the white response to the emergence of black political power restricted the range of options available to black leadership. First, the white voters who helped to elect West in 1982 brought about a clear division in the outlook of African American officials. Put simply, West's election ended Marsh's five-year reign. The Marsh faction no longer controlled city policy and West's resounding reelection in 1984 signified a permanent split in Richmond's black political community. With West on the council, it became much more difficult to define the "African American interest" in terms of city policy. Divisions within the African American community would have eventually emerged even if West had not been elected, but it is evident that the whites who provided his margin of victory hastened the arrival of the split.

The growing antitax sentiment in Richmond's white community also restricted the range of options available to black political leadership. The city's property tax rate was significantly higher than in the surrounding counties, a fact not lost on many citizens and commentators. As retail sales stagnated, the city became even more reliant on property taxes as a source of revenue, yet these could not be raised because it would put Richmond at an even greater competitive disadvantage with the adjacent counties. The collapse of the real estate market in the late eighties made this reality even more painful because it removed the option of simply increasing the assessed value of property as a means of obtaining more revenue without an official tax increase. By the early 1990s, the city manager proposed various user fees, coupled with an actual property tax reduction. These, however, never received council approval because the burden would have fallen more heavily on low- and middle-income home owners than on the more affluent taxpayers.

The compromise reached with the Main Street establishment also limited the available options for the black political leadership. In a formal sense, the compromise ceded control over city decisions about key economic development opportunities to a body (Richmond Renaissance) that was not publicly elected. Perhaps more importantly, the choice of one's partners always precludes other options and alliances. In Richmond, the alliance between City Hall and Main Street worked against the development of a neighborhood-based agenda, as city officials poured more than $20 million into the failing Sixth Street Marketplace. Moreover, elected officials often exhibited a narrow understanding of African American interests, which was largely defined by affirmative action set-asides in various construction projects (see chap. 4).

White flight from the city and the growth of the suburbs have posed formidable problems for Richmond, as for other metropolitan areas. On the one hand, the city would like to compel suburban residents to pay for their use of Richmond's amenities and for services the city provides which the county does not. (There have been, for instance, accusations that the county has actually "dumped" homeless and mentally ill people across the boundary line so that these people could utilize city services.) But proposals to do so through the implementation of a city income tax or other "commuter tax" are not politically feasible because of the threat that even more businesses will simply move their operations to the counties. County leaders often publicly express their commitment to a thriving core city, but they are rarely in a position to follow up with actual money.

One solution that business leaders and some academics have offered to the dilemma—regionalization of services—has been only tentatively embraced. Evidence of cooperation exists in projects such as the regional airport. It may also be possible to promote regionalization of services such as water supply and fire protection where cost savings are evident. Beyond this, however, the prospects are much more tenuous. Many county residents moved to escape the urban problems; they have no intention of paying for Richmond's troubles or of supporting a regional school system. For their part, city officials are often wary of proposals for regionalization and metropolitan government. They worry that such plans may be embraced by the Main Street establishment as a means of restoring white control, by taking key decisions out of the hands of black officials.

Polls conducted in 1994 indicate the ambivalence of county residents about working cooperatively with the city. On the one hand, there was near uniform agreement that the condition of the counties was related to the strength of the city. County residents acknowledged that the problems of the city had an effect on their well-being. They also said that there should be more substantial city-county cooperation than evident at the time. On the other hand, a majority of county residents were opposed to a plan to establish a regional government to deal with water supply, transportation, and public safety issues. A vast majority of county residents also maintained that the principal explanation for the city's problems was the activities and behavior of the residents.[26]

One of the best indicators of the manner in which the county residents view the city emerged in a series of questions in which they were asked to rate their local government. More than 85 percent of the residents in Henrico and Chesterfield Counties rated the quality of their government as excellent or good. Residents were also asked to rate the quality of the government in surrounding jurisdictions. In both Henrico and Chesterfield Counties, about 50 percent of the residents said that they did not know enough about the government of the other county to rate it, but of those who offered a rating, about 80 percent viewed the other county's government as excellent or good. Seventy-five percent of county residents, however, claimed to know enough about the city of Richmond to rate its government—and only 15 percent of those felt that the government of Richmond was excellent or good. In short, county residents recognized the connection between their quality of life and conditions in the city, but they did not have sufficient confidence in the city to support bold measures of cooperation that might be mutually beneficial.[27]

In any case, the combined effects of flight from the city, partial secession, and antitax sentiment have left the city government in a bind. Clearly, African Americans exercise more power in Richmond than at any previous time. Yet the city's economic base—despite efforts at downtown revitalization—has become an increasing problem. The downtown retail district is marked by empty storefronts and no longer has a national chain as an anchor store. There was significant office construction in the 1980s, but the resulting overdevelopment has left the city with a glut of space. Local political figures have come to realize that the mere possession of power does not mean necessarily that they can wield it efficaciously.

Conclusion

We do not intend to imply that Richmond is an inhospitable place to live for all its residents. For middle-class people, both black and white, Richmond provides a relatively high quality of life. Taxes may be higher than in the surrounding counties, but the city remains a relative bargain compared to many metropolitan areas. Although most residential areas are informally segregated, race relations are generally civil. Richmond is a city with much appeal for black professionals and businesspeople. And middle-class whites—especially those without school-age children—still find the city a comfortable and interesting place to reside.

The major problems fall into two categories. First, Richmond does not necessarily have the political capacity to address its problems. To some extent, all metropolitan areas face this incapacity. But to some degree it is also a consequence of the political dynamics that have accompanied the rise of black power in the city. Second, the city's political shortcomings threaten its future possibilities. To what extent can Richmond economically match the growing metropolitan areas of the Southeast? To what extent can the city avoid becoming the dumping ground for all the problems inside a prosperous periphery of predominantly white counties?

SIX

Richmond v. Croson in the Courts

Richmond's efforts to confront political issues with significant racial dimensions often wound up in the court system. In the years prior to *Croson*, two controversial matters in the city were ultimately the object of scrutiny by the U.S. Supreme Court. In the early 1970s, U.S. District Court Judge Robert Merhige ordered that the county and city schools be consolidated for the purpose of ending segregation. After the decision was reversed by the U.S. Court of Appeals, the Supreme Court upheld the reversal on a 4-4 tie vote. Only eight justices voted (Lewis Powell abstained because of his former position as chair of Richmond's school board). Earlier we described how Richmond's attempt to annex part of Chesterfield County also received Supreme Court attention in the mid-1970s (see chap. 2). Maintaining that the annexation was racially motivated, the Court eventually approved a compromise proposal that allowed the annexation to stand but changed the electoral system from an at-large to a ward-based process.

Richmond's set-aside program never generated the emotional and political turmoil in the city that accompanied the busing and annexation controversies. Many U.S. cities were torn asunder by plans to promote integration through court-ordered busing, and Richmond was no exception. Annexation was controversial because in reality it was a question about whether whites or blacks would control political power in Richmond in the 1970s and beyond. By contrast, the set-aside program elicited only a few complaints before city council and, with this exception, was passed and implemented with little fuss. The court challenge to the program was politically earthshaking for this very reason. Set-aside ordinances had simply become a routine (and sometimes essential) instrument by which urban leaders conducted politics. To challenge set-asides was both to threaten business as usual in American cities and to undermine policy directions that were taken for granted.

This chapter begins by describing the origins of the *Croson* challenge and the conflicting lower court decisions on it. We show how divergent opinions by Judges Robert Merhige and J. Harvie Wilkinson III defined the controversy that had emerged in the 1980s about the appropriate meaning of civil rights. The second part of the chapter explains the significance of *Croson* by locating it within the Supreme Court's affirmative action jurisprudence since *Regents of the University of California v. Allan Bakke. Croson* was the first time that a majority of the Court agreed on the necessity of utilizing a strict scrutiny standard in the examination of affirmative action policy. The final section of the chapter describes the response to *Croson* in Richmond, other U.S. cities, and the courts. We examine the various instruments that have been used to temper its effects and suggest that on a number of key issues—particularly the means by which cities demonstrate historical discrimination and the standards for narrow tailoring of affirmative action policy—the Court will have to rule again in order to clarify the present confusion.

The Supreme Court's *Adarand v. Pena* decision (1995), which overturned a federal set-aside program, has received substantial attention since this book was written. The importance of the *Adarand* decision was that it broadened the scope of the principles underlying the Court's opinion in *Croson* by arguing that *federal* set-aside programs were to be examined with the same "strict scrutiny" standard that had been established for local and state programs in the Richmond case.

Croson in the Courts

Richmond's decision to develop a set-aside ordinance was based on the results of an examination of city contracts that revealed a striking discrepancy in the amount going to white and black firms (see chap. 3). During the five years prior to 1973, minority businesses had received only 0.67 percent (less than $1 million) of the city's construction contracts which had totaled more than $124 million.[1] When this statistic was combined with the previous exclusion of blacks from the mainstream of Richmond's political and business life and with knowledge of the discrimination that had historically been practiced in the construction trades, it seemed evident to the council majority that it had a moral and political responsibility to redress the inequity.

In 1983, the council thought that its desire to do so stood on a firm legal basis as well. Members were aware that other large cities had established set-aside programs. In addition, they believed that the Supreme Court's *Fullilove v. Klutznick* decision had provided a legal foundation for their effort to redress the inequities in city contracting. *Fullilove* was concerned with a challenge to the minority business enterprise provision of the Public Works Employment Act (1977), which required, absent an administrative waiver, that at least 10 percent of federal funds granted for local public works projects must be used by the state or local grantee to procure services or supplies from businesses owned by minority group members.[2] The major claim of those opposed to the set-aside legislation was that it violated the equal protection clause of the Fifth Amendment. The Court rejected that challenge and concluded that Congress had the authority to redress the present effects of past discrimination so long as the method chosen was narrowly focused and limited in size, impact, and duration. It asserted that the 10 percent set-aside was a reasonable figure insofar as it represented a midway point between the percentage of minorities in the U.S. population and the percentage of minority contractors in the nation.[3]

The six members of the Richmond City Council who supported the bill, as well as the city's legal advisors, believed that they were simply applying the principles of *Fullilove* to the local level. The key part of the Richmond ordinance was that, absent a waiver, "all contractors awarded construction contracts by the city shall subcontract at least thirty per cent to the contract of minority business enterprises."[4] In fact, in almost all of its significant features, the city attorney's office tailored the bill to what it understood *Fullilove* permitted, believing that the legality of the set-aside provision itself had been established in the case. The ordinance's definition of minorities (wording that returned to haunt the city in 1989), which extended beyond the black community to include "Spanish speaking, Orientals, Eskimos, or Aleuts," was derived simply by replicating the language of the Public Works Employment Act. Further, in the selection of 30 percent as the set-aside target, the city chose a point nearly midway between the percentage of contracts awarded to minorities in 1983 and the percentage of minorities in the general population of the city, precisely what it felt Congress had done in 1977.

The principal legal challenge to the city ordinance commenced within five months of its initial passage. On September 30, 1983, J. A. Croson Corporation, an Ohio-based business, received bid documents from the city to install stainless steel plumbing fixtures in the Richmond City Jail. In this particular contract, Croson concluded that the city's regulation could be met only if a minority contractor supplied the fixtures, because these would, as purchased products, consume 75 percent of the contract's value. A representative from Croson testified that the company had immediately contacted several minority businesses, informing them of the project and requesting them to submit quotes on the fixtures if they were interested. Croson testified that on October 12 (the last day to submit bids) it again contacted the minority businesses to see if any would be bidding. None were able to do so and Croson submitted a bid of $126,530 using a quote for the fixtures provided by a nonminority firm.[5]

On October 12, however, Melvin Brown of the minority-owned Continental Metal Hose had informed Croson's representative that he wanted to participate in the bid and that he had not been contacted previously. Brown attempted to obtain a price quote for the fixtures but was rebuffed when the distributor claimed that his company had not established its credit worthiness. At the bid opening on October 13, Brown told Croson's representative that his company would still attempt to supply the fixtures. But on October 19 Croson requested a waiver from the city's minority utilization requirement on the grounds that a qualified minority supplier was not available. On October 27, the day that Brown learned of Croson's waiver request, he called the city's director of purchases and stores and noted that he had obtained a price for the fixtures, though his markup was $6,183 higher than the quote Croson was using from the nonminority supplier.[6]

After reviewing the various documents and arguments, the city advised Croson that it was canceling the bid and rebidding the contract. Croson attempted to appeal the decision but the city had no provision for an appeal in such circumstances. Croson then filed suit, alleging that the city's program violated several state laws and protections inherent in the Fourteenth Amendment of the U.S. Constitution. Croson maintained that the set-aside ordinance violated a Virginia law stating that local procurement policies had to be based on "competitive principles."[7] More important for the subsequent litigation, Croson contended that the ordinance violated the equal protection clause of the Fourteenth Amendment by endorsing a race-conscious remedy for which there was no compelling government interest and that was not narrowly tailored.[8] In this regard, it should be noted that while Croson's suit was an explicit challenge to the Richmond

law, it was also part of a more general series of challenges to set-aside policies that were being brought to various courts of the nation under the
auspices of the Association of General Contractors.

J. A. Croson Company v. City of Richmond was heard in the U.S. District Court by Judge Robert Merhige. No stranger to civil rights litigation
concerning the city of Richmond, in the 1970s Merhige had been a key
figure in the controversy over integration and school busing. Merhige also
presided over the challenge to Richmond's annexation plan and over the
city's objections ruled that it was racially motivated and could not be upheld until the city changed its methods of selecting the council. Seen by
segments of the black community as one of its few potential allies in official government, Merhige was vilified in some white circles, and at one
time anonymous death threats compelled him to request police protection
for his home.

Merhige's 1984 decision on the set-aside program was grounded in an
interpretation of the applicability of Fullilove to the city's program. Rec-
ognizing that the Supreme Court decision in that case had not provided
a "clear, easily applied test" for evaluating set-aside programs, Merhige
employed an opinion from the Eleventh Circuit in South Florida that had
attempted to distill a common set of concerns from the majority's position.
This approach required that (1) the governmental body have the authority to construct the plan, (2) "the governmental body adopting a remedial plan make adequate findings to ensure that it is remedying the present
effects of prior discrimination and not advancing one racial group's interest over another," and (3) the "use of racial classifications not extend further than established need of remedying the effects of past discrimination."[9]

On these grounds, Merhige upheld the Richmond set-aside program.
He maintained that Croson provided no evidence to demonstrate that a
city council lacks the power to develop set-aside programs. Merhige also
contended that Richmond provided adequate findings of the need for a
remedial program. In this regard, he pointed to the paucity of minority
businesses in Richmond, the fact that the city's claims about the historical discrimination in the construction industry were unrefuted at the trial, and the evidence cited by Congress in passing the minority business
provision that was challenged unsuccessfully in Fullilove. Merhige also
concurred with the city's claim that its program did not extend too far. As
evidence, he cited the inclusion of a waiver provision and the temporally
limited duration of the plan. Merhige specifically addressed the charge that
the percentage of the set-asides in Richmond was set at an arbitrary and

unreasonably high level. He maintained that the city was acting reasonably in establishing the 30 percent set-aside figure insofar as a number of
lower court decisions had implied that "the percentage of minorities in the
community's general population, not the percentage of minorities in the
area's business community is the appropriate benchmark for evaluating the
reasonableness of a set-aside figure."[10]

Croson appealed the decision to the Fourth Circuit Court of Appeals.
Once again, the city's plan was upheld when a 2-1 majority rejected
Croson's arguments and affirmed the reasoning outlined in Merhige's
opinion, particularly his interpretation of the applicability of *Fullilove*. At
the same time, Judge J. Harvie Wilkinson's dissent laid the foundation for
what eventually became Croson's appeal to the Supreme Court.

A member of a prominent Richmond family and a one-time clerk for
Justice Lewis Powell, Wilkinson was a Reagan appointee who, as a law
professor at the University of Virginia, had written a book criticizing the
logic inherent in the Court's landmark *Brown v. Board of Education* decision. In his dissent in *Croson*, Wilkinson maintained that the city's plan
violated state law which demanded that procurement policies be consistent with competitive principles. Drawing his reasoning from the free
market critiques of affirmative action policies, Wilkinson argued that the
Richmond plan predetermined results "in a way that does not comport
with savings in the public fisc or quality in the public product." More
significantly, Wilkinson contended that the factual findings of discrimination were inadequate and that the 30 percent set-aside figure "emerged
from a vacuum." Wilkinson's summary maintained that while he recognized the need to "overcome the legacy of discrimination," his colleagues
on the circuit court had actually harmed civil rights by approving "the
casual adoption of a crude numerical preference that can only impair the
ideal that all stand equally before the door and postpone the day of human
fellowship that transcends race."[11]

Wilkinson's vigorous dissent left Croson with more than a glimmer of
hope that his appeal to the Supreme Court might result in a different
outcome. His hopes were enhanced when the Supreme Court remanded
the case to the Circuit Court of Appeals with specific instructions to reconsider its decision in light of *Wendy Wygant v. Jackson Board of Education*, a case recently heard by the Court. *Wygant* arose from a collective
bargaining agreement between Jackson, Michigan, and a teachers' union
after the city was threatened with a suit for discrimination in employment
procedures. The agreement provided that "if it became necessary to lay off

teachers, those with the most seniority would be retained, except at no time would there be a greater percentage of minority personnel laid off than the current percentage of minority personnel employed at the time of the layoff." When a budget crunch forced the school district to make staff cutbacks, some nonminority teachers were laid off while minority instructors with less seniority were retained. When the appeal by the nonminority teachers reached the Supreme Court, their position was upheld and the Court overturned the collective bargaining agreement on the grounds that it penalized innocent nonminority parties and that findings calling for such a drastic remedy had not been adequately demonstrated.[12]

On the face of things, the instruction to reconsider *Croson* in light of *Wygant* was odd because the two cases appeared dissimilar. The Richmond set-aside ordinance did not directly prevent any individual from holding a job, while the other clearly prevented at least some individuals from temporarily practicing their vocation. But what the Supreme Court appeared to be doing by its instruction was challenging the entire basis of the Richmond ordinance, namely, the applicability of *Fullilove* to local programs. In other words, the Court was telling the circuit court that it should examine the set-aside policy in light of the Court's recent decisions which did admit the possible legality of affirmative action but which had been tightening the requirements that had to be met before race-conscious policies would be upheld.

The significance of the Supreme Court's instruction was evidenced by the circuit court's reversal of its own decision upon reconsideration. With Judge Hall of the three-member appeal panel changing his vote, Wilkinson's position became the majority opinion. Wilkinson argued that for set-asides to be justified, adequate findings of identifiable discrimination must be made and that the set-aside percentage cannot be based on comparisons with the entire population of the area. In Wilkinson's mind, the Richmond program was now illegitimate in concept inasmuch as its findings were based on notions of societal discrimination. He claimed that it was too sweeping in its application insofar as there was no justification for the 30 percent set-aside and because the definition of minorities included people (e.g., Aleuts and Eskimos) who had never resided in Richmond in substantial numbers. Ultimately, Wilkinson felt that the liabilities of the Richmond program opened affirmative action to possible abuse as nothing more than a racial pork barrel. As to *Fullilove*, Wilkinson acknowledged that some aspects of the plan followed it "to the letter." Yet the city's premise "was in error" because he contended that the Congress has much broader power in addressing violations of the Fourteenth Amendment than city governments.[13]

The city of Richmond appealed the circuit court's decision to the Supreme Court but most observers of the case's development recognized that the city was fighting a losing battle. Richmond's brief before the Court emphasized once again its contention that *Fullilove* was the controlling precedent and that it was misguided to apply *Wygant* in circumstances that were so completely different.[14] The city was joined in its efforts by amicus briefs from a number of organizations, including the National League of Cities. Their arguments, along with those put forward by Justices William Brennan, Harry Blackmun, and Thurgood Marshall, failed to persuade a majority of the Court. Justice Sandra Day O'Connor's opinion (joined by Rehnquist, White, and Kennedy), echoed Wilkinson's dismissal of *Fullilove* as the controlling precedent by noting that it was a special case applicable only to the U.S. Congress as a coequal branch of the national government and not to municipalities. O'Connor also repeated most of the major arguments that Wilkinson had made. She contended that (1) the Richmond plan was not justified by a compelling governmental interest since the record revealed no prior discrimination by the city in awarding contracts and (2) the 30 percent set-aside was not narrowly tailored to accomplish a remedial purpose.[15]

Affirmative Action and the Supreme Court: From *Bakke* to *Croson*

Observers of the Supreme Court would not suggest that its treatment of affirmative action in the past fifteen years has been a model of lucid exposition and logical analysis. Since it first addressed the issue by declaring that Allan Bakke was unfairly denied entrance to medical school by the University of California's use of racial quotas while simultaneously maintaining that race-specific remedies could possibly be constitutional, the Court has been sharply divided. It has argued about whether affirmative action is permissible and, if it is, what kind of findings of discrimination are necessary to legitimate a policy of race-conscious relief. Opinions have disputed what statistical measures may serve as an adequate indication of serious discrimination. Even in cases where the Court has agreed that race-conscious relief might be justified, justices have disagreed about whether a particular program is legitimately remedial and narrowly tailored. Moreover, there has been controversy about whether the same criteria should be employed to evaluate programs mandated by governmental units and those undertaken by private employers. And, at least until *Croson,* the justices disagreed on the level of judicial scrutiny that should be applied to affirmative action cases. Nonetheless, we must try to make some sense out of these divisions if we are to come to a genuine understanding of *Croson's* implications.

The difficulty of accomplishing this has been aggravated by a number of factors. First, affirmative action cases that have come before the Court have frequently resulted in a proliferation of opinions that have not permitted a definitive interpretation of the decision. For example, in the Bakke case six separate opinions were published. Matters are further complicated because while most justices have held fast to the position they originally adopted, the stance of others has undergone a considerable evolution. Justice John Paul Stevens, for example, believes that the precedents established in *Bakke* and *United Steelworkers of America v. Brian F. Weber* ought to be respected even though he personally does not agree with the constitutional interpretations made in those cases. On the other hand, (now retired) Justice Byron White wrote in the late 1980s that he would vote to overturn *Weber* even though he was a member of the majority that approved the affirmative action program contested at the time. Finally, the Court's decisions in particular cases have been rendered, at times, on relatively narrow grounds that have not always explicitly addressed the major legal and constitutional questions raised by affirmative action. Indeed, in *Bakke,* five justices felt that constitutional issues were involved while four others believed that they need not address them.

This context makes it difficult but not impossible to clarify the discussion of the Court's treatment of the issue. An examination of the voting patterns in affirmative action cases demonstrates that the Court's disagreement was structured in ways that have significant political implications.[16] In addition, the very proliferation of opinions that have made it difficult to interpret the meaning of any individual decision may, in fact, enable us to specify the pattern of disagreement in the Court with more accuracy than if the majority and dissenting opinions on every case had been univocal. In the period from *Bakke* to *Croson,* most justices expressed a position on the more general or theoretical aspects of affirmative action. They commented, for example, on whether they believed that the equal protection clause of the Fifth and Fourteenth Amendments permits affirmative action and whether the Civil Rights Act of 1964, especially its Title VII provisions, allows employers to develop plans that give preferential treatment to minorities, as well as what level of scrutiny should be given to affirmative action plans. The justices also expressed positions on the methods employed to apply race-conscious relief and elaborated on the relationship between their general stance on the constitutionality of affirmative action and the particular applications of it.[17]

Three of the justices that were on the Court from *Bakke* to *Croson*— Blackmun, Brennan, and Marshall—voted in favor of affirmative action plans every time a case was granted certiorari and was the subject of an official opinion. They also maintained a consistent position throughout the period. None of the three published separate opinions staking out a distinctive position on the constitutional issues raised by affirmative action policies. When one wrote a separate concurrence or dissent, it was typically used as a vehicle for expressing a personal opinion about a particular aspect of a case rather than for developing a position about the constitutionality of race-conscious relief that differed substantively from the other two. In this regard, we might think of Blackmun's dissent in *Croson*, in which his purpose was not to distance himself from Marshall's scathing critique of the majority's outlook but to express amazement that a Supreme Court in 1989 would overthrow an effort by leaders in the former capital of the Confederacy to make amends for its history of discrimination.[18]

The essence of the Blackmun-Brennan-Marshall position was that eliminating racial subjugation in the real world of contemporary America requires the use of race-conscious policies or, in the words they were fond of using, "in order to get beyond racism, we must first take account of race." The constitutional defense of their position was grounded in a distinction between racial classifications that stigmatize and those that are appropriately remedial.[19] For Blackmun, Brennan, and Marshall, legalized segregation stigmatized; set-asides rectified past discrimination. The implication of this distinction is that affirmative action is perfectly legitimate and does not violate the equal protection clause, which they argued is directed primarily against classifications that stigmatize. In addition, they believe that the Civil Rights Act clearly permits the voluntary adoption of affirmative action programs by private employers and that it is a cruel misreading of its intent to utilize this landmark legislation on behalf of American blacks as a way of prohibiting efforts to remedy racial discrimination.

Blackmun, Brennan, and Marshall thus argued that affirmative action programs should be judged by what they label "intermediate scrutiny." That is, do these plans further an important governmental purpose, and are they reasonably constructed so as to fulfill this goal?[20] The use of the intermediate scrutiny standard led them to be relatively tolerant of the development of affirmative action programs by local governments and private employers in terms of both the numerical goals employed and the policy's extension beyond the hiring process to promotion and layoff policies as well as matters such as economic set-asides. They suggested that other members of the Court who were willing to overturn these programs, on the grounds that adequate findings of discrimination had not been made or that local governments had used improper statistical comparisons in establishing target quotas, were willfully naive about how American society functions and the continuing effects of discrimination. In political terms, it might be said that Blackmun, Brennan, and Marshall echoed the standard liberal argument by asserting that affirmative action is a logical extension of the civil rights movement and that it is an integral element in the "task of moving our society toward a state of meaningful equality of opportunity, not an abstract version of equality in which the effects of past discrimination would be forever frozen into our social fabric."[21]

During the period from *Bakke* to *Croson*, the opposite voting bloc on the Court included Justices William Rehnquist, Byron White, and in later years Antonin Scalia. Rehnquist voted against affirmative action plans in each of the ten cases that came to the Court during this period. Scalia denied affirmative actions claims in each of the three cases that have been considered since his installation. White's voting pattern was more checkered because he was actually part of the majority that supported affirmative action in *Weber* and *Fullilove*, but both his voting and thinking changed over time. In each of the last seven cases in which the Court published an opinion prior to *Croson*, White voted against affirmative action. Perhaps more importantly, he also expressed a desire to overturn *Weber* and suggested that his belief about the meaning of affirmative action turned out to be quite different from those on whose side he had originally voted.[22]

The Rehnquist-Scalia-White voting bloc was characterized by several common features. They contended that affirmative action plans should be subjected to "strict scrutiny" to ensure that equal protection guidelines are not violated. The standard of strict scrutiny holds that any policy based on racial classification is inherently suspect and must be subject to the most rigorous judicial examination to determine whether the governmental interest involved is not merely important but "compelling," and whether the means chosen to implement this interest are "narrowly tailored."[23] In addition, Rehnquist, Scalia, and in later years White argued that the Civil Rights Act of 1964, especially Title VII, does not permit race-conscious policies in the areas of hiring, promotions, and layoffs. Their opinions often referred to the legislative history of the act to defend their stance that the vision of civil rights legislation was that of a color-blind, not a race-conscious, society. Indeed, they suggested that current defenders of affirmative action have subtly but almost completely transformed the meaning of civil rights in their attempts to "replace the goal of a discrimination-free society with the quite incompatible goal of proportionate representation by race and by sex in the workplace."[24] Rehnquist, Scalia, and White also agreed that the standards applied to private employers do not substantively differ from those that governmental units must meet, but they drew much less permissive conclusions from this assumption than did the more liberal wing of the Court.

Given these positions on the major theoretical questions raised by affirmative action, it is not surprising that Rehnquist, Scalia, and White were so critical of the specific plans brought to the Court for judgment. While Blackmun, Brennan, and Marshall supported most uses of affirmative action as government policy, the most conservative wing of the Court examined the policy's utilization with extraordinary rigor to see if the specific applications of affirmative action were incompatible with the guiding principle of race neutrality. In almost every instance, the conservative justices found that the programs formulated by municipalities, unions, and employers violated equal protection guarantees, subverted the meaning of the Civil Rights Act, harmed innocent nonminorities, promoted legitimate social goals by unjustified means, or provided advantage too widely to nonvictimized minorities.

The theoretical position of the Court's right flank was not as clear-cut and uniform as its voting record. Scalia's position was clearly more extreme than that of White and even Rehnquist. In essence, Scalia does not believe in anything that could remotely be called affirmative action. He argues that relief can only be granted to identified victims of discrimination on an individual basis. He contends it is unconstitutional to go beyond this to include race-specific measures that benefit members of a group who did not personally experience discrimination.[25] Rehnquist and White at least minimally assert that activities called affirmative action can be permissible. Rehnquist's opinions suggest that affirmative action policies that are narrowly tailored to remedy past discrimination could possibly be permissible. White concurs with Rehnquist and suggests that in particularly egregious cases he could even support affirmative action aid for individuals who are nonvictims.[26] It also remains true that Rehnquist has not seen an affirmative action plan that he could support and that White was, in the years before his retirement, increasingly less inclined to support such such policy. Analysts such as the *New York Times* reporter who observed that Scalia "is alone on the right flank of the Court" were somewhat misleading because the practical effects of his theoretical isolation, at least with respect to affirmative action, were negligible.[27]

Perhaps the critical case to illustrate this point is the 1986 decision in *Local 28 of the Sheet Metal Workers International Association v. Equal Employment Opportunity Commission.* A local union in New York had attempted to maintain what was essentially a whites-only policy by nepotistic recruitment practices. In 1964, the New York State Commission on Human Rights and the New York Supreme Court ordered the union to change its method of selecting apprentices. When the union persisted in efforts to circumvent the order, the United States initiated suit against it, and in 1975 the district court found the union guilty of discrimination, in violation of Title VII of the Civil Rights Act. The union was ordered to adopt an affirmative action plan with numerical quotas for membership, and a court-appointed administrator was chosen to facilitate implementation. In 1982, the federal government again took the union to court, where it was found guilty of contempt of the 1975 order. The court "imposed [a] $150,000 fine to be placed in a fund designed to increase nonwhite membership in the apprentice program and the union."[28] At this time, the union filed suit appealing the contempt order, the requirement to initiate the fund, and the original affirmative action plan dictated by the first ruling.

It is not likely that a more clearly defined justification for affirmative action or an example of what Justice Powell called "egregious discrimination" would be available to the Court. While acknowledging the seriousness of discrimination, both Rehnquist and White (Scalia had yet to join the Court) felt that the remedies extended beyond the legitimate reach of the Constitution. White argued that the effects of the lower court's actions "established not just a minority membership goal but also a strict racial quota that the union was required to attain. We have not heretofore approved this kind of racially discriminatory hiring practice and I would not do so now." Rehnquist's argument was even more restrictive, maintaining that the plan was invalid because Title VII of the Civil Rights Act did not allow the union or the court "to sanction the granting of relief to those who were not victims at the expense of innocent non-minority workers injured by racial preferences."[29] If the facts of this case—twenty years of resisting court orders added to decades of discrimination—were insufficient for Rehnquist and White to support an affirmative action plan with numerical quotas, it is hard to see how the theoretical differences between Rehnquist and Scalia, for example, had consequences for the manner in which they voted on the cases that came before them.

Although Justice Anthony Kennedy only ruled on affirmative action in *Croson* during this period, his opinion hints that his voting behavior may well follow that of the more conservative members of the Court on this issue. Kennedy has suggested that he agrees with Scalia's claim that "the moral imperative of racial neutrality is the driving force of the Equal Protection Clause" and that it might be beneficial to "strike down all preferences which are not necessary remedies to victims of unlawful discrimination." Ultimately, however, Kennedy did not join Scalia's opinion in *Croson* primarily because he believes that its practical effects can be accomplished by a less sweeping claim that does not actually require the Court to overturn precedents established in the recent past. Kennedy notes that he interprets the majority's adherence to the strict scrutiny standard to already forbid "the use even of narrowly drawn racial classifications except as a last resort."[30]

The swing vote on the Court during the *Bakke* to *Croson* period was comprised of Powell, Stevens, and O'Connor. Powell endorsed affirmative action in slightly more than half of the cases (five of nine) that came to the Court while he served. Stevens supported affirmative action policies in five of the eight cases that he heard during this time frame. In the seven cases regarding affirmative action that she has heard, O'Connor voted in favor of plans on two occasions.[31]

The evolution of Stevens's position follows a path almost directly opposite that of White. Stevens voted against affirmative action plans in *Fullilove* and *Memphis Fire Department v. Carl Stotts*. Moreover, he disagreed with the interpretation of the Civil Rights Act of 1964 made by the majority in *Weber*. Yet since 1984, *Croson* has been the only case in which he has voted against an affirmative action plan. Arguing that the interpretations of the equal protection clause and the Civil Rights Act in *Bakke* have become part of American law, Stevens became more willing to defer to affirmative action plans created by employers and legislatures. In one opinion, he quoted approvingly an article from the *Harvard Law Review* that contended that affirmative action can be a forward-looking policy and need not be justified by referring to previous acts of discrimination.[32] Yet he voted against *Fullilove* and continued the line of reasoning in that case to *Croson*, by arguing that set-asides are neither an adequate remedy for discrimination nor an especially effective plan for helping those most harmed by previous discrimination.

O'Connor has been much less supportive of affirmative action than Stevens, which her opinion for the majority in *Croson* clearly demonstrates. She believes that "strict scrutiny" needs to be applied to the examination of affirmative action plans, yet she has been a bit more lenient than Rehnquist and White in the application of the standard, suggesting that certain narrowly tailored plans can be legitimately employed to remedy past discrimination. Indisputably, O'Connor's interpretation of narrow tailoring is more rigorous than the Blackmun-Brennan-Marshall understanding or even than that of Stevens and former Justice Powell. In some of O'Connor's opinions, for instance, she has argued that affirmative action plans that utilize statistics to prove discrimination by comparing the percentage of minorities in the particular job to the percentage in the population at large are often invalid. In addition, O'Connor has adamantly insisted that affirmative action cannot be justified as an effort to remedy "societal discrimination" but must instead be premised on tangible, visible examples of discrimination.[33] O'Connor's reluctance to support affirmative action might best be noted in the fact that, besides the egregious discrimination case of the Sheet Metal Workers Union in New York, she has supported an affirmative action plan on only one other occasion—and it dealt with a plan based on gender, not race. Whereas Powell "swung" in favor of affirmative action plans five out of nine occasions, O'Connor's record shows that she "swings" to support the policy much less frequently.

Prior to the *Croson* decision, most commentators on the Court's treatment of affirmative action issues emphasized its continued willingness to acknowledge the policy's constitutionality. As late as 1988, Bernard Schwartz, a noted scholar of constitutional law, maintained that even with Ronald Reagan's two terms in office, the Court's position on the issue was still best captured by Marshall's quote in *Bakke*: "Despite the Court's inability to agree upon a route, we have reached a common destination in sustaining affirmative action against constitutional attack."[34] Some commentators have gone even further, claiming that decisions in *United States v. Philip Paradise* and *Johnson v. Transportation Agency, Santa Clara County, California* amounted to nothing less than a repudiation of the Reagan perspective on civil rights by a markedly conservative Court.[35]

These commentators were not necessarily mistaken in their claim that the Court had shown its willingness to uphold certain kinds of affirmative action policies. Yet they did not always explore the full implications of the statistical measures of discrimination that the Court felt were appropriate or the consequences of the manner in which "narrow tailoring" was being interpreted. In addition, they neglected to portray how precarious and vulnerable the Court's support for affirmative action really was. They rarely if ever mentioned the evolution of White's position or compared O'Connor's record on the issue to the other swing votes. Nor did they always discuss how a single change on the bench could easily reverse the outcome in a number of important cases. At a minimum, the *Croson* decision should prompt a serious reconsideration of the direction of the Court.

The Post-*Croson* Era

Although the *Croson* decision effectively ended Richmond's set-aside program, it did not settle the broader controversy over set-asides and the affirmative action policy of local governments. In the years following the Supreme Court's ruling, local governments across the nation examined their set-aside programs. Officials frequently attempted to provide a new justification for the policies grounded in concrete evidence of discrimination, and they often refashioned their policies to meet the tests that the Court's majority had articulated in its opinion. In addition, further litigation over local set-aside programs was brought to the federal court system, and these cases required that the implications of *Croson* be spelled out more precisely. Finally, changes in the personnel of the Supreme Court have implications for the review of future cases.

Richmond after *Croson*

The city of Richmond spent a considerable amount of time studying the Court's decision with the intent of rewriting the set-aside ordinance. Initially, Richmond City Councilman (now State Senator) Marsh claimed at a public forum that the Court's recent decision would not significantly detract from the city's effort to devise a set-aside policy. But as the implications of *Croson* became more clear, Marsh and his colleagues on the council recognized that the task was more difficult than they had originally envisioned. For this reason, a special commission was established to study the city's options in light of the Court's strict scrutiny mandate about local set-aside programs.

Appointed by the city manager and city council, the eight-person commission consisted of representatives from the Virginia Office of Minority

Business Enterprise, the legal profession, the city manager's office, and the local construction industry. The commission was charged with the tasks of determining (1) which racial minorities as defined by the Equal Employment Opportunity Commission (EEOC) were most appropriately the object of study in Richmond, (2) the extent to which minorities participated in the construction industry in the Richmond area, (3) the impediments that may have prevented a higher level of participation, and (4) the means that could remedy identified discrimination, including methods that were nonracial and, if necessary, those with a racial component. The commission met numerous times with city staff, conducted a public hearing, and employed outside consultants in the process of compiling information that could enable the city to construct a post-*Croson* policy.

As a preface to its legislative proposals, the commission presented a paper entitled "The Richmond Minority Construction Contracting Ordinance: Historical Context." The paper described Richmond as a city that had been permeated by the segregationist philosophy, the capitol of the Confederacy in the nineteenth century, and the "symbolic capitol for southern white resistance to school integration in the 20th Century." The paper maintained that segregationism was embedded in institutions such as the local school for the skilled trades, the Virginia Mechanics Institute, which offered a wide-ranging curriculum in mechanical training and broader business skills. By contrast, the construction training in the black high schools covered only a "relatively paltry curriculum." The paper noted that both informal and formal city practices had made it impossible for blacks to obtain a city license that would enable them to compete effectively for available employment in city contracting. Further, the essay maintained that the city had an "unwritten policy that it would not hire any black contractors during segregation."[36]

The ordinance that the city council passed as a result of the study differed considerably from that challenged in *Croson*. Premised on the assumption that minorities had been subjected to "discriminatory exclusion both as individuals and as subcontractors," the ordinance stated that "it shall be the official policy of the City of Richmond to increase the number of minorities who participate meaningfully in all city construction contracts." The crux of the new legislation was twofold. First, it was the "goal of the City to have twenty percent minority employment by all construction firms contracting with the City."[37] Second, the ordinance maintained that majority contractors had to demonstrate "good faith" efforts to involve minority firms in the work. The means of accomplishing this was to institute a prequalification phase in the bidding process that rewarded firms for their previous efforts in enhancing minority participation and awarding twenty points during the bidding process based on the proposed plan to utilize minority firms in the work.

The Nation after *Croson*

The process that occurred in Richmond was repeated in cities across the nation. As George R. LaNoue has noted, at the time of *Croson* "there were 234 minority set-aside programs in states, counties, cities, and special districts across the country."[38] It was evident that without effective counteraction, *Croson* threatened to undermine the vast majority of these programs. Cities that were making efforts to rewrite their set-aside policies were aided by the work of the National Association of Minority Contractors (NAMC). In the pre-*Croson* era, the Association of General Contractors (AGC) had aggressively led the fight against minority set-asides. On multiple levels and in many parts of the country, the AGC pursued a tactic of "strategic opposition" to set-aside plans in various cities. In association with its affiliated members, the AGC targeted for legal challenge those set-aside programs thought to be most vulnerable to judicial scrutiny for being in violation of the equal protection clause of the Fourteenth Amendment.

In the post-*Croson* era, the NAMC initiated an aggressive strategy of molding the thinking of local government officials about how to overcome the chilling effects of *Croson* and to help them understand, in the words of Ralph Thomas, the NAMC's executive director, the "new opportunities" for minority economic development that *Croson* created. Shortly after the Court overturned the Richmond plan, Thomas wrote that "opponents of government sponsored minority business utilization programs may be in premature celebration of their supposed 'victory' in the recent U.S. Supreme Court ruling in *City of Richmond v. J. A. Croson*. State and local minority business programs will fall like dominoes because of the ruling. But when the dust settles, new ones will be stronger than before, much less prone to attack."[39]

Under the banner of a national campaign, the NAMC unfurled a multidimensional plan of action. One part of the campaign focused on providing education to local governments about the *Croson* decision. The NAMC sponsored regional workshops for local officials, developed a "Richmond Compliance Manual" for use by states, counties, and municipalities in assessing their programs, and provided direct assistance to localities interested in assessing the legal viability of their existing programs.[40]

A second feature of the campaign consisted of providing information and assistance to cities that were interested in actually rewriting their programs. Finally, the NAMC planned to coordinate its efforts with other groups, such as the NAACP, the National Hispanic Association of Construction Enterprises, the United Indian Economic Development Association, and the Asian Pacific Chamber of Commerce, with the ultimate goal of encouraging Congress to pass legislation requiring state and local governments to adopt minority business enterprise (MBE) utilization programs based on congressional findings of past discrimination in specific states and localities.

At the urging of the NAMC, many localities responded to the Court's decision by commissioning disparity studies that attempted to demonstrate the extent of discrimination that might justify the utilization of preferential treatment under the strict scrutiny, narrow tailoring standards that the Court had established in *Croson*. George R. LaNoue and John Sullivan report that by March 1991, "29 states and local jurisdictions had completed some sort of post-*Croson* MBE study at a total cost of over $5,491,162 . . . [and] that another 37 studies were underway at costs totalling over $7,029,929." Utilizing a mix of historical analysis, anecdotal testimony, and statistical reasoning, such studies were almost uniformly intended to buttress the policy that had been in place prior to the Court's 1989 decision.[41]

The Georgia Supreme Court, for example, had overturned Atlanta's Women and Minority Business Enterprise Program (WMBE) in light of the *Croson* decision. The city of Atlanta responded by commissioning a study that focused on the economic experiences of black-owned and white-owned construction firms. Written by Andrew Brimmer, the noted black economist, and Ray Marshall, secretary of labor in the Carter administration, the Atlanta study was "1,034 pages long and cost $532,000."[42] It indicated that in 1982 black-owned firms had less than 1 percent of the total business sales, that black-owned construction firms relied on the public sector for 97 percent of their revenue, and that only 32 percent of minority-owned construction firms had bonding capacity. Brimmer and Marshall interpreted the data to suggest that discrimination continued to exist in Atlanta and that there was sufficient evidence to reinstate some type of minority business program.[43]

Chicago, Illinois, also revisited its set-aside program. In 1985, the city had established a set-aside program that required 25 percent of the contracts to be channelled to minority-owned businesses and an additional 5 percent to female-owned businesses. In the uncertain aftermath of the *Croson* decision, Chicago's program was attacked. The dialogue was highlighted in the city's print media, which intensified the struggle over affirmative action. Mayor Richard Daley Jr. proclaimed that the city's commitment to affirmative action was intact and, on the advice of the city legal's office, asserted that Chicago's program met the constitutional requirements dictated by *Croson*. The city began, however, to conduct disparity studies to buttress the claims undergirding the establishment of the program.

Similar efforts were undertaken in other places as well. Hoping to salvage its set-aside program, which had a goal of 35 percent minority participation in city building contracts, Birmingham, Alabama, held a series of public hearings. In Atlanta, William Bell, the city council president, sent letters to the chairpersons of several commercial banks headquartered in the city, seeking data on the extent of black participation in those institutions as board members, officers, and employees.

In New Haven, Connecticut, hearings were held to gather detailed information on discrimination in the area's construction business and to identify weaknesses in the city's plan. The New Haven Commission on Equal Opportunities, which organized the hearings, was warned by Ralph Thomas, the executive director of the National Association of Minority Contractors, not to rely solely on testimony. Instead, he urged the commission to "go back and look for patterns of discrimination such as a closed community of 'good old boy' contractors, construction lawyers, bonding agents, and bankers."[44]

The Courts after *Croson*

The impact of a Supreme Court decision, even one as apparently straightforward as *Croson*, is always dependent on the manner in which it is interpreted by the government officials who are charged with enforcing it, by the judges in the lower courts who are initially responsible for settling the controversies that arise about its meaning, and by the commentators and pundits who help to shape public opinion. Outright defiance of the Court, such as that practiced in the nineteenth century by Andrew Jackson ("John Marshall has made his decision, now let him enforce it") is rarely seen today given the prestige accorded to the institution by the public. But efforts to reverse the thrust of the Court's decisions legislatively, to define its reach in the narrowest of terms, and to mitigate its capacity to alter existing policies are common responses by those whose activities are placed under critical scrutiny.

Once the decision in *Croson* was made, the struggle to shape the decision's impact began. On one side, individual contractors and contractors' groups such as the AGC brought suit against existing set-aside programs in a number of localities, asking that these policies be overturned in concert with the arguments made in *Croson*. On the other side, local officials, organizations such as the NAMC, and ad hoc groups of legal scholars undertook activities designed to legitimate set-aside programs and inoculate them from *Croson*-type challenges. Part of this effort was the development of a legal strategy that could withstand the challenges put forward by individual contractors and the AGC.

The dimensions of the legal struggle took shape relatively quickly. Contractors and other industry groups went to court and demanded that set-aside programs be rescinded on the grounds that these violated the strict scrutiny standards outlined in the *Croson* decision. The defense of set-aside programs assumed multiple forms. In some cases, supporters simply argued that the plaintiffs did not deserve standing because they could not prove that they were individually harmed by the existence of the program. In other cases, set-aside proponents argued that their policy had done a better job of demonstrating the historical predicate of discrimination than had Richmond's. Finally, and perhaps most importantly, disparity studies were employed to indicate that the basis for establishing the policy had been placed on firmer ground.

State courts and federal district courts around the nation began the process of adjudicating the conflicting claims about the meaning of *Croson*. In a number of instances, the courts threw out set-aside programs on the grounds that they did not meet the strict scrutiny standard established in *Croson*. Yet a decision by a federal district court in the state of Washington furnished hope to set-aside supporters. The case, *Coral Construction Company v. King County, Washington* was initiated when a major construction company and the Association of General Contractors of Washington challenged an ordinance that amended the county's set-aside programs for minority- and women-owned business enterprises (WMBEs). King County had provided two methods by which WMBEs could receive preference in bidding on city contracts. Under the first method, contractors whose bids were within 5 percent of the lowest responsive bid were given preference if they were a WMBE or if the bids demonstrated that WMBEs should be used on a contract. A second method required, with certain exceptions, that successful bidders on county contracts of more than $10,000 use WMBEs for a specified percentage of the work.

The Coral Construction Company claimed that the county's program violated its equal protection rights and this assertion was grounded in an interpretation of *Croson*. Coral Construction had been the low bidder on a guardrail contract but did not receive approval to do the work as the county awarded the contract to a minority business enterprise that had made a higher bid. The district court, however, upheld King County, arguing that its set-aside program, unlike the Richmond policy, had a strong basis in evidence of past discrimination. The court maintained that King County had provided evidence of greater weight, detail, and specificity and that its program was more flexible than Richmond's.

In other instances, supporters of set-aside programs were buoyed when lower federal courts refused to give standing to plaintiffs who wanted the programs overturned. In Jacksonville, Florida, for example, the Northeastern Florida Chapter of the Association of General Contractors of America had brought suit against the city's minority business enterprise program, maintaining that the 10 percent set-aside provision unlawfully discriminated against white men. The federal district court used *Croson* as the basis for striking down the program. But the Eleventh U.S. Circuit Court of Appeals overturned the lower court, contending that the group should have never obtained standing because "it has not demonstrated that but for the set-aside program, any member would bid successfully for any of these contracts."[45]

Eventually, the Supreme Court granted standing to the petitioners and sent the case back for arguments on its merits. What has become evident in the years following *Croson* is that the decision, despite its clear statement about the strict scrutiny standard, has not ended the legal confusion about affirmative action. Although the Supreme Court apparently resolved the dispute over standing in its June 1993 decision, other key issues remain unresolved. First, what kind of evidence is necessary to demonstrate that historical discrimination warrants a race-conscious remedial policy? To what extent were the disparity studies produced by scores of cities sufficient grounds for the continuation of race-conscious affirmative action? Second, what standards would be utilized to judge whether the remedial plans were "narrowly tailored"?

With the addition of David Souter, Clarence Thomas, Ruth Bader Ginsberg, and Stephen Breyer and the departure of Thurgood Marshall, Byron White, William Brennan, and Harry Blackmun, the Supreme Court that will ultimately address these issues is markedly different from that in the 1980s. Moreover, the political environment in which such disputes are occurring is markedly different as well. In the 1990s, jurisprudence about affirmative action does not occur with a vital civil rights movement as a backdrop but takes place in a period in which conservative arguments about preferential treatment and national and state activities to prohibit it are moving to the forefront of our politics. Unless President Bill Clinton is able to gain reelection, appoint additional justices, and utilize scarce political capital to move the Court in a leftward direction, the basic lines of *Croson* are likely to remain intact. Legal disputes will probably focus on questions of what constitutes adequate proof of discrimination and how expansive "narrow tailoring" can actually be. Given the political capital that has been invested in set-aside programs, it is clear that a single decision cannot entirely end the controversy, but it is unlikely that program supporters will find much consolation in the nation's highest court.

SEVEN

Urban Politics after *Croson*

Our research into the background of *Richmond v. Croson* and the manner in which the set-aside policy was related to the strategy for black political progress in Richmond has led to four main conclusions. First, we argued that the set-aside program was the principal means by which African American officials demonstrated their loyalty to a black agenda while at the same time adopting a program for downtown revitalization. Second, we demonstrated that the program had some positive effects, materially benefiting two well-positioned entrepreneurs and perhaps altering the business climate for minority entrepreneurs by indicating that the city was interested in their success. But the reach of the set-aside policies was limited and by no means fulfilled the goals that defenders of such programs have often articulated. Third, we suggested that the broad framework of "set-aside politics" as a strategy for black political advance did not necessarily foster either the economic and political development of the African American community or successfully address some of the emergent problems in urban Richmond. Finally, our analysis implies that the limited effects of set-asides demand a reconsideration of the strategy for black political advancement.

This description of the limitations of the set-aside policy and the approach of which it was a constituent element is not intended to suggest that Richmond's African American leadership acted irrationally. Politics is typically a matter of making choices among many options, each of which has advantages and drawbacks. Many of the key decisions made by Richmond's black officials were perfectly defensible when considered individually. Adopting the agenda for downtown revitalization was rational given the presumptions voiced by black elected officials in the late 1970s about the imperative of economic growth.[1] The decision to attempt to shape the agenda for downtown revitalization in a manner that would benefit black Richmonders through set-aside policies was part of a nationwide strategy for using urban power to the advantage of African American constituents. The utilization of elite negotiation as the principal approach to politics was drawn from the relatively successful practices of the Crusade for Voters, once seen as a model for black politics in the United States. In short, Richmond's African American leadership adopted a mix of policies, elements of which had been either utilized elsewhere or previously successful in Richmond.

Yet black elected officials in Richmond can be faulted for the manner in which they responded to both the effects of their adopted policies and the new circumstances that they faced during the 1980s. While the supporters of the set-aside program vigorously defended it, they did not appear equally interested in examining its problems and limitations.[2] The majority of African American council members resisted all calls for popular election of the mayor, arguing that it was either a plot by whites to reassert control or a well-intentioned but naive recommendation that would have the same consequence. They did little to address the emerging problems to which set-aside programs were increasingly irrelevant.

Our analysis of developments in Richmond raises a number of questions. First, to what extent is this city's story consistent with experiences elsewhere? Is Richmond representative of developments in urban politics across the country? Or is it an aberrant case not only in terms of its set-aside policy but also in the manner in which its elected officials responded to the challenges in contemporary urban America? Second, if our analysis of Richmond politics is generally accurate, what alternatives might have been more successful? Are the choices of urban leaders so constrained by political and economic trends that it is foolish to engage in detailed criticisms of their decision making? Or could they indeed respond to the economic and political forces that influence their choices with more creativity and imagination in order to increase the range of local options available?

This chapter begins by addressing the issue of representativeness. We indicate the principal ways that politics in Richmond both reflects and diverges from key trends in urban America more generally. Albeit with important qualifications, we believe that lessons relevant to other cities can be drawn from the Richmond experience. The second and third parts of the chapter identify the key elements of the new trends that have emerged in urban American politics and in Richmond since *Croson*. The final section argues that these trends are preliminary steps in the formation of what could be labeled a "politics of development," which could potentially serve as an alternative model to the set-aside approach. We examine the principal components of the emergent approach and describe the tensions that it will have to resolve to become successful.

Richmond and the Nation

Perhaps it is best to examine the extent to which Richmond is representative of broader trends in urban politics by first acknowledging the areas in which it does *not* reflect emergent developments. In many other U.S. cities, neighborhood-based political associations were more visible and more active than in Richmond. Neighborhood-based political organizations were often vocal participants in the debates about the future of a city, protesting, criticizing, and suggesting alternatives to those pursued by the established leadership. Studies in a number of cities have noted that neighborhood organizations, with varying degrees of success, raised substantial objections to the downtown development priorities that were the centerpiece of the growth coalition's program.[3] One might have thought that the ward-based electoral system implemented in Richmond would have fostered the growth of such organizations, but it had the opposite effect of allowing a few individuals to dominate city politics and to stifle the effective development of a critical or alternative agenda. Neighborhood groups have occasionally arisen in Richmond and sometimes exercised a reactive influence on policy, but these did not really shape the manner in which the major political choices were defined.

In addition to the relative absence of neighborhood organizations, Richmond did not develop the liberal coalitions that have been prominent in other urban areas. As we have seen in chapter 5, white liberals exercised little influence in Richmond politics. In a city that was historically conservative, liberals have concentrated primarily on providing services to those who have fallen almost completely outside the safety net. Liberals have worked with churches and social service agencies to provide food and shelter to the homeless, offender aid to the imprisoned, and health clinics to those without access to medical care. But the combination of a ward-based electoral system, the historic difficulty of building grassroots interracial coalitions, and the fact that many white liberals themselves lived in the surrounding counties left Richmond without the kind of progressive white presence that has characterized politics in places such as New York and San Francisco.

Richmond is also not fully representative of the emerging trends in ethnic politics across the country. In many American cities, ethnic politics has become increasingly diversified as minority groups other than African Americans have taken a more active and visible role. Urban politics in Chicago, Los Angeles, San Antonio, Miami, and numerous other cities includes more than one minority group striving for influence and power. Although there has been some tension in Richmond between the Korean merchants and parts of the African American community, multicultural politics in Richmond is almost entirely defined by the enduring issue of black-white relationships.

Finally, we should note that the situation of midsized urban areas such as Richmond may be qualitatively different from the megacities that are often the subject of urban political scholarship. Although it is the state capital and the hub of a metropolitan region, Richmond does not exercise the unquestioned economic dominance in its area that Chicago, Houston, New York City, and Los Angeles do in their respective regions. For this reason, Richmond's relationship with its adjacent counties and the manner in which it shapes a beneficial intergovernmental environment may be more critical to its future. Questions about the interjurisdictional provision of services, regional strategies for economic development, and creative efforts at resource sharing may be more important to Richmond's leadership than to officials in larger areas who operate what scholars have come to label "world cities."[4]

Yet even given these qualifications, we still assert that this study of Richmond has ramifications that extend far beyond its environs. First, most of the efforts to measure the efficacy of construction set-aside programs in other cities have produced results that corroborate our findings. Set-aside programs do not distribute benefits across a wide range of minority entrepreneurs. For example, a highly publicized study in Washington, D.C., discovered that four contracting companies received more than 50 percent of the set-aside dollars in its program. In Seattle, Washington, only a handful of companies benefited from its minority set-aside policy. The reasons that the programs work in this manner—the difficulty of obtaining bonding for start-up entrepreneurs and the manner in which the "old boy" system expands to meet the set-aside requirements—are also probably similar across jurisdictions.[5]

A second way that the Richmond case is broadly representative concerns the manner in which affirmative action and set-aside programs have been elevated to the top of the agenda of the African American elite and urban leaders, respectively. We have argued that affirmative action was the means by which Richmond leaders justified their activity to their African American constituents. This, too, we would argue has been the case elsewhere. As Clarence N. Stone has demonstrated in his perceptive study of Atlanta, set-aside programs were the glue that held together the entire governing coalition.[6] Indeed, the heated response across the nation to the Court's decision in *Croson* indicates the extent of the political investment that urban black leadership had made in these programs.[7]

Finally, the set of urban problems that remain unaddressed by the forms of set-aside politics are depressingly similar across jurisdictions. While Richmond's murder rate, levels of teenage pregnancy, and number of high school dropouts may not be matched or exceeded in every city around the country, almost every major urban area struggles with the issues of crime, poverty, drugs, youth violence, and alienation — issues that have not been successfully addressed in Richmond or anywhere. In addition, most cities contend with these problems with relatively limited resources even when, as is the case in Richmond, the city is managed in a fiscally responsible manner according to national standards. Indeed, the prevalence of these issues is helping to alter the public mood and redefine the parameters of urban politics.

We might summarize our position about the representativeness of the Richmond case as follows. Richmond has not developed the full array of political associations and exhibited the range of pressure politics that have been evident in other cities. In general, Richmond politics has been less diverse and less subject to disruption by neighborhood groups and non-establishment coalitions than other urban areas. Further, it has yet to experience the tensions that have arisen in other locales because of the proliferation of ethnic politics. But in terms of affirmative action and the function of set-aside programs, Richmond mirrors many other urban areas. The manner in which it formulated the policy, the public justification for the program, and the role affirmative action played in the self-identification of political officials are relevant in urban arenas far beyond this midsized city.

New Trends in Urban Politics

Our conclusion about the need for a reorientation of African American urban politics is undoubtedly widely shared. The precise form that this reorientation should take, however, is subject to vehement contention, often dependent on the participant's ideological vantage point. Market conservatives such as Walter Williams and Thomas Sowell have called for the repudiation of almost every policy supported by contemporary black urban leaders and have recommended the development of an entrepreneurial ethic. Neoliberal critics such as James Sleeper have deplored the racial polarization in urban America and have endorsed a politics premised on Martin Luther King's notions of integration and community.[8] Liberal authors have called for a "Marshall plan" for U.S. cities in which a federal jobs policy would provide greater opportunity for inner-city residents. Scholars with a social-democratic bent have been unrelenting in their criticism of "growth politics," which they contend has disproportionately benefited the affluent and large-scale business institutions. Black nationalist writers complete the circle of criticism by maintaining that the historic unreliability of white institutions and white Americans demands that African Americans develop their own institutions and rely on the virtues of self-help, entrepreneurialism, and cultural revival.[9]

The intensity with which various positions have been advanced and defended has made common ground in the debate difficult to find. For example, some of the free market conservatives have not only called for the cultivation of personal responsibility and an entrepreneurial ethos but have denigrated the reliance on political solutions as inherently counterproductive. On the other hand, some liberal and progressive authors have argued that strategies emphasizing personal values and a communal ethos are simply a means of diverting attention from the structure of economic inequality that causes and maintains the conditions that need to be changed in urban America.

Recently, the debate about urban revitalization has become much less academic in tone as elections have taken a surprising turn. In the past few years, cities such as New York, Los Angeles, Philadelphia, Indianapolis, and Jersey City have turned to either white Republicans or white Democrats who have promised to change the status quo considerably. Successful mayoral candidates tout a more vigorous attack on crime, the improvement of schools through the introduction of voucher systems, experiments to reduce government spending through the privatization of services, and a renewed commitment to economic growth. In a number of cities where blacks retained their position as mayors, such as Atlanta, reports have focused on a generational change in African American leadership in which pragmatic, nonideological candidates have replaced an older generation of leaders with a different political style. Although the particular elements of the new urban politics differ from city to city, they have exhibited a number of common features.

A Return to Fundamentals

Urban elections of the 1990s have been characterized by campaigns in which the theme of "back to the basics" has been extremely prominent. In terms of the role of government, this has typically meant that candidates have emphasized the importance of using the power of government to reduce citizens' vulnerability to crime. In almost every major urban area, the prevalence of crime and the apparent inability of government to prevent it have become the staple of attacks against incumbent officials by challengers who promise to be tougher, more determined, and more visible in fighting the criminal element. The back to basics theme has implications for the expectations that government ought to have for the people who utilize its services. In the urban elections of the 1990s, successful candidates emphasized the personal responsibility of citizens and appealed to the frustrations of taxpayers who believe that too much aid and too many services have been provided without a commensurate obligation on the part of the recipients.

Pragmatic Experimentation

The call for a return to fundamentals has often been accompanied by an expressed willingness to experiment with market-oriented reforms in providing basic services. This too has its origins in citizens' frustrations with the effectiveness of government. A growing number of citizens appeared to believe that urban governments were not only incapable of fighting crime but were also ineffective in educating children, training people for employment, and in keeping the streets clean and the garbage picked up. To some citizens, conditions had deteriorated to the point that almost any kind of change was worth considering. In response, candidates pledged to improve (and sometimes revolutionize) the schools, expressed a willingness to consider privatization of numerous services, and called for experiments in promoting the economic development of their city and region.

Political Disaffection of the African American Community

In a number of cities, the campaigns have indicated that the African American community is increasingly disenchanted with the capacity of the political system to address its needs. Large numbers of African Americans

did not join the coalitions that elected Rudolph Giuliani and Michael
Riordan. In New York, the vast preponderance of African American voters supported David Dinkins for reelection. But it was evident that voter
turnout rates among African Americans were down, and they did not
mobilize in the kind of numbers necessary to reelect Dinkins or to prevent
the election of candidates who were opposed by the established black leadership. Clearly, the optimism that had accompanied the elections of black
mayors in the 1970s was almost exhausted, and many African Americans
either were poised to turn out the leaders in whom they had once placed
their hopes or were relatively indifferent to the prospect of their removal.

The New Urban Politics in Richmond

The trends that were shaping American urban politics appeared in Richmond as well. From 1990–95, crime rocketed to the top of the city's agenda. Citizens became increasingly skeptical of the intentions and capaci-
ties of the city's political leadership. Richmonders expressed a desire for
change by replacing almost all of the those officials who had been elected with the city council's first black majority in the 1970s and the early
1980s. Moreover, Richmond's leaders tentatively moved toward placing the
issue of city-county relations on the table once again as a way of improving its economic development position.

Crime

The principal impetus to the political shake-up in Richmond was height-
ened public concern about the city's homicide rate. During the early
1990s, the city was consistently ranked in the nation's top ten in murders
per capita, far exceeding any other locale in Virginia. A record was set in
1992 when the city witnessed more than 125 murders and, despite a de-
crease in 1993, 1994 saw the murder rate skyrocket and the city move to
second in the nation behind New Orleans in the per capita homicide rate.
One of the daily papers, the *Richmond Times-Dispatch*, kept a running tab
of the human destruction and the various crime "packages," anticrime
rallies, and public pronouncements designed to indicate that everyone
"had had enough." The local television stations consistently ran murder
stories as their lead and also promoted town meetings, summits, and other initiatives to address the problem as the paramount example of their
commitment to the community.

In one sense, Richmond's status as one of the country's homicide capitals was a statistical artifact. Since Richmond is an independent city with no formal relationship to its surrounding counties, its murder rate appears to be much higher than other cities that are formally part of a county jurisdiction. For instance, a number of the North Carolina cities to which Richmond is often unfavorably compared actually have higher homicide rates when the metropolitan statistical area (MSA) is the basis of comparison. In other words, the highly concentrated pockets of homicide activity in Richmond are simply undiluted by the large suburban populations that are typically included in the population base of many of Richmond's competitor cities. If the two most populous surrounding counties were included in the comparison, Richmond's homicide rate would be considerably lower.

But in another sense, it is small comfort to most Richmonders to know that they were really ranked 45th rather than second in murders per capita, because the escalating homicide rate and the increase in youth violence are nonetheless undeniable. Each year the stories become increasingly outrageous, the perpetrators and the victims become younger, the capacity to prosecute becomes more difficult because of intimidation of potential witnesses, and the political response appears increasingly inadequate to the task at hand. Richmonders who live in the neighborhoods where the violence is concentrated fear for their own lives and worry that their children will be unable to avoid the carnage taking place on the streets. More than any other issue, Richmond's homicide rate is a vivid reminder of how life in certain sections of the community has deteriorated.

Elections

The electoral system in Richmond has made it more difficult for citizens to express politically their desire for a reorientation of city priorities. Unlike many cities, Richmond does not elect its mayor. As a city with a council-manager form of government, Richmond has opted for a system in which an officially "weak mayor" is selected by the city council at the first meeting of the new council following an election. Despite the official strictures against strong mayors, not all of Richmond's mayors were "weak." Henry L. Marsh III demonstrated how a mayor could be an extremely powerful figure in city politics and, for a time, Roy West did so as well. Indeed, many of the complaints about the former was that he had become "Boss" Marsh or "King Henry," a man who utilized the mayoralty to impose his personal vision on a divided city.

During the 1980s and again in the early 1990s, movements arose to change the manner in which Richmond selected its mayor, invariably recommending that the city move to a popularly elected mayor. On each occasion, most of the traditional African American politicians opposed the movement on the grounds that it was a cleverly disguised maneuver for reasserting white dominance. Pointing to the facts that the voting age population was only 51 percent black, that a major proponent of the change was a white good government organization, that blacks voted less frequently than whites, and that a citywide election would be biased in favor of those with access to money, African American leaders opposed the change. They successfully prevented an amendment to the charter brought to the Virginia General Assembly, though they themselves petitioned the same body year after year for an extension of their own terms to four years.[10]

A public opinion poll conducted by the Survey Research Laboratory at Virginia Commonwealth University indicates that while a greater percentage of whites than blacks supported the change to a popularly elected mayor, the *overwhelming* majority in both communities believed it was a good idea (mayoral election was supported by 75 percent of blacks and 84 percent of whites). The poll did not ask people why they supported the proposal, but the reasons were often enunciated when the issue was raised publicly. First, citizens believed that they had the right to an election in which citywide problems and not merely ward-based concerns were the explicit focus of attention. Second, there was a growing belief that politicians—both white and black—who held a citywide position ought to be accountable to a citywide electorate. As one African American activist noted at a public hearing before the city council, "At least if we elect a bum, we can throw the bum out a few years later."[11]

Although the mayor is selected by the city council, Richmond holds citywide elections for its constitutional officers—sheriff, commissioner of revenue, and commonwealth attorney. During the early 1990s, the crime problem in the city transformed the election of the commonwealth attorney into a major event. In 1993, David Hicks, a young African American lawyer without ties to the black establishment challenged the white incumbent, Joe Morrissey, who had carefully cultivated his connections to the established black leadership. Yet council members who publicly expressed concern that a white could be elected citywide supported the incumbent in the commonwealth attorney election, and they continued to support him even when he was indicted on five felony counts prior to the primary election. To many observers, the reason for opposing the African American candidate was simply that he had few ties to the black establishment and could not be depended on to be a loyal follower.

While this situation contradicted public statements about the consequences of citywide elections, it was perfectly consistent with the practices that contributed to the demobilization we described in chapter 5. A citywide mayoral election would have required the established leadership to remobilize ordinary citizens and would have demanded the formation of new, citywide, interracial coalitions. Moreover, it would have required the establishment to put their policies up for discussion and review. In all likelihood, it would have been difficult for the black establishment to control or even guide the outcome. One can easily imagine that, just like the commonwealth attorney's race or the mayoral election in Jersey City, a newcomer who pledged to revitalize the city could have been elected. Given the choice between business as usual and greater democracy, they acted as establishments normally do, taking the path of least resistance and protecting their interests.

The commonwealth attorney campaign demonstrated that there was a pent-up political demand in Richmond that was unmet. The structure of city politics and the interests of those who held political office conspired to stifle it. Only the officeholders themselves—entrenched within a particular ward—could fail to acknowledge that Richmonders, both black and white, wanted more citywide accountability than they were receiving and desired to play a more substantial role in establishing its priorities. Such a change would be accompanied by more uncertainty about the identity of the mayor. But with the ward system protecting the election of a black majority city council, the possibility of a reinvigorated local politics made the at-large election of a mayor worth the risks that accompany democracy.

The commonwealth attorney's election in 1993 was sandwiched between two councilmanic elections that transformed the Richmond City Council. After the elections of 1992 and 1994, there was only one council member, Henry "Chuck" Richardson, who had been elected prior to 1990. While African Americans maintained a 6-3 majority on the council, both white and black Richmonders expressed their frustration with the body by removing almost every representative who did not exit gracefully through retirement. The 1994 election was especially shocking because it resulted in the removal of Mayor Walter Kenney, a stalwart of the Marsh faction, and West, the former mayor who had opposed Marsh from 1982–88. Turnout in both elections was disturbingly low (12 percent in 1992 and 20 percent in 1994) but the results proved that those Richmonders who had not given up on the political system altogether were in no mood to continue business as usual.

In 1995, the new council put the issue of a popularly elected mayor to a referendum, where it passed, not surprisingly, by a 2 to 1 margin. While people of good will could disagree about whether the specific proposal adequately clarified the relationship between the mayor and the city manager, the overwhelming vote was one more indication of the public's interest in staking out a new direction for the city.

Cooperation between City and County

In the aftermath of the Richmond annexation battle and other city-county controversies, the Virginia General Assembly passed legislation granting the state's nine largest "urban counties" immunity from annexation in 1978. At first, such legislation appeared to be to the advantage of everyone in the Richmond area. The legislation effectively placed a lid on simmering racial controversies. For African Americans, it guaranteed that they would not see their political power diluted by racially motivated annexation schemes, such as the one that had provoked such bitterness in the past decade. For whites in the counties, it guaranteed that they would not be subjected to the higher property tax rates in the city and would not have to send their children to the city schools. In addition, the legislation ensured that they would not face higher tax rates expressly to pay for solutions to the urban problems that afflicted Richmond proper.

Nearly fifteen years later, the negative consequences of the bargain were more apparent. While authors such as David Rusk were arguing that "elastic cities" flourished, Richmond was landlocked, without significant prospects for growth.[12] Faced with paying to address its urban problems, Richmond had neither sufficient population to spread the burden nor sufficient land to attract and build the economic development projects that were needed. By the standard measures of fiscal stress, Richmond was suffering terribly in comparison to a city such as Charlotte. While the counties, by comparison to the city, remained better off, it was becoming apparent that a spillover effect had materialized. Despite the growth of "edge cities" such as those in northern Virginia's Fairfax County, urban areas are primarily recognized by conditions in the signature locale. So as long as Richmond failed to flourish, Virginia's other cities would be less competitive than their rivals throughout the Southeast.

The situation was compounded by what was apparently a hardening of political lines between Richmond and Henrico County, one of the principal neighboring counties. Given city leadership's expressed concern about the election of a mayor from inside the city boundaries, it was almost impossible to think that proposals for consolidation or for reopening the annexation question on a statewide level would be received positively and not perceived as a means of diluting African American political strength. The Henrico County leadership appeared to be equally if not more intransigent in their reaction to the prospect of greater cooperation with the city. The county's board of supervisors insisted on proceeding with plans to build their own water treatment plant instead of continuing to purchase water from the city. When other counties and the city convened a summit to discuss cooperation on common problems, Henrico County's leadership refused to attend, contending that the meeting would be a platform for Richmond's leadership to bash them. Clearly, they viewed cooperation largely as a subterfuge by which Richmond attempted to get the county to pay for the city's problems.[13]

Several problems resulted from the lack of city-county cooperation. On the most obvious level, the area was plagued by inefficiencies and an excessive amount of social irrationality. Throughout most of the 1980s and early 1990s, the city and counties struggled to provide public transportation from the city to the available jobs in the counties for people who did not own cars. Political leaders jerry-rigged some temporary solutions but were unable to develop a workable, reliable metropolitan transportation system. Similar problems arose in the battle between the city and the counties over the water supply and other services where efficiencies were possible but not achieved.

The barriers to cooperation were less visible but perhaps even more important in the area of economic development. With a different set of attitudes and even actors, it might have been possible for the entire metropolitan area to develop a strategic plan for economic development. In addition, a study might have identified the area's key features and major strengths and then marketed the region accordingly. For many years, however, this cooperation was simply not achieved. While the surrounding counties did well economically, conditions might have improved for everyone if the city and county governments had established a more unified approach.

At root, the barriers to governmental consolidation or even functional cooperation lay in very different conceptions of self-interest as well as suspicions about what cooperation would mean for the respective governments. These conceptions would not be completely dissolved, even if the leadership changed. What was needed was a reconsideration of self-interest and the development of confidence-building measures between the city and counties. By the beginning of the 1990s, it was evident that at least some of the actors involved were beginning to rethink the entire city-county issue. Some elected city leaders were calling for studies of metropolitan consolidation. More visionary people in the area were extolling the possibilities of regional development that would capitalize on the richness of Richmond as a historical site. Further, leaders in state government had come to recognize the enormous fiscal drain that continued core city problems meant for the state.

A Politics of Development across America

In one sense, the new urban electoral outcomes appear to be an ominous sign for African Americans. In some of the cities that we have mentioned, the electorate was racially polarized, and this has often worked to the detriment of African American candidates. Moreover, black turnout was generally low in all of these elections. Perhaps it could be argued that the emergence of mayors such as Michael Riordan and Brett Schundler simply indicates the precariousness of the hold on political power that African Americans actually have and why strategies designed to conserve it should not be excessively criticized. Do the fears expressed regularly in Richmond about the reassertion of white political dominance have merit?

But the results of elections in the 1990s could also be viewed as a salutary challenge to African American leadership, not as a rejection of black leaders per se but of the results generated by a particular political approach. Minority communities in some locations have embraced leaders who promise major reforms. The issues at the heart of these campaigns—crime, education, and economic development—are thought by many urban residents, regardless of race, to be absolutely vital to the pursuit of serious urban revitalization. In this sense, these electoral outcomes reinforce our argument—that the limited benefits achieved from set-aside politics and the legal challenges to which such a strategy is presently vulnerable should generate a significant reorientation in the approach developed by African American leadership.

It is possible that the electoral outcomes in places such as Los Angeles and Philadelphia will only lead to a hardening of positions. But these results may give added impetus to the forces calling for a reconsideration of the theory and practice of urban politics. Indeed, we believe that it is significant that responses to the recent outcomes in urban elections focus not simply on this issue or that problem but instead reevaluate the conceptual framework that animates African American leadership. In fact, it appears that "development" is emerging as a unifying theme for a revitalized commitment to addressing urban issues, a commitment that ultimately might constitute more than an ad hoc response to the latest election.[14]

The emergent ideas about development are by no means fully formed. But it is possible to discern some common features that appear to be present in most approaches to an alternative framework for urban policy. As we see it, the metaphor of development is intended to focus attention on four areas.

Fostering the Values and Behaviors That Would Enable Individuals to Expand Their Life Choices and Communities to Become More Livable.   Until recently, the promotion of community reconstruction in urban America through entrepreneurship, self-help, and changed values was perceived as the essence of a conservative position. Contrasting their position with a liberal emphasis on black advancement through governmental action (a domestic "Marshall plan") and African American political representation, proponents of self-help, such as Thomas Sowell, Walter Williams, and Robert Woodson, contend that directing energy to the political arena is useless and perhaps counterproductive. Sowell, for example, maintains that successful immigrant groups who have faced discrimination typically focus on obtaining the skills that will let them advance in the capitalist marketplace and leave politics for later generations. Moreover, conservative proponents of self-help argue that the content of black politics—an emphasis on discrimination, victimization, and the imperative of remedial policies—teaches a brand of fatalism that is destructive of the habits that are necessary to foster an entrepreneurial, achievement-oriented spirit.[15]

Activists and scholars to the left of the conservatives often respond vituperatively to their assertions. Considering the conservative position as essentially a vehicle for blaming the victim, liberals, progressives, and social democrats denounce the conservatives (especially the black conservatives) as people who have become the mouthpieces of the racist and capitalist white establishment that caused the problems in the first place. They argue that a direct attack on covert and overt racist practices constitutes the first step in making significant improvements in the condition of black America. Moreover, they tend to suggest that the value orientation and behavioral practices that the conservatives want to remedy are either understandable responses to social conditions or behaviors exhibited across the income structure.

The conflict between the two groups actually emerged, however, from their shared assumption that cultural and political approaches to black progress are incompatible. For conservatives, politics is synonymous with paternalism and dependence, promoting precisely those values that stifle black progress. For liberals, any talk of cultural renovation is a means of bringing racist assumptions to the debate through purportedly neutral assessments. Defense of these positions requires each side to remain adamant and ignore any inconvenient evidence. Conservatives rarely speak of ethnic groups that have used political advance as a means of achieving economic success, and liberals find any defection from the operative assumptions, even that of William Julius Wilson, to be suspect and open to criticism.[16]

As statistics on teenage pregnancy, youth involvement in violent crime, and the pervasiveness of drug use have become more widely publicized, urban political figures and national activists have begun to speak with more passion about the critical importance of values in responding to the problems of urban areas. Albeit with notable exceptions, these arguments entered the ideological spectrum with Jesse Jackson, Louis Farrakhan, and conservative academics such as Charles Murray, all of whom identify particular policies that would enable young people to develop the self-respect and personal incentives needed to avoid behaviors that are increasingly destructive to themselves and the community.

Responding in a Determined and Measurable Manner to the Basic Issues that Citizens Expect Government to Address.   Citizens, political candidates, and commentators on urban politics have spoken of the need for government to set priorities and be held accountable for meeting its goals and addressing its problems. Of course, public safety is at the top of the list, but the broader point is that governments must define their goals more precisely, devote the resources to achieving them, and be judged on their performance by the public. In this sense, the politics of the 1970s and 1980s, which were motivated by the possibility of achieving equal or proportional representation in ethnic and racial terms, was replaced in the 1990s by a politics in which leaders and officials were judged on performance in first stabilizing urban areas and then contributing to revitalization.

Creating a Political Environment in which the Will of the Citizens Could Be More Easily Expressed and Acted Upon.   Concern about crime and economic development are ultimately related to citizens' lack of commitment to and power over their own choices. The notion of citizen empowerment is an alternative to the cynicism and frustration rife in urban areas. Again, the particular form that this would take differs according to one's chosen ideological perspective. Typically, conservatives see the empowerment agenda in terms of school choices, home ownership for people in public housing, and tax breaks for small businesses in enterprise zones. Others define it as neighborhood crime watches, citizen review boards, and new forms of neighborhood associations. But there seems to be a growing movement for finding ways in which ordinary citizens can reclaim their communities.

Taking the Necessary Steps to Ensure That Urban Economies Will Remain Central to the Plans of the Region and State.   Copying a popular corporate practice, cities and urban regions have started to develop benchmarks against which they could locate their position and evaluate their progress. It is increasingly common for cities to evaluate their efforts in job creation, business retention, and crime prevention against other urban areas. Beyond this, city leaders are reaching out to state governments and surrounding counties to develop regional economic development plans. Here, they place a greater emphasis on the importance of signature cities to the growth of a region, an expressed desire to address common problems such as water supply and transportation, and the development of clearly defined strategies to promote regional development that would benefit an entire area.

Tensions

The emergent politics of development represents an alternative model to urban progress than that defined by its emphasis on various forms of set-aside politics and equal representation. Any political strategy will have obstacles to overcome and be shaped by its characteristic tensions. Problems as complex and multifaceted as those besetting America's urban areas are unlikely to be resolved by simply turning to an alternative approach. Indeed, it is relatively easy to foresee several major tensions that will arise as cities struggle to define and practice a developmental approach.

Conflict over Values

The presumed need to promote and nurture value orientations that will lead to responsible individual and social behavior is certainly widely acknowledged. From ministers in core cities, to elected officials charged with leading urban areas, to scholars who investigate city problems, citizens generally recognize that minimal standards of social decency, personal responsibility, and concern for future generations are vital to the capacity of urban areas to function. Most people would probably agree on a basic list of responsible behaviors that ought to be socially encouraged, rather than rewarded through a poorly developed system of governmental incentives.

Moreover, when governments go beyond moral exhortation, beyond "nurturing" and "fostering" values, to change the incentive structure through social policies, the result is likely to have punitive and controversial overtones. Social policies often become a way to punish people, defining them as moral inferiors, rather than a means to enhance the historical traditions that may have animated a community. One can imagine, for instance, a much more aggressive law enforcement stance in the nation and in many urban areas, designed to root out drug dealers and monitor known criminals. Yet such a stance could, in short order, generate an opposite reaction that would draw upon long-standing concerns about both the appropriate use of police power in urban communities and the violation of cherished constitutional rights. In a number of cities, such as Los Angeles, concern about police abuse sometimes rivals the concern about the extent of crime. Moreover, at the national level we have seen conservative Republicans agitate about the threat to liberty posed by the legislative solutions to gun violence in urban neighborhoods.

These controversies may be only the beginning of a series of bitter debates about the extent of governmental authority, especially under the broad rubric of family policy. A number of years ago the conservative scholar Edward Banfield asserted that any solution to the social malaise in urban America was politically unthinkable because it would require an unacceptable intrusion into the prerogatives of parents.[17] But as liberals today call for "early intervention" programs and others demand an end to "welfare as we know it," these issues may become items of practical import. How far should a profamily policy go in extending the reach of government, social workers, and teachers into the lives of children? What should be taught in the schools about drugs, sexual behavior, and personal responsibility? And how much should government be involved with the provision of Norplant, vasectomies, and sterilization?

The actual debate could be very healthy and force Americans to confront these critical issues. Of course, the values debates of the past fifteen years have been heated, persistent, and often immune to the kind of compromises that politicians are often so creative at inventing. As values become part of government policy on urban issues, avoidance of these seemingly intractable conflicts will be a formidable challenge.

The Conflict over Power

Numerous scholars of urban politics have called for greater experimentation with metropolitan governments, regional authorities, and planning districts as a way to address the pressing social and economic needs in urban America. In the past few years, their ideas have seemingly been more favorably received by many of the opinion leaders within metropolitan areas and by state legislative officials who are concerned about the drain that urban problems could pose for state financial coffers. But the recommendations for the rationalization of metropolitan government will always meet with resistance, ranging from gentle skepticism to "over my dead body" opposition.

At the level of basic self-interest, political officials are being asked to loosen their control over important institutions such as school systems. Moreover, they are told that they ought to grant power to larger bodies in which they will necessarily have a less powerful voice. For this reason, it is no surprise that in the Richmond area both city and county officials have resisted efforts initiated at the state level to study the feasibility of an elected metropolitan government charged with the responsibility for specified functions such as water supply and transportation.

Beyond the level of electoral self-interest, urban leaders are often skeptical of these proposals because of a legitimate concern about the fate of their constituents when their own power is diluted. In the Richmond area, some African American leaders believe that regionalization is a covert means of diluting the political power that it took black residents decades to gain. In other words, the rhetoric of cooperation is a means for restoring white dominance. They worry about the parameters of any deal that will require African American officials to cede direct control of institutions to other bodies. County leaders oppose the proposals because they are concerned that the changes are a covert way of making the counties pay for the problems that the city has not been able to address and, perhaps, not only confront issues such as water supply and transportation but also reopen the more politically volatile matter of the school system. Thus, county leaders view cooperation as a means for having the counties utilize tax revenues to respond to the social crisis in the inner city.

This tension does not mean that cooperative efforts are doomed from the outset. But cooperation demands creative leadership on both sides of the partnership, one that deals imaginatively and successfully with the tensions inherent in the situation. Depending upon the history and previous levels of cooperation, urban areas will likely move on a continuum, ranging from confidence-building measures to more formalized institutional arrangements. It will be the task of political leadership to recognize what is possible, to push the boundaries of cooperation, and to structure the negotiations so that benefits accrue to all the concerned parties.

The Conflict over Community

Some of the ideas that inform scholars and officials concerned with urban revitalization are inspired by the concept of "community." While everyone seems to believe that we need more "community," this agreement is predicated on widely different understandings of what it means and what it entails in urban and metropolitan areas. A sampling of the way the term has been used includes (1) an effort to stabilize and revitalize neighborhoods as the linchpin of urban reconstruction, (2) a commitment by people living in African American neighborhoods to utilize the traditions of self-help and group solidarity to address the issues that confront them, (3) the construction of interracial urban-suburban partnerships that view the entire metropolitan area as a "community," and (4) the promotion of class integration in metropolitan areas by federal social policies designed to address the geographical concentration of poverty by dispersing the poor.

The consensus on the need for more "community" can easily dissolve in the face of its specific manifestations. Consider, for example, the effort by the U.S. Department of Housing and Urban Development (HUD) to improve the opportunities of poor people by locating public housing in suburban neighborhoods. Despite the argument that such programs have proven to be effective, proposals for this form of class and racial integration of the suburbs will continue to meet strenuous political opposition. Most suburbanites left the cities to avoid the attendant problems and are unlikely to be happy about proposals to locate low-income housing projects in their areas or to accept a considerable number of subsidized low-income tenants in rental housing. Further, some African American officials do not agree that the dispersal of the black population into the suburbs is a workable answer to inner-city poverty.

Some of the initiatives to promote community revitalization in the African American community illustrate a different side to the problem of
defining community. In recent years, Louis Farrakhan's followers have
increased their presence and appeal in many distressed neighborhoods.
Given their commitment to reducing the drug trade, explicit avowal of
spiritual reconstruction in the reorientation of one's life, revival of the
African American tradition of self-help, and willingness to be active in the
community, they have obtained a respect unmatched by other groups in
troubled neighborhoods. Yet it cannot be said that in the short term this
kind of community revitalization can be reconciled easily with the notion
that neighborhood, community, city, and metropolitan area are a series of
concentric circles organized around similar principles. The notion of
community practiced by Farrakhan's adherents is very different from the
kind of elite racial reconciliation foreseen by proponents of metropolitan
government.

Again, the conflicts that arise over the practical implications of differing
conceptions of community will not necessarily impede either cooperation
or the development of shared purposes. But successful political leadership
must be both sufficiently courageous to counter those who simply want to
exploit these tensions and adequately inventive to demonstrate how enlight-
ened self-interest is compatible with varying ideas about community.

––––––––

In addition to the tensions sketched above, there are many reasons—
from global trends to neighborhood deterioration—to be skeptical about
the new direction of urban politics. First, economic trends that exacerbate
the earnings gap between the highly skilled and the poorly educated appear to be proceeding unabated. Indeed, studies of so-called world cities
(e.g., New York and Tokyo) indicate that the forces which create concentrated pockets of business affluence and which are serviced by low-paid
workers, are global, not merely national in scope. It is difficult to imagine
how local decision making can begin to reverse what are apparently inexorable structural trends in the world economy.

Analysts also note that the lack of a federal urban policy will make it
even more difficult for cities to successfully confront their challenges.
Pessimists will find that as voting power has become increasingly concentrated in the suburbs, there has been little incentive for national candidates
to make the revitalization of the core cities a significant component of their
campaign strategy, let alone their governance. And they will contend that

this omission is reflected in the governing priorities of a national government that has silently enshrined "benign neglect" as the dominant national urban policy.

Others might argue that the continuation of racial tensions or, at a minimum, the persistence of racial distrust will continue to make it difficult for metropolitan areas to address their problems honestly and effectively. In Richmond, they might note that after fifteen years of coexistence, the tensions between some of the surrounding county governments and the city leaders have remained remarkably high—and it is not uncommon for racial epithets to be hurled in both directions. Even within the city, the cooperative relationship between the predominantly white business leaders and the black civic elite remains precarious, and racial divisions regularly reappear in discussions of educational policy.

Still others might suggest that, regardless of the reason for its appearance, the level of social pathology in cities such as Richmond has made them essentially irreparable. They would observe that the breakdown of family ties, violence in the schools, appeal of criminal enterprise as a means of upward mobility, apparent ruthlessness of the criminal behavior of the young, and vast increase in out-of-wedlock births have damaged the cities in irreversible ways. Observers might predict that families will continue their exodus from these conditions, economic development will be impeded by the existence of crime, and most young people will not be able to obtain the educational foundation that would enable them to fulfill their aspirations.

The daunting problems that face cities such as Richmond will not be resolved in the foreseeable future. Local governments cannot redirect such national and global forces. Unlike the widely quoted adage of Tip O'Neill, all politics is *not* local. Perhaps some day the set-aside strategy will be seen as a relatively workable approach to a host of difficult problems. Undeniably, as is the case today, some cities will be better off than others and some urban areas will react more effectively to the new set of challenges and opportunities. Those cities are likely to be the home of leaders and citizens who acknowledge the full dimensions of the circumstances to which they must respond, who will establish carefully considered strategies for shaping conditions in the most advantageous way, and who will do so by enlisting the hopes, energies, and ingenuity of the entire community. Leaders in places such as Richmond cannot solve the "urban crisis," but they can enable more of its citizens to weather its effects while they also expand citizens' choices.

For a variety of reasons, it is unlikely that affirmative action will be as crucial to the urban political strategies of the next twenty years as they have been to the past two decades. It is more probable that ideas about "development" and the conflicts that these engender will be more salient in the cities than efforts to implement various policies that can be traced to specific affirmative action programs. But to the extent that the concept of affirmative action is related to fundamental notions about fairness, it will remain relevant to a host of emerging issues in urban politics. Dissatisfaction with current trends has fed a desire for change and a willingness to experiment. This willingness can only be sustained if citizens and leaders believe that the process and results are consistent with a genuine commitment to development and to the fair treatment of all citizens.

Notes

Introduction

1. Richmond, Va., ordinance no. 82-294-270 (1983), 10.
2. Tom Campbell, "Minority Business Ordinance Voted by City Council," *Richmond Times-Dispatch*, Apr. 12, 1983, A1; Alan Cooper, "Minority Contracts Rule Passes," *Richmond News Leader*, Apr. 12, 1983, 1. The *Richmond Times-Dispatch* and the *Richmond News Leader* are hereinafter abbreviated as *RT-D* and *RNL*, respectively.
3. Cooper, "Minority Contracts Rule Passes."
4. Martin Tolchin, "Officials in Cities and States Vow to Continue Minority Contractor Programs," *New York Times*, Jan. 25, 1989, A18.
5. "Constitutional Scholars' Statement on Affirmative Action after *City of Richmond v. J. A. Croson Co.*," *Yale Law Journal* 98 (June 1989): 1712.
6. Charles Fried, "Affirmative Action after *City of Richmond v. J. A. Croson Co.*: A Response to the Scholars' Statement," *Yale Law Journal* 99 (Oct. 1989): 155–56.
7. "Almost Home" (editorial), *RNL*, Jan. 25, 1989, 14.
8. Michael Kinsley, "Equal Lack of Opportunity," *Harper's*, June 1983, 8.

Chapter 1: The Affirmative Action Debate

1. Hugh Graham, *The Civil Rights Era: Origins and Development of National Policy, 1960–1972* (New York: Oxford University Press, 1990), 41.
2. Quoted in Charles Murray, *Losing Ground: American Social Policy* (New York: Basic, 1984), 93. Murray offers a concise history of affirmative action, though we do not necessarily agree with his analysis and conclusions. Information in the rest of this paragraph is also from this source.
3. Ibid.
4. Ibid.

5. Bernard Boxill, *Blacks and Social Justice* (Totowa, N.J.: Rowman and Allan-held, 1984), 153.

6. Boxill includes a description of utilitarian arguments in his chapter on affirmative action (*Blacks and Social Justice*, 168–72). For an analysis advocating the use of utilitarian arguments in Supreme Court discussions, see Kathleen Sullivan, "Sins of Discrimination," *Harvard Law Review* 100 (Oct. 1986): 78–99.

7. Ronald Dworkin, *Taking Rights Seriously* (Cambridge, Mass.: Harvard University Press, 1977), 227.

8. Ibid., 239.

9. See Jonathan Rieder, *Canarsie: The Jews and Italians of Brooklyn against Liberalism* (Cambridge, Mass.: Harvard University Press, 1985); Earl Black and Merle Black, *Politics and Society in the South* (Cambridge, Mass.: Harvard University Press, 1987), 271.

10. Nathan Glazer, *Affirmative Discrimination: Ethnic Inequality and Public Policy* (New York: Basic, 1975), 196–97.

11. See Thomas Sowell, *Civil Rights: Rhetoric or Reality* (New York: William Morrow, 1984), 39. See also Sowell, *Race and Economics* (New York: Longman, 1975) and *Markets and Minorities* (New York: Basic, 1981); Walter Williams, *The State against Blacks* (New York: McGraw-Hill, 1982).

12. Sowell, *Civil Rights*, 37–60.

13. Ibid., 57.

14. Ibid., 51–52.

15. Williams, *State against Blacks*, 126.

16. See, for instance, Sowell, *Ethnic America: A History* (New York: Basic, 1981).

17. Shelby Steele, *The Content of Our Character* (New York: St. Martin's, 1990), 34.

18. Lincoln Caplan, *The Tenth Justice: The Solicitor General and the Rule of Law* (New York: Vintage, 1988), 81–114, 172–84.

19. See William Bradford Reynolds, "Individualism versus Group Rights: The Legacy of Brown," *Yale Law Journal* 93 (May 1984): 996–98.

20. We should note that our examination of Adolph Reed Jr.'s work draws primarily on his research and essays concerning urban politics. In a review of Sowell's work, Reed tempers somewhat his criticism of affirmative action and notes that "preferential politics" has historically operated in ways that have damaged both American cities and urban residents' opportunities.

21. Reed, "The Liberal Technocrat," *Nation*, Feb. 6, 1988, 166–70.

22. William Julius Wilson, *The Declining Significance of Race: Blacks and Changing American Institutions* (2d ed., Chicago: University of Chicago Press, 1980), 2.

23. Wilson, *The Truly Disadvantaged: The Inner City, the Underclass, and Public Policy* (Chicago: University of Chicago Press, 1987).

24. Reed, "The Black Urban Regime: Structural Origins and Constraints," *Comparative Urban and Community Research* 1 (1987): 1–72. See also his "Critique of Neo-Progressivism in Theorizing about Local Development Policy: A Case from Atlanta," pp. 199–215 in *The Politics of Urban Development*, edited by C. N. Stone and H. T. Sanders (Lawrence: University Press of Kansas, 1987).

25. Reed, "Critique of Neo-Progressivism," 213.

26. Reed, "Black Urban Regime," 15.

27. Reed, "Critique of Neo-Progressivism," 212.

28. Reed, "Black Urban Regime," 20.

29. See Wilson, *Truly Disadvantaged*, esp. chap. 7.

30. Harold Cruse, *Plural but Equal: A Critical Study of Blacks and Minorities and America's Plural Society* (New York: Quill Books, 1987), 25–69.

31. Ibid., 350, 379.

Chapter 2: Black Politics in Richmond, 1945–89

1. Our discussion in this paragraph of the reform movement is drawn from Christopher Silver, *Twentieth-Century Richmond: Planning, Politics, and Race* (Knoxville: University of Tennessee Press, 1984), 176–82.

2. Ibid., 179.

3. Overton Jones, "Only Living Negro City Councilman Recalls Local Political Highlights of Bygone Days," *RT-D*, June 9, 1948, 4.

4. "Candidates for Council Give Views," *RNL*, May 17, 1948, 15.

5. "DeCuennois Is Nosed Out by 263 Votes," *RT-D*, June 9, 1948, 1, 5.

6. Silver, *Twentieth-Century Richmond*, 184.

7. "Separate but Equal Held," *Richmond Afro-American*, July 23, 1955, 1.

8. Numan V. Bartley, *The Rise of Massive Resistance: Race and Politics in the South during the 1950s* (New York: Columbia University Press, 1969), 110–11.

9. Ibid., 134.

10. Quoted in ibid., 134.

11. Our discussion of the origins of the Crusade for Voters relies heavily on A. J. Dickinson, "Myth and Manipulation: The Story of the Crusade for Voters in Richmond, Virginia" (honors thesis, Yale University, 1967), and Robert Arthur Rankin, "Black Power Politics: The Crusade for Voters in Richmond, Virginia" (master's thesis, University of Virginia, 1974).

12. A description of the efforts of the Richmond Civic Council can be found in Rankin, "Black Power Politics," 10–16.

13. Dickinson, "Myth and Manipulation," 25.

14. Ibid., 31.

15. Rankin, "Black Power Politics," 35–36.

16. "Hill's Defeat Is Attributed to Negro Vote," *RT-D*, June 18, 1950, B1.

17. This paragraph is a summary of Dickinson, "Myth and Manipulation," 31–34.

18. Ibid., 38.

19. "Council Approves Resolution for Fair Employment," *Richmond Afro-American*, June 2, 1962, 1.

20. "Voters' Crusade in City Job Drive," *Richmond Afro-American*, Mar. 31, 1962, 1.

21. "Council Approves Resolution."

22. Robert E. Baker, "Richmond Quietly Leads Way in Race Relations," *Washington Post*, July 29, 1962, E1.

23. Virginius Dabney, "Richmond's Quiet Revolution," *Saturday Review*, Feb. 29, 1964, 18.

24. "Voters' Voice Seeks to Add Vigor to Political Campaigns," *Richmond Afro-American*, Mar. 14, 1964, 1.

25. Ed Grimsley, "Negroes to Back Full Slate," *RT-D*, Mar. 4, 1964, 1.

26. "Voters' Voice Slate Urges Training, Jobs," *RT-D*, Apr. 17, 1964, 2.

27. Ibid.

28. The Crusade pamphlet is cited in Rankin, "Black Power Politics," 55.

29. Quoted in Dickinson, "Myth and Manipulation," 47.

30. Ibid., 49.

31. Quoted in ibid., 49–50.

32. Dickinson, "Myth and Manipulation," 68.

33. Rankin, "Black Power Politics," 75.

34. Dickinson, "Myth and Manipulation," 70–72.

35. Ibid., 68–69.

36. "Marsh to Run for Council," *Richmond Afro-American*, Apr. 16, 1966, 6.

37. *RT-D*, June 9, 1966, 18.

38. Ibid.

39. Dickinson, "Myth and Manipulation," 95.

40. John Moeser and Rutledge Dennis, *The Politics of Annexation: Oligarchic Power in a Southern City* (Cambridge, Mass.: Schenkman Publishing, 1982), 53.

41. "RF Must Go," *Richmond Afro-American*, June 8, 1968, 1.

42. "Council Candidates State Views," *RT-D*, June 9, 1968, C1.

43. "5 Endorsed by Crusade for Council," *RT-D*, June 10, 1968, A1.

44. Barry Barkan, "Cephas, Mundle Played RF Game, but White Voters Let Them Down," *Richmond Afro-American*, June 22, 1968, 1.

45. "Richmond's Most Vital Election in Decades," *RT-D*, June 11, 1968, A12.

46. Grimsley, "What Happened in Tuesday's Vote," *RT-D*, June 14, 1968, C1.

47. Milton L. Randolph, "Power Structure Can't Pick Our Leaders," *Richmond Afro-American*, June 22, 1988, 5.

48. See Moeser and Dennis, *Politics of Annexation*, 86. Our discussion of the annexation issue is drawn from Moeser and Dennis's examination of the issue.

49. Ibid., 141.

50. Bill Miller, "Marsh Continues to Run Campaign of Reassurance," *RT-D*, Apr. 17, 1977, B1.

51. "Text of Marsh's Statement on Leidinger," *RT-D*, Aug. 15, 1978, B1.

52. "Still a Bad Move," *RT-D*, Aug. 16, 1978, A6.

53. Miller, "5-4 Vote Sets Date of September 11," *RT-D*, Aug. 29, 1978, A1.

54. Miller, "Firing Plan Termed Months Old," *RT-D*, Aug. 28, 1978, A11.

55. See Miller, "5-4 Vote," A5.

56. "A Sham, A Shame," *RT-D*, Aug. 22, 1978, G6.

57. Henry L. Marsh III, interview by Margaret Edds, Richmond, Feb. 21–22, 1985. Edds furnished the authors with a transcript of her interviews.

58. Moeser and Dennis, *Politics of Annexation*, 183.

59. This is discussed in Silver, *Twentieth-Century Richmond*, 315–20.

60. A good description of the genesis of the project was presented by Clarence Townes in a speech entitled "Richmond Renaissance" and presented at a conference in Gainesville, Florida, May 4, 1988. An interesting study of the role of the arts community in revitalization plans is J. Allen Whitt, "The Arts Coalition in Strategies of Urban Development," pp. 144–56 in *Politics of Urban Development*, edited by Stone and Sanders.

61. Campbell, "City Renaissance Plan Unveiled," *RT-D*, Mar. 25, 1982, A1.

62. "Renaissance," *RNL*, Mar. 25, 1982, 1.

63. Campbell, "City Renaissance Plan Unveiled," A6.

64. Campbell, "Upset Has Factions Guessing," *RT-D*, May 6, 1982, B1.

65. Ibid.

66. Ibid.

67. Henry L. Valentine, interview by Margaret Edds, Richmond, Feb. 6, 1985.

68. Campbell, "West Willing to Negotiate Tightrope," *RT-D*, July 4, 1982, C1.

69. Ibid., C12.

70. Campbell, "New Council Elects West," *RT-D*, July 2, 1982, A1.

71. Campbell, "West Willing."

72. Ibid., C12.

73. Ibid., C1.

74. "West-Marsh Conflict Widens Council Rift," *RT-D*, July 18, 1983, A1.

75. Ibid.

76. Henry "Chuck" Richardson, interview by authors, Richmond.

77. Ibid.

78. Ibid.

79. Campbell, "Battle in West's District Is for More than Council Seat," *RT-D*, Apr. 30, 1984, C1.

80. Ibid.

81. Ibid.

82. Campbell, "West Defeats Ms. Dell by 1028 Votes," *RT-D*, May 2, 1984, A1.

83. Campbell, "West Charges Marsh Dominates Crusade," *RT-D*, Apr. 10, 1986, B1.

84. Carolyn Wake, interview by Margaret Edds, Richmond, Feb. 7, 1985.

Chapter 3: Set-Aside Politics

1. An excellent summary of the historical plans for the revitalization of downtown Richmond can be found in Silver, *Twentieth-Century Richmond*.

2. For an analysis of the Byrd organization's political orientation, see J. Harvie Wilkinson III, *Harry Byrd and the Changing Face of Virginia Politics, 1945–1966* (Charlottesville: University Press of Virginia, 1968), 23–61.

3. Silver, *Twentieth-Century Richmond*, 184–86.

4. This alliance was especially evident when urban renewal plans were proposed. Some conservative whites objected to the use of government funds for such undertakings while black citizens were angered at the prospect of eviction from their homes and neighborhoods.

5. "Hill Discusses Negro Vote against Expressway Plan," *RT-D*, June 27, 1950, 3.

6. See James E. Davis, "Crusade Reverses Stand on Expressway," *RT-D*, Jan. 16, 1973, A1; and "The Crusade's Contribution" (editorial), *RT-D*, Jan. 17, 1973, A14.

7. Marsh, interview.

8. Dickinson, "Myth and Manipulation"; see also the series of articles published in the *Richmond Afro-American* from April to June 1966.

9. Marsh's original opposition to the expressway is described in Davis, "Council Authorizes Pact on Expressway Segment," *RT-D*, Dec. 19, 1972, A1. The position of the editorial page of the *RT-D* is expressed in "Death of Downtown?" Jan. 10, 1973, A14.

10. See Davis, "Crusade Reverses Stand."

11. Marsh, interview.

12. The debate on the convention center is presented in Miller, "Debate Increasing on Site for Convention Center," *RT-D*, July 6, 1975, A1; and Campbell, "Center Debate Still On," *RT-D*, Aug. 29, 1976, C1.

13. Jerry Lazarus, "Views Differ on Number of Hotel Rooms City Can Support," *RT-D*, Sept. 10, 1981, A1.

14. See "Hilton Proposal Rejected," *RT-D*, Nov. 27, 1981, A1; and Campbell, "Planner Says Hilton Would Delay City Hotel," *RT-D*, Dec. 10, 1981, A1.

15. See Tom Campbell and Mike Grim, "Hilton Charges Conspiracy in Suit," *RT-D*, Dec. 24, 1981, A1; and Grim, "Hilton Site Owners Sue City, *RT-D*, Dec. 30, 1981, B1.

16. Marsh, interview.

17. Ibid.

18. Reed, "Critique of Neo-Progressivism," 209. See also, Mack H. Jones, "Black Political Empowerment in Atlanta: Myth and Reality," *Annals*, Sept. 1978, 90–117.

19. Reed, "Critique of Neo-Progressivism," 210.

20. In the weeks following the *Croson* decision, the construction of the airport and Atlanta's more general set-aside program were still cited as a model of a major commitment to affirmative action. Ralph Thomas, executive director of the National Association of Minority Contractors, called Atlanta "perhaps the most effective affirmative action city nationwide." Quoted in Ronald Smothers, "Affirmative Action Booms in Atlanta," *New York Times*, Jan. 27, 1989, A10.

21. Richmond, Va., ordinance no. 82-294-270 (1983), 10.

22. *City of Richmond v. J. A. Croson Co.*, 109 S.Ct. 706 (1989), 706–757.

23. Charles Taylor, chief of purchases and stores, interview by authors, Richmond, May 5, 1990.

24. We also searched city records from the time that the set-aside program was instituted to check the home base of the minority firms that were awarded contracts.

25. Dwight Snead, interview by authors, Richmond, Aug. 8, 1991.

26. Curtis Harris, interview by authors, Richmond, Aug. 17, 1991.

27. Ibid.

28. John Kramer, interview by authors, Richmond, Aug. 10, 1991.

29. Paul Smith, interview by authors, Richmond, Aug. 10, 1991.

30. Richardson, interview, Richmond, June 6, 1991.

31. Clarence Stone, *Regime Politics: Governing Atlanta, 1948–1988* (Lawrence: University Press of Kansas, 1989).

32. Our interviews with corporate officers involved in affirmative action programs continually elicited comments about the importance of being a good corporate citizen in Richmond. See chap. 5 for an extended discussion of corporate-initiated affirmative action.

Chapter 4: Set-Asides and the Broader Strategy for Black Progress

1. See also, W. Avon Drake and Robert D. Holsworth, "Richmond and the Politics of Calculated Cooperation," pp. 87–108 in *Dilemmas of Black Politics: Issues of Leadership and Strategy*, edited by Georgia Persons (New York: Harper-Collins, 1992); Drake and Holsworth, "Electoral Politics, Affirmative Action and the Supreme Court," *National Political Science Review* 2 (1990): 65–91.

2. For an example of such concerns, see "Cops Use Dogs against Children," *Richmond Afro-American*, July 10, 1971, 1; "Marsh Hits Use of Dogs as Probe of Clash Begins, *Richmond Afro-American*, July 17, 1971, 1; Preston Yancy, "Review of Cops Crucial Need," *Richmond Afro-American*, July 31, 1971, 5; "Blackwell Residents Exhibit Distrust of Cops at City Hall," *Richmond Afro-American*, Aug.

7, 1971, 1; Peter Lee and Carolyn Harris, "Blackwell Incident Sparks More Fire," *Richmond Afro-American*, Aug. 28, 1971, 1.

3. Yancy, "Review of Cops."

4. Raymond Boone, "City of Richmond Has Official Policy of Black Exclusion," *Richmond Afro-American*, Oct. 2, 1971, 5.

5. Robert W. Waitt, "Figures Indicate Widespread Discrimination in City Jobs," *Richmond Afro-American*, Dec. 29, 1973, 3.

6. Ibid.

7. Ibid.

8. This perspective was evident in our interviews with various council members.

9. "City's Budget Outlook," *RT-D*, Nov. 23, 1979, A12.

10. See Richmond, Va., Equal Employment Opportunity Program, Employment Profiles, Dept. of Personnel, 1988.

11. Ibid.

12. This finding is consistent with the analysis of trends in the international economy by scholars who argue that "symbolic analysts" are the kind of people who will prosper in the global economy. See, for example, Robert B. Reich, *The Work of Nations: Preparing Ourselves for 21st Century Capitalism* (New York: Alfred A. Knopf, 1991).

13. See Richmond, Va., Equal Employment Opportunity Program, Employment Profiles, Dept. of Personnel, 1988.

14. Sowell, *Civil Rights*, 48–53.

15. It should be noted that some of the blacks elected to the city council were the same people who were applying the pressure before they were elected. Our point concerns the kind of politics that was successful and is not a commentary about particular individuals.

16. All budgetary figures come from the Richmond, Va., Annual Budgets, and information provided by the Richmond, Va., Dept. of Budget and Strategic Planning.

17. The history of downtown revitalization in Richmond and its connection to African American politics is described in our essay entitled "Richmond: The Politics of Calculated Cooperation," 93–95.

18. See Silver, *Twentieth-Century Richmond*, 153–56, 184–99.

19. These characteristics of Jackson Ward are described in "Jackson Ward Vision 2000: Technical Report," a project commissioned by Richmond Renaissance and the City of Richmond, May 1988.

20. Ibid.

21. See "Jackson Ward Opinion Survey," in "Jackson Ward Vision 2000."

22. Our analysis of city voting records and census data indicates that registration levels decreased in the 1980s, even when taking into account the slight decline in eligible adult voters.

23. Our analysis of neighborhood groups indicates that, with a few notable exceptions, they tended to be very short-lived and were typically unsuccessful in putting forward new leaders who could make fresh contributions to political debate in the city.

24. See Dickinson, "Myth and Manipulation."

25. Yancy's columns appeared weekly in the *Richmond Afro-American* and remain one of the most thoughtful and interesting bodies of commentary produced about Richmond politics during this period.

26. Since Richmond's mayor was elected by the council and its council members elected in wards, there was little opportunity for the electoral process to address citywide issues, particularly the economic development policies that the council had adopted.

27. See Drake and Holsworth, "Affirmative Action and Elite Racial Reconciliation," *Research in Race and Ethnic Politics* 7 (1994): 57–82.

Chapter 5: White Responses to Affirmative Action

1. Albert Karnig and Susan Welch, *Black Representation and Urban Policy* (Chicago: University of Chicago Press, 1980), 9.

2. Richard Morin and Dan Balz, "Shifting Racial Climate," *Washington Post,* Oct. 25, 1989, A1.

3. Lee Sigelman and Susan Welch, *Black Americans' Views of Racial Inequalities* (New York: Cambridge University Press, 1991), 129.

4. James R. Kluegel and Eliot R. Smith, "Affirmative Action Attitudes: Effects of Self-Interest, Racial Affect, and Stratification Beliefs on Whites' Views," *Social Forces* 61 (1983): 804.

5. W. Richard Merriman and Edward G. Carmines, "The Limits of Liberal Tolerance: The Case of Racial Policies," *Polity* 20 (spring 1988): 525.

6. Thomas Silver, ed., "The Polling Report," Feb. 20, 1995, 1. Taken by Princeton Survey Research Associates, this poll indicates that 54 percent of whites "completely" or "mostly" agree with the statement, "We have gone too far in pushing equal rights in this country."

7. Sigelman and Welch attempt to demonstrate the similarity between the structure of white and black public opinion by noting that support for affirmative action diminishes among both groups when the issue of preferential treatment is raised. While this is certainly true, we have emphasized the gap that remains between the two groups on this issue.

8. See Morin and Balz, "Shifting Racial Climate."

9. Sigelman and Welch, *Black Americans' Views,* 164–65.

10. Williams quoted in Morin and Balz, "Shifting Racial Climate," A1.

11. See Black and Black, *Politics and Society*; and *The Vital South* (Cambridge, Mass.: Harvard University Press, 1992).

12. Rieder, *Canarsie*, 112.

13. Glazer, *Affirmative Discrimination*.

14. See Thomas and Mary Edsall, *Chain Reaction: The Impact of Race, Rights, and Taxes on American Politics* (New York: W. W. Norton, 1991), 86–87.

15. Peter T. Kilborn, "A Company Recasts Itself to Erase Decades of Bias," *New York Times*, Oct. 4, 1990, A1. See also, Marilyn Much, "Affirmative Action Still Alive: Companies Tailoring Plans Despite Apparent White House Apathy," *Industry Week*, Aug. 6, 1984, 47–48; Anne B. Fisher, "Businessmen Like to Hire by the Numbers," *Fortune*, Sept. 16, 1985, 26–30. Fisher writes, "Some corporate management, no doubt, push affirmative action only because government pushes them. But persuasive evidence indicates that most large American corporations want to retain their affirmative action programs, numerical goals and all."

16. Gus Thomas, former director of VRMSDC, interview by authors, Richmond, Oct. 16, 1991.

17. Ibid.

18. Tom Willis, director of general services, Crestar Bank Corporation, interview by authors, Richmond, Nov. 8, 1991.

19. Bernie Kosakowski, director of minority business development, Philip Morris Corporation, interview by authors, Richmond, Nov. 15, 1991.

20. Mary Jackson, minority business program administrator, Virginia Power, interview by authors, Richmond, Mar. 12, 1991; Eva Teig, vice president for governmental relations, interview by authors, Richmond, Mar. 28, 1991.

21. Kosakowski, interview.

22. Survey Research Laboratory, "The Metropoll," Virginia Commonwealth University, Dec. 19, 1990, 7.

23. Interestingly, William Leidinger, former city manager and the white council member most closely allied with the Main Street business community, voted for the ordinance in 1983. See Campbell, "Minority Business Ordinance Voted by City Council," *RT-D*, Apr. 12, 1983, A1.

24. Data on real estate tax rates were taken from the *Virginia Statistical Abstract* (Charlottesville: Center for Public Service, University of Virginia, 1992), 642–47.

25. These data are contained in census figures published in the ibid., 536–41.

26. Survey Research Laboratory, "Richmond Regional Cooperation Survey," Virginia Commonwealth University, Oct. 1994, and "The Urban Partnership Survey," Virginia Commonwealth University, Nov. 1994.

27. Survey Research Laboratory, "Richmond Regional Cooperation Survey."

Chapter 6: *Richmond v. Croson* in the Courts

1. This statistic is cited in Merhige's opinion in *Croson v. Richmond*, U.S. District Court for the Eastern District of Virginia, Richmond Division, No. 84-

0022-R, p. 28. This opinion will be cited hereinafter as Merhige, U.S. District Court.

2. *H. Earl Fullilove et al. v. Philip M. Klutznick*, 100 S.Ct. 2758 (1980), 2763.

3. Ibid.

4. Richmond, Va., ordinance no. 82-294-270 (1983), 10.

5. Testimony in U.S. District Court revealed a disagreement between Croson and the city of Richmond about the sincerity of Croson's effort to contact minority firms (see Merhige, U.S. District Court, 6).

6. Ibid., 9.

7. Ibid., 16–17.

8. Ibid., 15. See also *Richmond v. Croson*, U.S. Supreme Court, Brief on Behalf of the Appellee, p. 11.

9. Merhige, U.S. District Court, 26–27.

10. Ibid., 28–29.

11. *J. A. Croson Company v. City of Richmond*, U.S. Court of Appeals for the Fourth Circuit, No. 85-1002, 48–49, 60, 62.

12. *Wendy Wygant v. Jackson Board of Education*, 106 S.Ct. 1842 (1986), 1843.

13. *Croson v. Richmond*, United States Court of Appeals for the Fourth Circuit, No. 85-1041 (on remand from the U.S. Supreme Court), 15, 11.

14. *City of Richmond v. J. A. Croson Co.*, U.S. Supreme Court, 1988, Reply Brief of Appellant City of Richmond, 3–7.

15. *Richmond v. Croson*, 109 S.Ct. 706 (1989), 4139–43.

16. There are some obvious limitations to examining voting patterns of Supreme Court justices. As we have noted, justices may not agree on the issues raised by a particular case, so their votes on any single case may not be properly comparable. In addition, scholars have argued that certain justices may sometimes vote with the winning side not because they believe in the principle articulated but in order to tone down the majority's argument. We do not think that these limitations are decisive in examining the affirmative action cases because of the number of votes and because of the number of highly individualized opinions.

17. Besides *Richmond v. Croson*, in our analysis we use the nine other cases that are typically referred to in the scholarly literature as affirmative action cases. These are *Regents of the University of California v. Allan Bakke* (98 S.Ct. 2733 [1978]), *United Steelworkers of America v. Brian F. Weber*, (99 S.Ct. 2721 [1979]), *Fullilove v. Klutznick* (100 S.Ct. 2758 [1980]), *Firefighters Local Union No. 1784 v. Carl Stotts* (104 S.Ct. 2576 [1984]), *Wendy Wygant v. Jackson Board of Education* (106 S.Ct. 1842 [1986]), *Local 28 of the Sheet Metal Workers' International Association v. Equal Employment Opportunity Commission* (106 S.Ct. 3019 [1986]), *Local Number 93, International Association of Firefighters v. City of Cleveland* (106 S.Ct. 3063 [1986]), *United States v. Philip Paradise* (107 S.Ct. 1053 [1987]), and *Johnson v. Transportation Agency, Santa Clara County, California* (107 S.Ct. 1442 [1987]).

18. *Richmond v. Croson*, 109 S.Ct. 706 (1989),4157–58.

19. This assertion was first employed by Blackmun in his opinion in *Bakke*. It was then quoted by Marshall in his opinion in *Fullilove*. See 100 S.Ct. 2758 (1980).

20. Ibid.

21. Marshall, in *Fullilove v. Klutznick*.

22. White's willingness to overrule *Weber* is stated in his opinion in *Johnson v. Transportation Agency*, 1465 ("I also would overrule *Weber*").

23. An interesting discussion of the evolution of the "strict scrutiny" standard from a guideline used to promote a liberal, activist jurisprudence to the basis for a conservative attack on liberal policies such as affirmative action is found in Archibald Cox's *Court and the Constitution* (New York: Random House, 1987). See also, Bernard Schwartz, *Behind Bakke: Affirmative Action and the Supreme Court* (New York: New York University Press, 1988), 66–67, 72–75, 85–87; and Judith A. Baer's discussion of "suspect classifications" in *Equality under the Constitution: Reclaiming the Fourteenth Amendment* (Ithaca, N.Y.: Cornell University Press, 1983), 105–52.

24. This statement is in Scalia's opinion in *Johnson v. Transportation Agency*, 107 S.Ct. 1053 (1987), 1466.

25. See Scalia's opinion in *Richmond v. Croson* (109 S.Ct. 706 [1989], 4148): "Nothing prevents Richmond from according a contracting preference to identified victims of discrimination. While most of the beneficiaries might be black, neither the beneficiaries nor those disadvantaged by the preference would be identified *on the basis of their race*. In other words, far from justifying racial classification, identification of actual victims makes it less supportable than ever."

26. White notes that he could still possibly accept relief for nonvictims in his opinion in *Local 28 of the Sheet Metal Workers' International Association v. Equal Employment Opportunity Commission*, 106 S.Ct. 3019 (1986). We argue below, however, that it is significant that White judged the affirmative action plan in this case unconstitutional.

27. This analysis appears in Linda Greenhouse, "Court Bars a Plan Set Up to Provide Jobs to Minorities," *New York Times*, Jan. 24, 1989, A19.

28. *Local 28 v. EEOC*, 106 S.Ct. 3019 (1986), 3029.

29. Ibid., 3062–63.

30. *Richmond v. Croson*, 109 S.Ct. 706 (1989), 4145–46.

31. Tallying O'Connor's vote is complicated by the fact that her opinion in *Local 28 v. EEOC* concurred in part with the plurality while not concurring in the judgment. We have counted this as a vote against an affirmative action plan not only because of the refusal to concur in judgment but also because so much of her opinion is itself directed against the plurality's position.

32. *Johnson v. Transportation Agency*, 107 S.Ct. 1442 (1987), 1460.

33. "In the employment context, we have recognized that for certain entry level positions or positions requiring minimal training, statistical comparisons of the racial composition of an employer's workforce to the racial composition of the relevant population may be probative of a pattern of discrimination. . . . But where special qualifications are necessary, the relevant statistical pool *must be the number of minorities qualified to undertake the task*" (emphasis added, *Richmond v. Croson* (109 S.Ct. 706 [1989], 4141. See also 4136). The Court's use (or misuse) of statistics and the curious logic embodied in such use could be the subject of an entire article on its own.

34. Schwartz, *Behind Bakke*, 163.

35. This perspective is argued in Lincoln Caplan, *The Tenth Justice*.

36. "The Richmond Minority Construction Contracting Ordinance: Historical Context," 6–7, 11.

37. Richmond, Va., ordinance no. 93-91-91 (1993), 2–4.

38. George R. LaNoue, "Social Science and Minority 'Set-Asides,'" *Public Interest* 10 (winter 1993): 51.

39. Ralph Thomas, "The Impact of the Supreme Court's Decision in *City of Richmond v. J. A. Croson* on Federal/State/Local Minority Business Utilization Programs" (Washington, D.C.: NAMC, 1990).

40. An example of the NAMC's effort is the booklet noted in n. 39. Among other items, the booklet includes the facts of the case, the Court's decision and rationale, and strategies by which localities could ensure the legality of their own programs.

41. George R. LaNoue and John Sullivan, "'But for' Discrimination: How Many Minority Businesses Would There Be?" *Columbia Human Rights Law Review* 24, no. 1 (winter 1992–93): 99.

42. LaNoue, "Social Science," 53.

43. Andrew Brimmer and Ray Marshall, *Trends, Prospects, and Strategies for Black Economic Progress* (Washington, D.C.: Joint Center for Political Studies, 1995).

44. Thomas, "Impact."

45. "Court Reinstates Case Challenging Affirmative Action," *Washington Times*, June 15, 1993, A3.

Chapter 7: Urban Politics after *Croson*

1. Indeed, we have serious reservations about the criticisms of "growth politics" that are sometimes voiced by academic critics of urban leaders. While we agree that growth is not a magical answer to the problems of the most disadvantaged populations, we also do not think that the critics have articulated an alternative to a growth-oriented politics that would be beneficial to those citizens at the bot-

tom of the income ladder. From our perspective, the question is not so much growth or no-growth policies but identifying the best kind of economic development strategy with which to address the challenges that confront cities.

2. It is difficult for all political leaders to shift course, rejecting approaches that they once advocated, particularly if their decisions have been subjected to debate and criticism. Indeed, those politicians who demonstrate this flexibility often see what they perceive to be "growth" labeled expedience and lack of backbone.

3. It should be noted that the actual success of these groups was often quite limited. Clarence Stone's study of Atlanta observes that the neighborhood movement was ultimately confined to a "reactive and defensive posture" (Stone, *Regime Politics*, 241).

4. Saskia Sassen, *The Global City: New York, Tokyo, and London* (Princeton, N.J.: Princeton University Press, 1991).

5. Howard Sanchez and James Ragland, "4 Dominated D.C. Minority Contracting," *Washington Post*, June 1, 1992, A1.

6. Stone, *Regime Politics*, 144–48.

7. We noted in chap. 6 that LaNoue's research has shown that more than 230 such programs had been instituted.

8. See James Sleeper, *The Closest of Strangers: Liberalism and the Politics of Race in New York* (New York: W. W. Norton, 1990), 312–16.

9. Harold Cruse, for example, calls for the development of a panoply of black institutions, ranging from a political party to a theater.

10. City council members could have also argued that the surrounding counties did not popularly elect the chair of their boards of supervisors. Yet it is also the case that numerous cities with the council-manager form of government had moved to popularly elected mayors as a means of promoting citywide accountability.

11. Survey Research Laboratory, "The Metropoll," Apr. 1991.

12. See David Rusk, *Cities without Suburbs* (Baltimore, Md.: Johns Hopkins University Press, 1993); and his presentation before the Governor's Advisory Commission on Revitalizing Virginia's Urban Areas, July 19, 1993.

13. The antipathy evident in the latest chapter of the Richmond-Henrico County association can be traced back at least thirty years to the consolidation battles of the 1960s. See Silver, *Twentieth-Century Richmond*, 233–55.

14. We recognize that the term "development" has a controversial past within the discipline of political science. Utilized in the 1960s to describe an approach to enhancing the economies of materially poorer nations, the term became synonymous with the ethnocentric biases of Western social scientists. We think that the term can be usefully refurbished and pared of its ethnocentric biases. In our minds, its principal virtue is that it can serve as a frame of reference for analyzing the actions of political leaders that differs from the vantage points presently employed.

15. See Sowell, *Civil Rights*, 21–35, 37–60.

16. Stephen Carter examines the response to Wilson's work in *Reflections of an Affirmative Action Baby* (New York: Basic, 1991), 105–6.

17. Edward Banfield, *The Unheavenly City Revisited* (Boston, Mass.: Little, Brown, 1974).

Bibliography

"Almost Home." *Richmond News Leader*, Jan. 25, 1989, 14.

Baer, Judith A. *Equality under the Constitution: Reclaiming the Fourteenth Amendment.* Ithaca, N.Y.: Cornell University Press, 1983.

Baker, Robert E. "Richmond Quietly Leads Way in Race Relations." *Washington Post*, July 29, 1962, E1.

Banfield, Edward. *The Unheavenly City Revisited.* Boston, Mass.: Little, Brown, 1974.

Barkan, Barry. "Cephas, Mundle Played RF Game, but White Voters Let Them Down." *Richmond Afro-American*, June 22, 1968, 1.

Bartley, Numan V. *The Rise of Massive Resistance: Race and Politics in the South during the 1950s.* New York: Columbia University Press, 1969.

Bell, Derrick A. *Race, Racism, and American Law.* Boston: Little, Brown, 1980.

Belz, Herman. *Affirmative Action from Kennedy to Reagan: Redefining American Equality.* Washington, D.C.: Washington Legal Foundation, 1984.

Black, Earl, and Merle Black. *Politics and Society in the South.* Cambridge, Mass.: Harvard University Press, 1987.

——. *The Vital South: How Presidents Are Elected.* Cambridge, Mass.: Harvard University Press, 1992.

"Blackwell Residents Exhibit Distrust of Cops at City Hall." *Richmond Afro-American*, Aug. 7, 1971, 1.

Boone, Raymond. "City of Richmond Has Official Policy of Black Exclusion." *Richmond Afro-American*, Oct. 2, 1971, 5.

Boxill, Bernard. *Blacks and Social Justice.* Totowa, N.J.: Rowman and Allanheld, 1984.

Brimmer, Andrew, and Ray Marshall. *Trends, Prospects, and Strategies for Black Economic Progress.* Washington, D.C.: Joint Center for Political Studies, 1995.

Bunzel, John. "Affirmative Re-Actions." *Public Opinion* 9 (Feb.-Mar. 1986): 45–49.

Campbell, Tom. "Battle in West's District Is for More than Council Seat." *Richmond Times-Dispatch*, Apr. 30, 1984, C1.

——. "Center Debate Still On." *Richmond Times-Dispatch*, Aug. 29, 1976, C1.

——. "City Renaissance Plan Unveiled." *Richmond Times-Dispatch*, Mar. 25, 1982, A1.

——. "Minority Business Ordinance Voted by City Council." *Richmond Times-Dispatch*, Apr. 12, 1983, A1.

——. "New Council Elects West." *Richmond Times-Dispatch*, July 2, 1982, A1.

——. "Planner Says Hilton Would Delay City Hotel." *Richmond Times-Dispatch*, Dec. 10, 1981, A1.

——. "Upset Has Factions Guessing." *Richmond Times-Dispatch*, May 6, 1982, B1.

——. "West Charges Marsh Dominates Crusade." *Richmond Times-Dispatch*, Apr. 10, 1986, B1.

——. "West Defeats Ms. Dell by 1028 Votes." *Richmond Times-Dispatch*, May 2, 1984, A1.

——. "West Willing to Negotiate Tightrope." *Richmond Times-Dispatch*, July 4, 1982, C1.

Campbell, Tom, and Mike Grim. "Hilton Charges Conspiracy in Suit." *Richmond Times-Dispatch*, Dec. 24, 1981, B1.

"Candidates for Council Give Views." *Richmond News Leader*, May 17, 1948, 15.

Caplan, Lincoln. *The Tenth Justice: The Solicitor General and the Rule of Law.* New York: Vintage, 1988.

Carmines, Edward G., and James A. Simson. *Issue Evolution: Race and the Transformation of American Politics.* Princeton, N.J.: Princeton University Press, 1989.

Carter, Stephen. *Reflections of an Affirmative Action Baby.* New York: Basic, 1991.

"City's Budget Outlook." *Richmond Times-Dispatch*, Nov. 23, 1979, A12.

"Constitutional Scholars' Statement on Affirmative Action after *City of Richmond v. J. A. Croson Co.*" *Yale Law Journal* 98 (June 1989): 1711–16.

Cooper, Alan. "Minority Contracts Rules Passes." *Richmond News Leader*, Apr. 12, 1983, A1.

"Cops Use Dogs against Children." *Richmond Afro-American*, July 10, 1971, 1.

"Council Approves Resolution for Fair Employment." *Richmond Afro-American*, June 2, 1962, 1.

"Council Candidates State Views." *Richmond Times-Dispatch*, June 9, 1968, C1.

"Court Reinstates Case Challenging Affirmative Action." *Washington Times*, June 15, 1993, A3.

Cox, Archibald. *The Court and the Constitution.* New York: Random House, 1987.

"The Crusade's Contribution." *Richmond Times-Dispatch*, Jan. 17, 1973, A14.

Cruse, Harold. *The Crisis of the Negro Intellectual.* New York: Morrow, 1967.

——. *Plural but Equal: A Critical Study of Blacks and Minorities and America's Plural Society.* New York: Quill Books, 1987.

Dabney, Virginius. "Richmond's Quiet Revolution." *Saturday Review,* Feb. 29, 1964, 18–28.

Davis, James E. "Council Authorizes Pact on Expressway Segment." *Richmond Times-Dispatch,* Dec. 19, 1972, A1.

———. "Crusade Reverses Stand on Expressway." *Richmond Times-Dispatch,* Jan. 16, 1973, A1.

"Death of Downtown?" *Richmond Times-Dispatch,* Jan. 10, 1973, A14.

"DeCuennois Is Nosed Out by 263 Votes." *Richmond Times-Dispatch,* June 9, 1948, 1, 5.

Dickinson, A. J. "Myth and Manipulation: The Story of the Crusade for Voters in Richmond, Virginia." Honors thesis, Yale University, 1967.

Drake, W. Avon, and Robert D. Holsworth. "Affirmative Action and Elite Racial Reconciliation." *Research in Race and Ethnic Politics* 7 (1994): 57–82.

———. "Electoral Politics, Affirmative Action and the Supreme Court." *National Political Science Review* 2 (1990): 65–91.

———. "Richmond and the Politics of Calculated Cooperation." Pp. 87–108 in *Dilemmas of Black Politics: Issues of Leadership and Strategy,* ed. Georgia Persons. New York: HarperCollins, 1992.

Dworkin, Ronald. *Taking Rights Seriously.* Cambridge, Mass.: Harvard University Press, 1977.

Edsu6l, Thomas. *Chain Reaction: The Impact of Race, Rights, and Taxes on American Politics.* New York: W. W. Norton, 1991.

Fisher, Annie B. "Businessmen Like to Hire by the Numbers." *Fortune,* Sept. 16, 1985, 26–30.

"5 Endorsed by Crusade for Council." *Richmond Times-Dispatch,* June 10, 1968, A1.

Fried, Charles. "Affirmative Action after *City of Richmond v. J. A. Croson Co.:* A Reponse to the Scholars' Statement." *Yale Law Journal* 99 (Oct. 1989): 155–62.

Glazer, Nathan. *Affirmative Discrimination: Ethnic Inequality and Public Policy.* New York: Basic, 1975.

Graham, Hugh. *The Civil Rights Era: Origins and Development of National Policy, 1960–1972.* New York: Oxford University Press, 1990.

Greenhouse, Linda. "Court Bars a Plan Set Up to Provide Jobs to Minorities." *New York Times,* Jan. 24, 1989, A19.

Grim, Mike. "Hilton Site Owners Sue City." *Richmond Times-Dispatch,* Dec. 30, 1981, B1.

Grimsley, Ed. "Negroes to Back Full Slate." *Richmond Times-Dispatch,* Mar. 4, 1964, 1.

———. "What Happened in Tuesday's Vote." *Richmond Times-Dispatch,* June 14, 1968, C1.

Hamilton, Charles V. *The Black Experience in American Politics.* New York: Putnam, 1973.

"Hill Discusses Negro Vote against Expressway Plan." *Richmond Times-Dispatch*, June 27, 1950, 3.

"Hill's Defeat Is Attributed to Negro Vote." *Richmond Times-Dispatch*, June 18, 1950, B1.

"Hilton Proposal Rejected." *Richmond Times-Dispatch*, Nov. 27, 1981, A1.

"Jackson Ward Vision 2000: Technical Report." Project commissioned by Richmond Renaissance and the City of Richmond, May 1988.

Jones, Mack H. "Black Political Empowerment in Atlanta: Myth and Reality." *Annals*, Sept. 1978, 90–117.

Jones, Overton. "Only Living Negro City Councilman Recalls Local Political Highlights of Bygone Days." *Richmond Times-Dispatch*, June 9, 1948, 4.

Karnig, Albert, and Susan Welch. *Black Representation and Urban Policy*. Chicago: University of Chicago Press, 1980.

Kilborn, Peter T. "A Company Recasts Itself to Erase Decades of Bias." *New York Times*, Oct. 4, 1990, A1.

Kinsley, Michael. "Equal Lack of Opportunity." *Harper's*, June 1983, 8–10.

Kluegel, James R., and Eliot R. Smith. "Affirmative Action Attitudes: Effects of Self-Interest, Racial Affect, and Stratification Beliefs on Whites' Views." *Social Forces* 61, no. 3 (1983): 797–824.

LaNoue, George R. "Social Science and Minority 'Set-Asides.'" *Public Interest* 110 (1993): 49–62.

LaNoue, George R., and John Sullivan. "'But for' Discrimination: How Many Minority Businesses Would There Be?" *Columbia Human Rights Law Review* 24, no. 1 (1992–93): 93–134.

Lazarus, Jerry. "Views Differ on Number of Hotel Rooms City Can Support." *Richmond Times-Dispatch*, Sept. 10, 1981, A1.

Lee, Peter, and Carolyn Harris. "Blackwell Incident Sparks More Fire." *Richmond Afro-American*, Aug. 28, 1971, 1.

Loury, Glenn. "The Moral Quandary of the Black Community." *Public Interest* 79 (1985): 9–22.

"Marsh Hits Use of Dogs as Probe of Clash Begins." *Richmond Afro-American*, July 17, 1971, 1.

"Marsh to Run for Council." *Richmond Afro-American*, Apr. 16, 1966, 1.

Merriman, W. Richard, and Edward G. Carmines. "The Limits of Liberal Tolerance: The Case of Racial Policies." *Polity* 20, no. 3 (1988): 518–27.

Miller, Bill. "Debate Increasing on Site for Convention Center." *Richmond Times-Dispatch*, July 6, 1975, A1.

———. "Firing Plan Termed Months Old." *Richmond Times-Dispatch*, Aug. 28, 1978, A11.

———. "5-4 Vote Sets Date of September 11." *Richmond Times-Dispatch*, Aug. 29, 1978, A1.

———. "Marsh Continues to Run Campaign of Reassurance." *Richmond Times-Dispatch*, Apr. 17, 1977, B1.

Moeser, John, and Rutledge Dennis. *The Politics of Annexation: Oligarchic Power in a Southern City.* Cambridge, Mass.: Schenkman Publishing, 1982.

Morin, Richard, and Dan Balz. "Shifting Racial Climate." *Washington Post*, Oct. 25, 1989, A1.

Much, Marilyn. "Affirmative Action Still Alive: Companies Tailoring Plans Despite Apparent White House Apathy." *Industry Week*, Aug. 6, 1984, 47–48.

Murray, Charles. *Losing Ground: American Social Policy.* New York: Basic, 1984.

Randolph, Milton L. "Power Structure Can't Pick Our Leaders." *Richmond Afro-American*, June 22, 1988, 5.

Rankin, Robert Arthur. "Black Power Politics: The Crusade for Voters in Richmond, Virginia." Master's thesis, University of Virginia, 1974.

Reed, Adolph, Jr. "The Black Urban Regime: Structural Origins and Constraints." *Comparative Urban and Community Research* 1 (1987): 1–72.

———. "A Critique of Neo-Progressivism in Theorizing about Local Development Policy: A Case from Atlanta." Pp. 199–215 in *The Politics of Urban Development*, ed. C. N. Stone and H. T. Sanders. Lawrence: University Press of Kansas, 1987.

———. "The Liberal Technocrat." *Nation*, Feb. 6, 1988, 166–70.

Reich, Robert B. *The Work of Nations: Preparing Ourselves for 21st Century Capitalism.* New York: Alfred A. Knopf, 1991.

"Renaissance." *Richmond News Leader*, Mar. 25, 1982, 1.

Reynolds, William Bradford. "Individualism versus Group Rights: The Legacy of Brown." *Yale Law Journal* 93 (May 1984): 995–1005.

"RF Must Go." *Richmond Afro-American*, June 8, 1968, 1.

"The Richmond Minority Construction Contracting Ordinance: Historical Context." Prepared by Commission on Minority Participation in Construction Contracting for the City of Richmond, June 1992.

"Richmond's Most Vital Election in Decades." *Richmond Times-Dispatch*, June 11, 1968, A12.

Rieder, Jonathan. *Canarsie: The Jews and Italians of Brooklyn against Liberalism.* Cambridge, Mass.: Harvard University Press, 1985.

Rusk, David. *Cities without Suburbs.* Baltimore, Md.: Johns Hopkins University Press, 1993.

Sanchez, Howard, and James Ragland. "4 Dominated D.C. Minority Contracting." *Washington Post*, June 1, 1992, A1.

Sassen, Saskia. *The Global City: New York, Tokyo, and London*, Princeton, N.J.: Princeton University Press, 1991.

Schuwerk, Robert. "The Philadelphia Plan: A Study in the Dynamics of Executive Power." *University of Chicago Law Review* 39 (1972): 732–39.

Schwartz, Bernard. *Behind Bakke: Affirmative Action and the Supreme Court.* New York: New York University Press, 1988.

"Separate but Equal Held." *Richmond Afro-American,* July 23, 1955, 1.

"A Sham, A Shame." *Richmond Times-Dispatch,* Aug. 22, 1978, A11.

Sigelman, Lee, and Susan Welch. *Black Americans' Views of Racial Inequalities: The Dream Deferred.* New York: Cambridge University Press, 1991.

Silver, Christopher. *Twentieth-Century Richmond: Planning, Politics, and Race.* Knoxville: University of Tennessee Press, 1984.

Silver, Thomas, ed. "The Polling Report." Princeton Survey Research Associates, Feb. 20, 1995.

Sleeper, James. *The Closest of Strangers: Liberalism and the Politics of Race in New York.* New York: W. W. Norton, 1990.

Smothers, Ronald. "Affirmative Action Booms in Atlanta." *New York Times,* Jan. 27, 1989, A10.

Sniderman, Paul M., with Michael G. Hagen. *Race and Inequality: A Study in American Values.* Chatham, N.J.: Chatham House, 1985.

Sniderman, Paul M., and Philip E. Tetlock. "Reflections on American Racism." *Journal of Social Issues* 42 (1986): 173–87.

Sowell, Thomas. *Civil Rights: Rhetoric or Reality.* New York: William Morrow, 1984.

——. *Ethnic America: A History.* New York: Basic, 1981.

——. *Markets and Minorities.* New York: Basic, 1981.

——. *Race and Economics.* New York: Longman, 1975.

Steele, Shelby. *The Content of Our Character.* New York: St. Martin's, 1990.

"Still a Bad Move." *Richmond Times-Dispatch,* Aug. 16, 1978, A6.

Stone, Clarence N. *Regime Politics: Governing Atlanta, 1948–1988.* Lawrence: University Press of Kansas, 1989.

Stone, Clarence N., and H. T. Sanders, eds. *The Politics of Urban Development.* Lawrence: University Press of Kansas, 1987.

Sullivan, Kathleen. "Sins of Discrimination." *Harvard Law Review* 100, no. 1 (Oct. 1986): 78–98.

Survey Research Laboratory. "The Metropoll." Richmond: Virginia Commonwealth University, 1990.

——. "Richmond Regional Cooperation Survey." Richmond: Virginia Commonwealth University, 1994.

——. "The Urban Partnership Survey." Richmond: Virginia Commonwealth University, 1994.

"Text of Marsh's Statement on Leidinger." *Richmond Times-Dispatch,* Aug. 15, 1978, B1.

Thomas, Ralph. "The Impact of the Supreme Court's Decision in *City of Richmond v. J. A. Croson* on Federal/State/Local Minority Business Utilization Programs." Washington, D.C.: NAMC, 1990.

Tolchin, Martin. "Officials in Cities and States Vow to Continue Minority Contractor Programs." *New York Times*, Jan. 25, 1989, A18.

Virginia Statistical Abstract. Charlottesville: Center for Public Service, University of Virginia, 1992.

"Voters' Crusade in City Job Drive." *Richmond Afro-American*, Mar. 31, 1962, 1.

"Voters' Voice Seeks to Add Vigor to Political Campaigns." *Richmond Afro-American*, Mar. 14, 1964, 1.

"Voters' Voice Slate Urges Training, Jobs." *Richmond Times-Dispatch*, Apr. 17, 1964, 2.

Waitt, Robert W. "Figures Indicate Widespread Discrimination in City Jobs." *Richmond Afro-American*, Dec. 29, 1973, 3.

"West-Marsh Conflict Widens Council Rift." *Richmond Times-Dispatch*, July 18, 1983, A1.

Whitt, J. Allen. "The Arts Coalition in Strategies of Urban Development." Pp. 144–56 in *The Politics of Urban Development*, ed. C. N. Stone and H. T. Sanders. Lawrence: University Press of Kansas, 1987.

Wilkinson, J. Harvie III. *Harry Byrd and the Changing Face of Virginia Politics, 1945–1966.* Charlottesville: University Press of Virginia, 1968.

Williams, Walter. *The State against Blacks.* New York: McGraw-Hill, 1982.

Wilson, William Julius. *The Declining Significance of Race: Blacks and Changing American Institutions.* 2d ed. Chicago: University of Chicago Press, 1980.

————. *The Truly Disadvantaged: The Inner City, the Underclass, and Public Policy.* Chicago: University of Chicago Press, 1987.

Yancy, Preston. "Review of Cops Crucial Need." *Richmond Afro-American*, July 31, 1971, 5.

Index

Adarand v. Pena, 139
Affirmative action: attitudes by race, 116–
19; in black progress strategies, 32–36;
business opposition to, 125–26; and civil rights, 13, 15–17; conservative criticisms of, 17–22; corporate support for,
120–25; defenses of, 12–17; and elite
racial reconciliation, 87, 90–91; nationalist perspective on, 28–31; and political
campaigns, 115, 119; political complex-
ity of, 115–16; progressive criticisms of,
23–28; shortcomings of conventional
debate about, 91–93; U.S. Supreme
Court voting patterns on, 146–53; white
responses to, in Richmond, 119–26
Almond, Lindsey, 40
Annexation, 51, 53–55, 138, 172
Antitax sentiment, 130, 133, 136
Association of General Contractors, 2, 87,
125, 142, 155, 158
Atlanta airport, 26, 70–71; as model for
Richmond, 79–80

Baer, Judith, 196n
Bagley, Phil, 50
Baker, Robert E., 45, 46, 47, 188n
Bakke, Allan, 139, 145, 146
Balz, Dan, 193n
Banfield, Edward, 178, 199n
Barkan, Barry, 188n
Bartley, Numan V., 41, 187n
Bell, William, 157

Bemiss, Fitzgerald, 48
Black, Earl, 118, 186n, 193n
Black, Merle, 118, 186n, 193n
Blackmun, Harry, 14, 145, 147, 148, 149,
152, 159, 196n
Bliley, Tom, 75
Bobb, Robert, 98
Boone, Raymond, 48, 49, 97, 192n
Booz-Allen and Hamilton, 75
Boxill, Bernard, 14, 186n
Brennan, William, 14, 145, 147, 148, 149,
152, 159
Breyer, Stephen, 159
Brimmer, Andrew, 156, 197n
Brown, Melvin, 141
Brown v. Board of Education, 30, 40
Budgetary priorities, 100–103
Byrd, Harry, 4, 8, 40, 41, 72, 110

Calhoun, John C., 41
Campbell, Tom, 185n, 189n, 190n,
194n
Caplan, Lincoln, 186n, 197n
Carmines, Edward G., 117, 193n
Carpenter, James, 55
Carter, Edward, 39
Carter, Jimmy, 76, 156
Carter, Stephen, 199n
Carwile, Howard, 48, 50, 51, 52, 74
Cephas, B. A., Jr., 46, 47, 48, 50, 52, 65
Citizen surveys: on Jackson Ward revital-
ization, 106–7; on regional cooperation,

134–35; on Richmond's set-aside program, 126

City-county cooperation, 172–73, 178–79

City of Richmond v. J. A. Croson Co.: aftermath of, 153–59; Blackmun's dissent in, 147; conservative commentary on, 4, 15–16, 20; in circuit court, 143–44; in district court, 142–43; liberal reaction to, 4; in U.S. Supreme Court, 143–47, 151–53, 195n, 196n, 197n

Civil Rights Act of 1964, 12; Title VII provisions of, 146–47, 149–50

Civil Rights Commission, 17, 21

Clinton, Bill, 1, 160

Cooper, Alan, 185n

Coral Construction Company v. King County, Washington, 158–59

Cox, Archibald, 196n

Crestar Bank, 122–24

Crime, 168–69

The Crisis of the Negro Intellectual, 29, 31

Croson v. Richmond, 194n, 195n

Crusade for Voters: emphasis on unity, 109–10; estrangement from rank and file, 111; and fair employment practices, 44–45; founding of, 42–43; original strategy of, 42–43, 162

Cruse, Harold, 6, 29–32, 35, 187n

Cultural politics, 175–78

Dabney, Virginius, 45, 46, 47, 50, 188n

Daley, Richard, Jr., 157

Davenport and Company, 63

Davis, James E., 190n

Davis, Jefferson, 37–38

The Declining Significance of Race, 23

Deese, Manuel, 60, 62, 98

Dell, Willie, 55, 62, 63, 65, 68, 128

Democratic party, 28, 34, 35, 38

Dennis, Rutledge, 53, 58, 188n, 189n

Dickinson, A. J., 42, 44, 47, 50, 187n, 188n, 190n, 193n

Dinkins, David, 168

Disparity studies, 156–57

Downtown revitalization: and African Americans, 71–77; and businessowners,

72; and Henry Marsh, 74–77; and the Hilton controversy, 75–77

Du Bois, W. E. B., 31

Dworkin, Ronald, 14, 15, 186n

Edds, Margaret, 57, 63, 77, 189n

Edsall, Mary, 194n

Edsall, Thomas, 194n

Elastic cities, 172

Employment (municipal): assessment of progress, 98–100; perception of discrimination in, 96–98

Equal Employment Opportunity Commission (EEOC), 13, 17, 21, 154

Equal Protection Clause, 151

Executive Order 10925, 12

Executive Order 11246, 12, 13

Farrakhan, Louis, 28, 29, 176, 181

Feinstein, Dianne, 115, 119

Fifth Amendment, 146

Fisher, Anne B., 194n

Fourteenth Amendment, 16, 31–32, 141, 146

Fried, Charles, 4, 20, 185n

Friedman, Milton, 18

Fullilove v. Klutznick, 70, 148, 195n, 196n; applicability to Richmond challenged, 144, 145; as precedent for Richmond set-aside program, 80–81, 140, 142, 143, 145

Gantt, Harvey, 119

Gayles, Franklin, 51

Gillespie, Andrew, 2, 58

Ginsberg, Ruth Bader, 159

Giuliani, Rudolph, 168

Glazer, Nathan, 17, 18, 19, 20, 23, 121, 186n, 194n

Godwin, Mills, 48

Golding, William, 130

Graham, Hugh, 185n

Greenhouse, Linda, 196n

Grim, Mike, 190n

Grimsley, Ed, 188n

Growth politics, 166

Guy, Buddy, 127

Hall, Judge, 144
Hamilton, Charles, 110
Harper's (magazine), 5
Harris, Carolyn, 192n
Harris, Curtis, 85, 191n
Harris, Louis, 117
Harvard Law Review, 17, 151
Helms, Jessie, 115, 119
Hicks, David, 170
Hill, Oliver, 39, 40, 42, 73
Hilton Hotel controversy, 58–59, 61
Holiday, Billie, 104
Holt, Curtis, 54
Houghton, James R., 122
Howell, Henry, 124
Hunter, Richard, 63, 64, 65, 102

Intermediate scrutiny, 147, 148

Jackson, Andrew, 157
Jackson, Jesse, 119, 176
Jackson, Maynard, 26, 79, 80
Jackson Ward, 40; revitalization of, 105–7
James, Alix, 49
Johnson, Lyndon B., 12, 119
Johnson v. Transportation Agency, Santa Clara County, California, 152, 195n, 196n
Jones, Dwight, 69
Jones, Overton, 187n

Karenga, Malena, 29
Karnig, Albert, 116, 193n
Kennedy, Anthony, 145, 151
Kennedy, John F., 12
Kenney, Walter T., 51, 55, 64, 171
Kilborn, Peter T., 194n
Kilpatrick, James J., 41, 47, 48
King, Martin Luther, Jr., 4, 35, 52, 96, 166
King, Rodney, 116
Kinsley, Michael, 5, 185n
Kluegel, James R., 117, 193n
Kool and the Gang, 127
Kosakowski, Bernie, 194n
Kramer, John, 191n
Kucinich, Dennis, 61

LaNoue, George, 155, 156, 197n
Laventhol and Horwath, 76
Lazarus, Jerry, 190n
Lee, David, 105, 107
Lee, Peter, 192n
Lee, Rex, 20
Leidinger, William, 56–61 passim, 70, 77, 98, 102, 131, 194n
Local Number 93, International Association of Firefighters v. City of Cleveland, 195n
Local 28 of the Sheet Metal Workers International Association v. Equal Employment Opportunity Commission, 150, 195n, 196n

Marable, Manning, 29
Marsh, Henry L. III, 190n; and downtown renewal, 74–77; as first black mayor, 56–62, 71, 169; quest for independent black political power, 49–52, 55; response to *Croson*, 153; and Richmond Renaissance, 78–79; rivalry with Roy West, 62–69, 88, 108–9, 134; and setasides, 78–79, 88; white resistance to, 128–31
Marshall, John, 157
Marshall, Ray, 156, 197n
Marshall, Thurgood, 12, 14, 145, 147, 148, 149, 152, 159, 196n
Marshall Tucker Band, 127
Massive resistance, 30–32
McDaniel, Claudette Black, 55, 57, 58, 63, 64, 66, 68, 112
Memphis Fire Department v. Carl Stotts, 151, 195n
Merhige, Robert, 54, 55, 138, 139, 142, 143, 194n, 195n
Merriman, W. Richard, 117, 193n
Miller, Bill, 189n, 190n
Moeser, John, 53, 58, 188n, 189n
Moore, T. Justin, 61, 62, 78
Morin, Richard, 193n
Morrissey, Joe, 170
Much, Marilyn, 194n
Mundle, Wilfred, 49, 50, 52, 65
Murray, Charles, 176, 185n

Narrow tailoring, 145, 148, 153
National Association for the Advancement of Colored People, 13
National Association of Minority Contractors, 155–57, 197n
National League of Cities, 145
Neighborhood politics, 109–10; weakness of, 163, 165
New Republic, 23
New York State Commission on Human Rights, 150
New York Times, 90, 150
Nixon, Richard M., 13, 17, 121

O'Connor, Sandra Day, 82, 145, 151, 152, 153, 196n
O'Neill, Tip, 182
Organization for a New Equality, 4

Pendleton, Clarence, 21
People's Political and Civic League, 41
Perkins, Charles, 129
Persons, Georgia, 191n
Philip Morris, 122–24
Police department, 95–97
Political demobilization, 107–14, 167–68, 171, 172
Political disaffection, 167–68
Politics of development, 174–83
Poll tax, 48–49
Population dynamics, 131–32
Powell, Lewis, 38, 55, 138, 143, 150, 151, 152
Pragmatic experimentation, 166–67
Prince, Adolphus, 69
Project One, 74–77
Public Works Employment Act, 140

Quail Oak Company, 83, 84

Race conscious relief, 145–53
Ragland, James, 198n
Randolph, A. Philip, 96
Randolph, Milton A., 48, 188n
Rankin, Robert, 48, 49, 187n

Reagan, Ronald, 4, 14, 16, 20, 21, 23, 32, 122, 143
Reed, Adolph, Jr., 5, 6, 23–28 passim, 35, 186n, 187n, 191n
Regents of the University of California v. Allan Bakke, 139, 145, 146, 148, 151, 195n
Regionalization, 135–36, 164
Rehnquist, William, 16, 122, 145, 148, 149, 150, 152
Reich, Robert B., 192n
Revitalization, 82, 134; of Jackson Ward, 104–6, 192n
Reynolds, William Bradford, 20, 21, 186n
Richardson, Henry "Chuck," 55, 60, 63, 65, 68, 80, 81, 82, 88, 171, 189n, 191n
Richmond Affirmative Action Plan, 97–98
Richmond Afro-American, 51, 52, 97, 111; revitalization of, 48–49
Richmond Civic Association, 38, 43–44
Richmond Civic Council, 41
Richmond Committee to Save Public Schools, 41–42
Richmond Forward, 38; and the African American community, 45–46, 49–52
Richmond Minority Construction Contracting Ordinance: historical context, 154, 197n
Richmond News Leader, 4, 41, 58, 62
Richmond Renaissance: origins of, 61–62; discontent in the black community with, 103–5
Richmond Set-Aside Ordinance, 2
Richmond Times-Dispatch, 50, 52, 57, 74, 168
Riddell, Joyce, 129
Rieder, Jonathan, 118, 186n, 194n
Riordan, Michael, 168, 174
Robinson, Norvell, 57
Rogers, Elijah, 97, 98
Rouse, James, 103
Rusk, David, 172, 198n

Sanchez, Howard, 198n
Sanders, H. T., 187n, 189n

Sassen, Saskia, 198n
Saturday Review, 45, 90
Scalia, Antonin, 148, 149, 150, 151, 196n
Schundler, Brett, 174
Schwartz, Bernard, 152, 196n, 197n
Set-asides: citizen indifference to, 126; court challenge to, 138–45; defended in U.S. Supreme Court, 147–48; initial use in Richmond, 70–71; operation of, 82–85; origins of official program, 80–81; perceptions of, 85–87; in places other than Richmond, 164; political functions of, 87–91
Sigelman, Lee, 118, 193n
Silver, Christopher, 40, 72, 104, 187n, 190n, 192n, 198n
Silver, Thomas, 193n
Sixth Street Marketplace, 78–79
Sleeper, James, 166, 198n
Small Business Act of 1965, 12
Smith, Eliot R., 117, 193n
Smith, Guy, 117
Smith, Paul, 191n
Smothers, Ronald, 191n
Snead, Dwight, 83–85, 191n
Souter, David, 159
Sowell, Thomas, 6, 18, 19, 22–27 passim, 30, 33, 34, 66, 91, 100, 114, 166, 175, 186n, 192n, 199n
Steele, Shelby, 20, 186n
Stevens, John Paul, 14, 151, 152
Stone, Clarence N., 91, 165, 187n, 189n, 191n, 198n
Strict scrutiny, 139, 148
Sullivan, John, 156, 197n
Survey Research Lab, 106–7, 194n, 198n

Tax rates, 130
Taylor, Charles, 83, 191n
Team of Progress, 55
Thomas, Clarence, 21, 159
Thomas, Gus, 194n
Thomas, Ralph, 155, 157, 197n
Tolchin, Martin, 185n

Townes, Clarence, 189n
Tribe, Laurence, 4, 8
The Truly Disadvantaged, 24, 34

United States v. Philip Paradise, 195n
United Steelworkers of America v. Brian F. Weber, 146, 148, 195n, 196n
University of California, 145

Valentine, Henry L., 63, 64, 189n
Virginia Commonwealth University, 106–7, 126, 194n
Virginia General Assembly, 172
Virginia Office of Minority Business Enterprise, 154
Virginia Power, 122–24
Virginia Regional Minority Supplier Development Council, 122–25
Vision 2000, 105–6
Voter registration, 108
Voters' Voice, 46–48

Waitt, Robert W., 192n
Wake, Carolyn, 67, 129, 190n
Walker, Maggie, 104
Waller, Fats, 104
Wall Street Journal, 59, 77
Washington, Booker T., 29, 30, 84
Washington Post, 45, 90, 116, 117, 118
Welch, Susan, 116, 118, 193n
Wendy Wygant v. Jackson Board of Education, 143, 144, 145, 195n
West, Roy, 103, 108, 109, 112, 126, 128, 129, 134, 169, 171; election of, 62–63; reelection campaign in 1984, 65–67; relationship with 1977 majority, 62–65; rivalry with Henry Marsh, 65–68, 69; support for set-asides, 82, 88–89
White, Byron, 145–53 passim, 159, 196n
White exodus, 131–32
Whitt, J. Allen, 189n
Wilder, L. Douglas, 46, 64, 108, 119
Wilkins, Roy, 96
Wilkinson, J. Harvie III, 139, 143, 144, 145, 190n

Williams, Geline, 129
Williams, Linda, 118, 193n
Williams, Walter, 18, 19, 22, 23, 25, 27, 66, 91, 166, 175, 186n
Willis, Tom, 194n
Wilson, Pete, 115, 119
Wilson, William Julius, 5, 6, 23–27

passim, 34, 35, 103, 176, 186n, 187n
Woodson, Robert, 175

Yale Law Journal, 4, 21
Yancy, Preston, 111, 112, 191n, 193n
Young, Andrew 26

W. AVON DRAKE is the director of the African American Studies Program and an associate professor of political science and public administration at Virginia Commonwealth University. He has written on black social thought and urban racial politics in the *Western Journal of Black Thought* and the *National Political Science Review*.

ROBERT D. HOLSWORTH is the director of the Center for Public Policy at Virginia Commonwealth University. He has written extensively on American social movements and contemporary U.S. politics, including *Public Interest Liberalism and the Crisis of Affluence* (1980) and *Let Your Life Speak* (1989).